DIALOGUES ≋ JERRY BROWN

Center for ATTitudinal
Healing :

Jerry Brown

DIALOGUES

JERRY BROWN

Berkeley Hills Books
Berkeley, California

Published by Berkeley Hills Books, P.O. Box 9877, Berkeley, California 94709.

Cover design by Elysium, San Francisco
Photograph by Janet Orsi/*Sonoma County Independent*

Manufactured in the United States of America

This book is printed on 100% recycled paper using soy-based ink.

All royalties from the sale of this work go to We The People Legal Foundation, Inc., 200 Harrison Street, Oakland, California 94607.

Grateful Acknowledgement is made to quote from the following:
In the Vineyard of the Text, by Ivan Illich. Copyright © 1993 by Valentina Borremans. Reprinted by permission of The University of Chicago Press.
Mountains and Rivers without End, by Gary Snyder. Copyright © 1996 by Gary Snyder. Reprinted by permission of Counterpoint.
Aftermath: The Remnants of War, by Donovan Webster. Copyright © 1996 by Donovan Webster. Reprinted by permission of Pantheon Books, A Division of Random House.
The Great Transformation, by Karl Polanyi. Copyright © 1944 by Karl Polanyi. Reprinted by permission of Holt, Rinehart & Winston, A division of Harcourt Brace.

1 3 5 7 9 10 8 6 4 2

Library of Congress Cataloging-in-Publication Data

Brown, Jerry, 1938-
        Dialogues / Jerry Brown
            p. cm.
Discussions from the nationally-syndicated radio program, "We the People," hosted by Jerry Brown.
        Includes bibliographical references
        ISBN 0-9653774-9-0 (paper)
        1. United States--Civilization--1970-   2. United States--Politics and government--Philosophy.   3. United States--Social conditions--1980-   4. Interviews--United States.   I. We the people (Radio program)   II. Title.
E169. 12.B74   1998
973.92--DC21   98-8389
                                                                                CIP

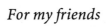

For my friends

CONTENTS

> "The thing that's important to remember is that for a
> baby, birth and the first hours, days and weeks
> afterwards are its first impressions. We know how
> important first impressions are, but neurologically,
> we are patterning people for insecurity and addiction
> and mistrust."

Acknowledgements

I would like to express my thanks to each of the people who appear in these conversations, to KPFA Radio in Berkeley, and to those in the We The People organization who made the broadcast of *We The People* possible. Particular thanks to John Strohmeier and Amy Boyd for having the idea and developing the concept of this book, and for their tireless editing. Thanks also to Linda Teixera for hours of transcription, and for valuable comments.

Note to the Reader

In the winter of 1994, I started a national call-in radio program, *We The People.* My plan was to take up contemporary ideas and controversies and explore them as honestly as I could. My hope was to clarify tacit assumptions and test them against common sense and democratic principles. In the beginning, the format involved an opening monologue followed by comments from listeners. Later, I invited guests and structured the show as a dialogue between myself and the person who joined me in conversation.

For guests, I sought out people whose writings or whose life exemplified unusual intelligence and honesty. I wanted to learn as much as I could about our society and the mental structures which shape it. I looked for people who had deep understanding, or perhaps a special vantage point from which they saw things many of us had missed. From hundreds of conversations that were broadcast, eighteen were chosen and edited for this book.

You will find that each dialogue illuminates the paradoxes of progress, and opens up cracks in the certitudes of our modern world view. The perspectives you will encounter here are not ideological or cynical. They are caring.

For example, Jonathan Kozol, in the opening dialogue, tells the story of Mott Haven, the poorest neighborhood in the South Bronx. Surrounded by pain and squalor, people live there in a daily struggle minutes away from the splendor of Manhattan. Kozol shows their despair, but also the grace and heroism with which they live. The last conversation in the book is with Suzanne Arms, who describes the modern way of birth as a process of alienating babies from their mothers. She takes issue with a culture where the more education a woman has, the less confidence she has in her body's natural ability to give birth.

My conversation with Ivan Illich makes explicit the link between the political and the personal. He says, "I believe that if something like a political life is to remain for us in this world of technology, then it begins with friendship." Illich is saying that "the good," which at one time had its source in community or political life, can be encountered today only in friendship.

Late last year, I decided to end my radio program in order to run for Mayor of Oakland. The *We The People* radio program had been an incredible opportunity to learn. It was a privilege to speak with so many thoughtful people. But after ranging over many ideas and probing their implications, I felt it was time to engage in action. It is one thing to conceptualize. It is quite another to take responsibility for where you live and for what lies within your grasp.

Jerry Brown
July 14, 1998

DIALOGUES ≋ JERRY BROWN

Apartheid in the Heart of New York City
Jonathan Kozol

> "I once asked a priest in the South Bronx, 'What is it
> like to be born in prison and know that you might die
> there?' And she wondered how different it was from
> being born in the South Bronx, and knowing that you
> might die there."

*Jonathan Kozol, a former teacher in the Boston Public School System, is
the author of several powerful critiques of American social policy and education, including* Death at an Early Age *and* Savage Inequalities. *Shortly
after the publication of his tenth book,* Amazing Grace, *he and I met to
discuss this study of the real people who dwell in Mott Haven, a little knot
of poverty in the middle of the South Bronx, the poorest neighborhood of
the poorest congressional district in the United States.*

*The facts about Mott Haven are not in dispute. Forty-eight thousand
people live there, with a median household income of $7,600 a year. In
1993, nearly fifteen percent of the adult residents were believed to be heroin
users; the homicide rate was among the highest in the nation, and the rate
of unemployment is so difficult to measure, it is often omitted from government reports. Many of the young men there are currently in prison,
and very few will attend college or trade school. But these are human beings. They're mothers and fathers, children growing up with hopes and
aspirations, heroes and villains. It's a human community reflecting an aspect of America that most Americans will never experience, but it is in
many ways a mirror of ourselves, of our attitudes and way of life.*

*Jonathan, tell me, how did your personal involvement with the Mott Ha-
ven neighborhood begin?*

I had heard about an Episcopal church in Mott Haven where a priest was doing some unusually good work with the kids and parents of the community. So I just got on the subway in the middle of Manhattan one day, right in front of Bloomingdale's. That's one of the richest urban neighborhoods in the world. I just got on the train, and rode ten stops, got off in the middle of the South Bronx, and walked up to St. Ann's Church. It drew me into months and months of deepening friendships with kids, and mothers, and grandmothers, and teachers and priests. I ended up spending most of two years talking to people in that neighborhood.

So the subject of Amazing Grace *is that in the midst of that squalor there is grace.*

Yes, that really is the point of the title. Mott Haven is a squalid neighborhood in many ways. First of all, it is one of the poorest neighborhoods of the South Bronx, which is the poorest congressional district in the country. Ninety-five percent of the kids there live in poverty. Many families in the neighborhood live on about the same amount of money that wealthy people spend to garage their cars in midtown Manhattan. Second, it is a very diseased neighborhood. About a quarter of the young mothers in the area, when I was working on my book, were said by doctors to be HIV-positive. So when you're with children there, visiting a school or kindergarten, as I did often, you count the children. You go: one, two, three, four—and you realize every fourth child might lose their mother to AIDS.

Is that something that's talked about in school, or is it just something that fills the background for children as they grow up?

Classroom teachers, naturally, are sensitive about what they will say in front of children. But it's very much part of the fabric of life. So many children have someone in their family—a mother, uncle or brother—

who's dying of AIDS, so it can't be avoided. And there's a lot of pediatric AIDS as well. A charitable group there run by the Dominican Sisters, a Catholic order, actually specializes in grieving services for children who anticipate losing their parents. So these things create a melancholy feeling that's often in the background.

There are also many more ordinary illnesses there that make life awfully tough. The neighborhood has the highest rate of child asthma in the United States. About two-thirds of the children are Puerto Rican and the rest are black—there are no white people in the neighborhood. When you're talking to some of these kids, if some subject arises that upsets them, you'll suddenly hear them start wheezing. And then you'll see the child reach into his or her pocket and pull out this little pump. They call it "the pump." It's really an inhaler. You get used to seeing the same little orange-colored pumps in the hands of many children. Some of the kids even have to sleep with what they call breathing machines next to their bed.

There's also a melancholy feeling because so many kids have parents in jail or in prison. Many children there have their daddy or their grandpa or their uncle or their brother in the New York City jail, which is on Riker's Island in the East River. Riker's Island is now the largest penal colony in the world. There are 20,000 people out there on any given day, and a large women's jail is part of the prison colony. In fact, the population of the female inmates there is so large that they have a nursery in the prison for the babies who are born there. I heard of a person who was born there and then died there, a child born with AIDS who later died of AIDS right on the island.

You don't even hear anything about this. I've been reading The New York Times *for years. I've been to Manhattan many times. And yet Riker's Island doesn't even show up as part of the dialogue or part of the reality. It's like a type of apartheid just carved out of the heart of New York.*

I'm glad you used that word because most of the press in New York

City would never dare to use one as accurate as that. But apartheid is what it is. This is not only a monstrously huge prison colony, but it's also almost entirely filled with people of color—black and Latino men and women—and they almost never speak of it. Riker's Island is sort of like a family secret, and yet it's very hard to miss. When you fly into La Guardia Airport, you go right over Riker's Island. If you're sitting on the right side of the plane when the wheels go down, just before they touch the ground, you look out the window and you're looking into New York's prison colony.

I once asked a priest in the South Bronx, 'What is it like to be born in prison and know that you might die there?' And she wondered how different it was from being born in the South Bronx, and knowing that you might die there. And that raised another point in my mind, which is that we not only doubled and quadrupled and quintupled our prisons in the United States in the past twenty years, but also whole neighborhoods feel like prisons now. Mott Haven is, for many children, like a prison without bars, because it's virtually impossible for most of the kids ever to get out. The segregated schools there—Jerry, when we talk about separate and unequal, this is it. This is like something that dates back before the Plessy decision of a hundred years ago.

So what you have here right in the middle of the most sophisticated city in the United States, with the most enlightened literary and journalistic communities, is a segregation tighter and more effective than anything that was developed in the South.

Well, certainly almost as effective. It's hard to imagine any place in America that is more totally segregated and closed in than this neighborhood. A twelve-year-old boy, whose name was Jeremiah, said to me, "Where we live it feels locked down." I was struck by that because locked down is a prison term. He was referring to the fact that there's no safe place to play, that parents have to keep their kids indoors all the time. Typically mothers tell their children to go outside and play, but what they mean is to go into the corridor of the building. The real outside is too dangerous.

When I repeated his words, "It feels like we're locked down," to a teenager, she replied—I don't have the text in front of me. I'm giving all these quotes from memory—she said, "It isn't exactly as though we're in a prison. It's more as if we'd been put in a garage." She used that word, garage. "That's a place where, if you don't have room for something, but you're not sure if you should throw it out, you put it there so you won't have to think of it again."

So people living there are very conscious of their rejection by this society.

The little kids aren't, but after the age of ten or twelve, they certainly understand that they are being rejected by our society. It's obvious in their schools; they never see any white children. It's obvious in the hospitals; you almost never see a white patient there, and sometimes no white doctors, either. You see many doctors from other countries like Haiti, or from African countries. In fact, there's now a group of French doctors called "Doctors Without Borders," a group who actually set out to work in the Third World, that has come in to help the South Bronx.

So there is a sort of colonial feeling there, and it's colonial in at least one other respect too. The best newspaper in New York, *The New York Times*, is virtually impossible to buy in the South Bronx. They obviously don't feel that people who live in the South Bronx are the kind of people whom their advertisers want to reach. This came up once while talking to a woman in the neighborhood who's a very important figure in my book. Alice Washington is the name I give her; she's very savvy and sophisticated. In fact, she's the kind of woman who, if she weren't black and weren't poor and had grown up in a just society, probably would have gone to Radcliffe or Harvard.

Even though she's self-educated, she has good taste and likes to read *The Times*. But she tells me that she can't get it in her neighborhood. She noted that I live near the New Hampshire border in New England.

And they have a big stack of *New York Times* at my store every morning." So she said, "If they can get their paper all the way to where you live three hundred miles away, why can't they get it to the Bronx?"

Once I told her what a teenager had said to me: "If white folks were to wake up and read in the news that all those people in the ghetto were gone, or dead, or went away somewhere, I think they'd be ecstatic." I repeated these words to Mrs. Washington. I used to measure everything I heard against her judgment. She fills the role of a Greek chorus in some ways, although I know that sounds pretentious. Anyway, I asked her, "What do you think?" She thought for a while, and she said, "How old was this girl?" I told her, sixteen. She said, "I'm three times her age and I feel the same way."

Months later, she brought that up again. I kept going back to people because I wanted to make sure that what I had written reflected their deepest beliefs. So I went back months later and she said something like this: "Remember that time we were talking about what that teenager said, and I told you I thought they'd be glad if we were all dead? I thought it over and I changed my mind. I don't think they wish that we were dead. I think they wish that we were never born."

And that, I happen to think, is true. What do you do when you've got this huge population of people, mostly black and Latino, who were of great economic importance to America in the past, but who today, because of the way our economy has been transformed, have come to be regarded as superfluous? Why would any manufacturer in New York City hire a poor man in the South Bronx for five dollars an hour when he can get the same thing done for three dollars a day in the Third World?

So although my book doesn't focus on economics, that theme keeps coming up. You get the horrible feeling that you're dealing with a population that's regarded not just as superfluous in economic terms, but maybe in some other ways as well.

Can you make a distinction in our social policy between economically superfluous and humanly superfluous?

Well, a distinction can surely be made on religious grounds.

But in a country that has separated church and state, you can't invoke religion as a criteria in defining policy.

No, you can't, not legally, not constitutionally. But you can invoke human terms.

But do human terms enter into discussions at that level? I know they are part of the political conversation. I engaged in that myself when I was in New York City in 1992, running for President against Bill Clinton. We had an open discussion at Gracie Mansion in front of fifteen television cameras, The New York Times, The Washington Post, Newsday. *There was this big commitment made to an urban social agenda that was supposed to cost thirty-five billion dollars—a drop in the bucket in a six trillion dollar economy.*

But after that highly publicized meeting, the whole subject was only mentioned one more time, in The Los Angeles Times, *before the election. And between then and now, I don't believe it's ever been discussed, even though there were all sorts of lights and cameras and hoopla and excitement in April of 1992, staged for the New York Democratic primary. That was all about saving the city and how we have to do something. But what we have done is become complacent with the idea of redundant, surplus people. When we talk about issues, it's all about economics and getting people equipped for global competition. The implied premise is that if they're not needed for competition, they're not needed at all. We may want to invoke something human, but that "something human" has no place in the world we're in now, according to the people who run it.*

I think that's true. Economic considerations govern social policy throughout the United States, but most vividly for me in New York City. About five years ago, I was raising this question in Washington, and I happened to stop by and talk with a Congressman from California who's since retired, Gus Hawkins. Gus was an elderly man by then, an African-American, and he looked at me sympathetically as I was describing the men I see hanging on the corners in these ghetto neighborhoods all day. He just sighed and asked, "What do you do with a former slave when you no longer need his labor?"

That comment has echoed through my mind ever since, and I think of it in New York all the time. The answer to this question seems to be that you put him, and people like him, as far out of sight as possible so they won't ruin tourism downtown, so you won't see children begging in front of Saks Fifth Avenue, so they won't spoil the pretty sight of Rockefeller Center at Christmas time, and so they won't upset people when they go to St. Patrick's to pray on Christmas Eve. You shove them off into the most isolated, segregated section of the city, and you put into the same neighborhood anything that you don't want in your own neighborhood—a waste incinerator, a sewage plant, a prison barge. Then you cut back health care, you cut back educational programs. And when people explode every so often, you decide it's time to build another prison.

In 1976, Jimmy Carter went to Charlotte Street in the South Bronx and stood in front of one of these abandoned buildings and said he was going to do something about our neighborhoods. So you have this history going back more than two decades. But it looks like people have settled into the idea that they can't do anything about it. The idea among both Republicans and Democrats seems to be to cut back expenses and do nothing. Places like Mott Haven have become accepted, if they are thought about at all.

And what we see there is not going to stop with the South Bronx. It's going to spread, and is spreading, beyond the so-called ghettos, because the criteria has become competition. We have opened our borders for this competition. There's billions of people out there, and the dirty little secret is that a huge number of Americans are redundant and no longer needed in the social organization that is upheld by those who have their hands on the levers of management and control. I believe that's what is going on now in Washington. They're doing the only thing they know how to do, and that's try to make economic sense out of something that only can be understood in theological or human terms.

That's exactly right. Whenever I listen to the debates in Washington, whenever I'm up on Capitol Hill, or I turn on C-SPAN, the word I hear is efficiency. But what are they trying to do? They're trying to create a more efficient system of exclusion, or a more efficient system of containment. They are not talking about a system that would open up possibilities for these children. When they talk about the ghetto nowadays, nobody talks about abolishing it. They talk about a ghetto with more drug-free zones around the public schools. They talk about a site-based ghetto school—that's a very trendy term in education now. They talk about defensible ghetto parks, defensible meaning they put up iron bars around them and they don't let the drug users in.

All the terminology has to do with how to make a more attractive ghetto, a less costly ghetto, a more manageable ghetto, but the ghetto itself as a permanent cancer on the body of this country isn't questioned any longer. That's not even on the agenda.

If you look at what's happening in Congress, it looks like there will be less funding for the state of New York, less funding for the city of New York, less money for Medicaid, less money for food stamps, less money for educational attainment and scholarships, less, less, less. The rhetoric is somehow that under the lash of economic pressure, people at the bottom are going to finally figure out for themselves the American Dream.

The nightmarish quality of that argument is that it somehow presumes if you just cut back nutrition enough, and cut back health care enough, and make people miserable enough, it will magically transform the economy, and bring back the jobs from Singapore and Mexico and Haiti and wherever else. It all rests upon the myth that it's the behavioral problems of the poor that have created this problem.

The fact is, there are lots of behavior problems in a poor neighborhood. If you made me live in South Central L.A. for two years, I'm sure I'd have behavior problems, too. But the behavior of the people in the neighborhood did not design the American economy. They did not design the school system. They did not design the ghetto. And making those people more miserable is not going to reverse any of those problems.

The bill now on the verge of being accepted by Congress gives states the right to make all sorts of adjustments in the levels of subsistence that they grant to poor people. In the version that's probably going to be passed after compromise, states will be able to reduce basic subsistence as much as twenty-five percent. If you take away twenty-five percent of what the children now have in the South Bronx, you are going to see a very grim scenario. Let me give you one example.

The woman I mentioned before who's at the heart of my book, Alice Washington, she's forty-nine years old. She was in a monogamous marriage, but her husband was a drug-user and she is HIV-positive. When she is sick, she goes to the local hospital. If she goes to another neighborhood, she's told she has to go to the hospital in her own zone, so they enforce racial segregation in that manner.

She goes to the hospital in her zone, and typically she waits four to ten hours; it's sometimes two days before she even gets examined. So she sits in a crowded waiting area. The last time she went, when she had a high fever, she was kept four nights sitting in a waiting room. I'm sitting in her kitchen, which is where a lot of the book takes place, and I ask her, "Where were you waiting?" And she says, "In the waiting area with everybody else—old men coughing up their guts, little children vomiting, people with TB, other people with AIDS, people bleeding." After four nights, they finally found a bed for her, and they sent her upstairs. The bed in the room they sent her to was covered with blood. It hadn't been made because they were short of staff. They'd been laying off staff, and she had to go out in the hallway and find her own linen and make her own bed.

Now, that's the way it is. You cut back twenty-five percent of the resources in that neighborhood, and you aren't simply going to make things a little tougher for poor people, you're going to push many over the edge. At some point, I don't think you're going to be able to contain the suffering. It is going to explode out into the neighborhoods in which the rest of us still lead our relatively comfortable lives.

Don't forget, if it only took me eighteen minutes on the subway to go from the richest to the poorest neighborhood in New York City, it'll only take eighteen minutes for angry young people to go the opposite direction someday.

If you look at this morning's newspapers, you'll see that the possible cuts in aid are more like thirty percent in the fourth or fifth year. Obviously, they're going forward because the poor are powerless; they have no place in the middle- or upper-class reality where decisions get made. The perversity is that at the same time, the business section of The New York Times *today has a report on how the Dow keeps going up. It's hitting record levels all the time at the very moment that you have degradation literally within minutes of Wall Street.*

That's what is extraordinary to me. I keep reading in the paper, and I keep hearing on TV, that our cities are bankrupt. In New York, you hear it all the time. Whenever there's another slashing cut, the newspapers editorialize and wring their hands and say, "Well, of course, this is going to cause pain, and we wish we didn't have to do it. But there's no choice because there's just no money." Then I look at the downtown areas, and I see affluent people who are leading richer lives than they ever have. Friends of mine, college classmates, people who came up with me during the same generation, they're talking about buying a third home. They already have one in Vermont and one in New York, and now, perhaps, they're going to buy one in the islands or Southampton.

You know, Jonathan, I was listening to Hugh Sidey being interviewed on C-SPAN. He's probably the longest standing commentator for Time *maga-*

zine in Washington; he's covered nine presidents. Sidey suggested that the reason Colin Powell didn't run for President was because there was no crisis. He could discern no mission like the Gulf War, and now that things were pretty well settled and there was no great, historic challenge, there was no real need that he could fulfill.

Now that's an incredible statement after what you have said. I presume Hugh Sidey does not know about Mott Haven and he doesn't know about what's going on in the inner reaches of the city of Washington, D.C.. We're like Marie Antoinette. Our consciousness is so bemused and obscured by the novelty, the action, the apparent successes of modern progress, or we've become so numb because of our entertainment, or our own neuroses and isolation, that the crises of our time go absolutely untold in a way that can be heard.

I once asked Mrs. Washington if she thinks rich people in New York know what she goes through, or what the children in her neighborhood go through. She looked at me for a long time and then said, "They know, and they don't know." I think what she meant is that they know the facts, because they see the data in the paper every so often. But they don't know, because it's never portrayed with the intensity and with the cumulative vividness that will make it real.

I have to ask you a question on another matter. As I was preparing for our meeting today, someone referred to your book Savage Inequalities. *You wrote there about the Monsanto company and the thousands of pounds of toxic chemicals it was spilling somewhere in the Midwest that affected young children in a school that you were studying. I want you to comment on that because I'm wondering if it's related to what we're talking about.*

It's closely related. What it was is the following: There's a huge Monsanto plant on the southern edge of East St. Louis, Missouri on the Mississippi River. East St. Louis is the only all-black city in America and is said to be the most destitute city in the United States. I could believe that. I was informed when I was there in 1990 that the Monsanto plant was spewing toxins into the air that, along with toxins from a nearby chemical plant and sewage plant, have poisoned the air and the soil of East St. Louis to the point that it has one of the highest rates of child asthma in the United States, and all sorts of other child illnesses.

But the thing that's insidious is that the Monsanto plant is technically not in East St. Louis. It's in an adjacent town, a tiny town which has a population of some two hundred people. And so it's sort of a municipal subsection, created, it seems, as a tax dodge so that the companies that spill their poison into the air of East St. Louis can't be taxed to support the schools or hospitals of East St. Louis.

Now, in certain ways, except for the tax aspect, this business of dumping filth on the poorest of the poor is the same phenomenon that you see in New York City. The city, for example, some years ago, needed to figure out a way to get rid of all the sewage that comes out of its millions of toilets. So what did they do? They made an arrangement whereby toilets in the affluent midtown area of Manhattan and, I think, in Greenwich Village also, connect directly with a pipe that brings the sewage up to Harlem. The huge sewage plant is right in Harlem, and people used to say that it gives off a terrible stink.

As I said before, the medical waste goes to the South Bronx. They send the homeless to the South Bronx, too. They send both trash and people conceived as trash to the same place.

So what you have here is such an imbalance of power that powerlessness turns into invisibility. It's the same as a hundred years ago when the U.S. sent troops to Manila to kill 200,000 Filipinos and take over that country, or the wiping out of the Indians that were trying to hold the Black Hills as part of their ancestral right in accordance with a signed treaty. The victims were viewed as not entitled to the same empathy, concern or respect as the white or the powerful are entitled to. Here we are, with a feminist movement, a civil rights movement, a lot of awareness, and yet the same injustice is going on in as powerful a way as it did fifty and a hundred years ago.

There's only one thing that makes it different and, in a way, more in-sidious. Because all this is done through structural arrangements, sys-tematically, nobody—no individual that I know, and none of my white friends in New York—has to feel responsible. In other words, no one person that I talk to about my book, or any editors in New York who talked with me while I was writing it, have to look in the mirror and say, "I did this to those children. I don't like black kids so I dumped my sewage on them." Nobody feels that way because the wheels are all spin-ning now and it happens automatically.

So you have all these folks in Manhattan, many of whom regard themselves as mildly liberal or centrist politically, who voice fairly pleas-ant sentiments about poor children, contribute money to send poor kids to summer camp, or something like that, and feel benevolent. That's the thing that makes it insidious. We're not nazis; we're nice people. We read sophisticated books. We go to church. We go to synagogue. Meanwhile, we put other people's children into an economic and envi-ronmental death zone. We make it hard for them to get out. We strip the place bare of amenities. And we sit back and say to ourselves, "Well, I hope that they don't kill each other off. But if they do, it's not my fault."

It reminds me of a word Vaclav Havel used in his essay, "The Power of the Powerless." The word is "automatism." He's talking about the automa-tism of the state, of the bureaucracy, of the technology in a world that's on autopilot. That's precisely what you're describing here, and we're watch-ing it accelerate.

Ultimately, there are people who can get a hold of the process. There's somebody who goes to work on Wall Street. There are people who make decisions at the government level. There's you, there's me. We're individu-als, not a system. Somehow the evil must be ascribable and somebody has to be accountable. And yet as we try to find out who that is—Is it the Mayor? Is it Clinton? Is it you and me for not being as articulate as we should be?—the system is reaching a level where no one can give it loyalty, and that is the beginning of a breakdown that is too horrible to even articulate.

All right. I agree with you when you ask, "Is it this person, is it that person, or is it all of us?" Ultimately, it is all of us. I don't feel exempt from responsibility myself. But if I could just end this discussion on maybe a tiny note of hope.

One thing has surprised me since *Amazing Grace* was published. I've been touring the country, and I'm not surprised to find very warm receptions in places like Cambridge, Massachusetts, and Berkeley, and Oakland, and San Francisco. But I've also had remarkable surprises in some other sections of the country. I was talking to conservative Christians in Texas on what I believe was a Baptist radio network. I expected they would be hostile to me and would simply peg me as a northern liberal from the 1960s. Instead, when the host, who was a preacher, read passages from my book, he got choked up. He got upset.

Somebody called in who, as I now recall it, wasn't really hostile, but he complained that I had not suggested exactly what we should do. The pastor interrupted at that point and said—this is from my memory again, so I'm not certain of the words he used—but he said, basically, "We know already what to do because we read the Gospel."

I happen to be Jewish, Jerry, as you know, and I didn't know what he meant. So I asked, and this was, more or less, his answer: "There is an exchange like this in the Bible, when Simon Peter keeps asking Jesus, 'What are we supposed to do? What are our obligations? What do you ask of us?' Finally, Jesus answers Simon Peter, 'If you love me, feed my sheep'." I thought there was an elegant simplicity there that has been lost, and I keep repeating those words to people as I go across the country. 'Feed my sheep.'

The Plunder of Nature and Knowledge
Vandana Shiva

"It wasn't progress to make agriculture chemical-
based and based on heavy energy subsidies. It was
crude science. It was crude technology. We have paid
a heavy price for it, and we should stop being foolish
trying to perpetuate those models of sophistication."

*In February 1996, on the occasion of her appearance at the International
Forum on Globalization in Berkeley, California, I had an opportunity to
meet with Vandana Shiva, one of the world's most challenging thinkers on
the environment, women's rights and international economics. Ms. Shiva
is from India, and is a physicist, ecologist and activist. A recipient, in 1993,
of the Right Livelihood Award, known as the alternative Nobel Peace Prize,
she directs the Research Foundation for Science, Technology and Natural
Resource Policy, and is Associate Editor of* The Ecologist. *Ms. Shiva has
written several books, including the recent* Biopiracy: The Plunder of Nature and Knowledge.

*As I read your book, Vandana, I was struck by the chapter title "Piracy
Through Patents: The Second Coming of Columbus," and I thought of all
the discussion in the United States and other countries about the protection of something now known as intellectual property. Kind of ironic, isn't
it, that concern for intellectual property has so far outrun our concern for
human well-being?*

The very notion of intellectual property, Jerry, is not that old. Patents
are old. But to define a group of ideas and knowledge as a new form of

property, and then to extend that form to cover animals and cows and sheep and seeds and medicinal plants, as if they were products of the human mind, this is an absolutely new human condition.

Not enough is heard about the arrogance of these American corporations, who worry about piracy of Michael Jackson music by Chinese record companies while claiming patents on forms of life. One U.S. corporation, for example, has taken patents on neem, a tree which produces pesticides that my mother has used, my grandmother has used, everyone in Indian society has used. Entire medicinal plants, even our soils are being claimed, and the people who protest most about piracy of intellectual property are the ones most engaged in the piracy of the biological diversity of the Third World and the indigenous knowledge of societies like India. Most of this indigenous knowledge has been generated, maintained, reproduced and continued over millennia in the hands of women as the caretakers of knowledge. So it's piracy from Third World women by the largest corporate powers in the world.

When was this term "intellectual property" first used?

It has only come up in the 1980s. Before that the concern was "industrial property" because it was recognized that you can have invention and innovation around industrial artifacts, around machines, around tape recorders, around radios. This shift from "industrial property" to "intellectual property" has taken place just over the last decade, and it has happened so quickly and powerfully that it was central to the property rights discussions within the World Trade Organization and the Uruguay round of GATT.

GATT has a whole chapter called "Trade-Related Intellectual Property Rights," through which now the whole world must follow a very perverse system that is promoting of monopolies. It has absolutely no ethical limits and ethical boundaries and has no social obligations of any kind. Extremely responsible regimes and laws around patents, around copyrights, around trademarks are being dismantled, under threats from the United States, under a special clause in the trade act, and under new laws.

For example, there was a law passed in the U.S. last year, the Economic Espionage Act of 1996, by which any transfer of knowledge regarded as economic espionage will be treated as a threat to national security, requiring mobilization of federal investigation agencies. So we have reached a very, very crazy situation in which sharing what has been shared most in society—knowledge, seeds, genetic resources, biodiversity—has been turned into a crime. This sharing has always been the basis of human well-being and human prosperity.

Is this the concept of commodification that Karl Marx wrote about?

It's way beyond the commodification that Marx would have imagined. When Marx talked of commodification, the reality of the industrial revolution was that the capacity of capital and those who controlled capital was merely to extract the surplus labor of people acting in the now, in the present. So, I can exploit you if I have capital and you have labor, and take away your surplus labor and leave you just enough to survive so that you can keep working for me. Through intellectual property, on the other hand, particularly in living things, capital now has the ability to appropriate surplus from the future, surplus from the future of nature.

By making a claim on future evolution in nature—through reproduction of animals, and plants and seeds, as if this were happening because someone invented a cow, or a seed—capital has now gained the ability to collect rents, and incomes, and royalties on the basis of that. So that the farmer who has labored on the land, instead of being able to save and plant his or her seed every year, must pay rents and royalties to a handful of seed companies. To me, that is way beyond the appropriation of labor surplus in the present. It is the appropriation of surplus of nature and labor into the future, thus denying both humanity and nature their best potential.

Is there any nation that opposes this?

India did oppose the drafting of intellectual property rights into the World Trade Organization and into the GATT. As a result, it took four years for the United States to get this agenda on there, but I can tell you the Indian people are definitely not accepting it.

I've just come straight out of a very remote village in Kerala, which has been very much in the public eye because of this best-selling book, *The God of Small Things,* which takes place there. The villagers invited me to into their community because for over two years they have been documenting its biodiversity. They had a ceremony they wanted me to attend, in which they declared that their biodiversity is both their collective trust and covered by their collective right. They will never allow any of its products to be patented, and any characteristic shared by that collective heritage is not up for appropriation.

Of course, one village can't stop this process. But there is a growing movement in India, where people are saying exactly what Gandhi said when the British put a tax on salt that the people collected from the sea in order to pay for their colonial armies. Gandhi went to the beach and picked up the salt and said, "This has been given by nature for free. It is necessary for us, for our survival. You can not tax it. Such a law is unjust and deserves to be broken."

In the very same way, we have a very wide and vibrant seed *satyagraha* going in our country. Satyagraha is Gandhi's word for non-cooperation with unjust laws. Intellectual property rights proposals, ranging from patents on life forms to monopoly rights on seeds, have been brought again and again to the Indian Parliament through the pressure of the United States and the World Trade Organization, and again and again they have had to be withdrawn. Interestingly, the United States Agriculture Secretary came to India and threatened us last year and said you had better revise your laws to protect our corporations. Of course, the Indian people instantly mobilized and said, "No. India's laws are meant to protect Indian people, India's environment, India's legacy and

India's heritage, not just to protect the profits of a handful of corporations."

And yet, there's a certain amount of progress being made, is there not, in defending the intellectual property of developing countries against corporate appropriation?

It depends on what you call progress. The progress we really need is protection of the collected legacies of indigenous societies that have found that certain medicinal plants have certain healing properties. Indigenous societies have evolved seeds that can tolerate saline water, they have evolved seeds that can survive in drought. These are the legacies that need protection.

In my valley, for example, we have the best rice, and another valley near by has the best basmati—basmati, the word itself means the rice with an aroma, the rice with a perfume. The other day someone brought me basmati seeds to save because I run a program in India that conserves native seeds and seeds that have been evolved by farmers through very dynamic and innovative processes. What we are basically saying is, the farmers have innovated; they should have rights. Innovation doesn't begin when the agricultural corporations enter the scene of breeding. Innovation is there all the time, as long as human beings are interacting with the wealth that has been given to them by nature. Seeds don't just come to us from the land. They come through a core of evolution.

I can't say I'm very familiar with seeds or hybrid seeds and the growing corporate control of that part of life. Can you just sketch out what is the state of the case? How much food derives from seeds that are handed down by farmers, and how much is in the control of seed corporations?

In India, eighty percent of the seeds are farmer's seeds. They are seeds that have been evolved by farmers, saved by farmers, exchanged between farmers. Of the rest, fifteen percent comes from the public sector, which means universities, agriculture laboratories, the publicly-sponsored seed enterprise. The remaining five percent comes from the private seed industry. Most of this has traditionally been in vegetables and floriculture, but since the arrival of new economic policies of globalization and liberalization, the seed sector has been greatly opened up for foreign corporations.

Cargill, which is the biggest private corporation in the world, has a big control over agriculture, not only in the United States, but also over the rest of the world. Cargill came into India in 1988, and in 1992 tried to introduce hybrid sunflower seeds. The seeds failed. The farmers literally tore down the Cargill offices and the Cargill seed plant, first because they had been misled, and then because of Cargill's refusal to accept liability—to take responsibility for the failed crops and the failed seed.

Companies like Monsanto are also trying to enter India in a very big way. They, of course, look at India as a market. We're told that without these corporations we're going to have famine, but this is not at all true. Most of the research that these corporations are doing is focused on selling their seeds more effectively, and selling their chemicals more effectively. Herbicide resistant seeds will enable Monsanto to sell their Round-Up herbicide better. It will not produce more food for the hungry.

It is very interesting that even though in India we have tremendous resistance to the new monopolies, and farmers have said they will not allow them to take root and take crown, Round-Up resistant soy, a genetically-engineered soy bean, was planted with an agreement that I would call high-tech slavery. Monsanto says the farmers can't save seeds for three years after planting; seeds must be purchased each year. Monsanto has the right to investigate the farmer, to make sure they have not saved seeds. The farmer cannot use chemicals other than Monsanto's, and if the farmer is caught using other companies' chemicals, he will be dismissed from the program. Even the farmer's heirs are liable in this agreement, but Monsanto is totally free and we know that the cotton crop failed last year and Monsanto had no liability, no responsibility.

I see this as a new system of absolute rights with absolute irresponsibility that leaves no space for democracy and accountability. And given that this is all happening around food, the most vital need that human beings have, I think it is time for people who love freedom, people who love democracy, people who love justice, to turn to agriculture, to food and to intellectual property rights to see exactly how totalitarian regimes are being created in the name of progress.

In the U.S. would it be the reverse? Would ninety percent of the seeds come from corporations?

I think one hundred percent of the seeds. There are a few smaller sources—there's Seeds of Change, there's Heirloom Seeds. But they're not in industrial food crops. They're in vegetables and they protect garden varieties. They're not in agricultural crops that account for major production. They're really for home gardening and small scale cultivation for self-use.

So would you say that U.S. farmers are totally dependent on those corporations?

I would say the U.S. farmer is a slave to American agribusiness. Production has increased. Many more bushels are produced per acre because of the pesticides and hybrid varieties that the big seed companies make available. That's the short-term "benefit" of the process that you're describing. But the entire equation of agricultural production has been so artificially engineered that it's very difficult to figure out when more is really more, and when it is less.

Take for example the fact that the biggest producer of rice in the world is increasingly becoming the California desert, where there is no water. Rice is a crop that has evolved in high rain zones where there is plenty of water, and societies like India, Thailand, Japan, where rice has has evolved accordingly to the ecological advantages of the land, are now being rendered non-competitive because of a strange combination of subsidies.

I was just studying figures—the rice cultivation in California has a water subsidy in the amount of something like $980 per ton. Now if that cost were internalized into the cost of rice, this would not be an efficiently producing system. But you can't object to that under the rules of the World Trade Organization. The World Trade Organization does not have a system of taking into account such environmental subsidies. It's only direct financial subsidies that are taken into the audit of the World Trade Organization. In fact, if you were to ask me what drives free trade, I would say it is running on massive hidden subsidies that make non-competitive, unproductive enterprise look like competitive enterprise.

I'll give you another very simple example. Tomatoes to be grown for Pepsico were introduced into Punjab because the Green Revolution—which was this miracle revolution that was supposed to have done all kinds of good things for India—had collapsed. In fact, the violence and terrorism in Punjab was linked to the collapse of the Green Revolution and the declining economic situation of farmers; the younger farmers took up arms in an effort to form a separate state. Well, the tomatoes were being sold by the farmers to Pepsico for one rupee fifty, which is next to nothing. One can't even translate it into a fraction of a dollar. Pepsico, meantime, was getting seven rupees fifty for transporting those tomatoes. Now quite clearly with that kind of subsidy on transporting, a subsidy made by buying cheap from farmers, it's wonderfully efficient for Pepsico to grow tomatoes in Punjab. But if you were to build in all the real costs, all the environmental costs, all the social costs, this system would not be the miracle it has been made to look like.

Vandana, could you talk a litle more about this Green Revolution?

Everything I am saying is related to this issue of the Green Revolution. The Green Revolution was projected as a miracle savior of India from the famines that had afflicted the nation from the early 1900s up to the middle of the century. But it's very important to recognize why these famines took place. Famine in India occurred during British rule because food became a tradable commodity, not a basic item of meeting a human need under the control of the peasants and the farmers who were the producers. They had no control of what they grew because two-thirds of what they grew was just taken over as taxes by the British rulers. In 1942, for example, while two million Indians were dying, India exported more rice than ever before, because the British were at war and needed more and more deployment of food to sell all over the world on international markets and they did not care if Indians died.

There was no famine after 1942 in India. In 1965 there was a drought and a small scarcity. India had to import wheat that year. But the United States put a condition on these imports and said, "You have to change your agriculture system, then we'll send you the shipments." The condition was to introduce a "Green Revolution," chemical agriculture with new plant varieties called dwarf varieties, sometimes called miracle varieties. These crops were engineered to be shorter, not higher yielding. The native varieties were not low yielding—that's a myth that has been propagated and it is a total lie. We conserved the old varieties, and some of them out-performed the Green Revolution varieties even in terms of yield. And in terms of nutrition, of course, they are much better.

The Green Revolution was really designed to sell more chemicals. The dwarf varieties were necessary because local varieties are tall and slender and fall down when they have too much uptake of instantaneous chemicals rather than the slow absorption of nutrients from organic manure. That problem was solved by shortening the varieties, turning them into dwarfs so that they could take up more chemicals. That was the real issue. The Green Revolution was made to look like it was about hunger, but it was about selling chemicals. The new biotechnologies are being promoted in a similar way, as if they were about hunger, but they too are about selling chemicals and gaining more control and dependence of the farmers. Farmers are compelled to buy inputs from companies, and then sell back their production to the the same companies, leading to really a very, very sophisticated and complex form of slavery, but slavery all the same.

Lester Brown from the World Watch Institute has put together figures showing that the rate of increase in the world-wide production of wheat and rice is falling. He suggests that we are looking at serious food shortages, particularly as China switches to a more industrial base, upscales from a more vegetarian diet to meat, puts more cars on the road, and paves over their agricultural land. Do you have any thoughts on that?

I definitely think there are going to be food shortages, but not because we are unable to grow food in adequate quantities. We're going to have food shortages because we are putting trade higher than need. India has had food abundance, food security, without any problem at all. But last year India opened up its food markets under pressure from the World Trade Organization and the World Bank, and we're already having food scarcity. We increased our exports of food on the grounds that we had enough, and now our imports have doubled. By importing twice as much, we are spending scarce foreign exchange, and before we know it, our international debt is going to deepen and an economic crisis will continue to grow.

We must recognize, first of all, that rice and wheat are not the only foods that people eat and live on. Most people of the Third World, in fact, live on crops other than rice and wheat—crops such as millet, sorghum, pearl millet—some of which have been forgotten because of what I call racism in food. White crops, you know—rice that is white, flour that is white—have been made to look superior. Crops that are more nutritious but darker have been pushed out as primitive crops, as backward crops, as marginal crops, even though, if you were to look at nutrition per acre, they give us far more. I think we need a whole rethinking around that. These crops are also prudent in resources, using one one-hundredth of the water that irrigated rice uses. They could produce so much more in terms of the nutrition human beings need.

The second problem with the tapering off of productivity gains made during the Green Revolution, even in the false way in which they were measured, is related to the fact that chemical inputs are totally nonsustainable. You can't keep pumping fertilizers into soil because fertilizers don't improve soil fertility You can't keep spraying crops with pesticides because pesticides increase pests rather than control them. These are non-sustainable options of growing food. Sooner or later this thing has to run out.

Rather than looking for a deepening and acceleration of this direction of technological change in agriculture—more chemical dependence, more monocultures, more uniformity and more centralized control—what we should be looking for to increase productivity is what I call biodiversity intensification. Which would mean that we should intensify our natural biological production. We should intensify our use of organic manures, intensify pest control through biological means on the farm, intensify the diversity of what we grow on the farm.

All of that will start taking care of both the environmental problems and the uprooting of the small farmer from the land. It will create decentralized food production, more healthy food production and will therefore undo the kind of monopolistic concentration we see now, in which five companies control the world's trade in food. Five or six companies control all the patents and seeds. That kind of concentration is the biggest threat to food security, and is the biggest reason we are going to see food scarcities in the future.

To get to more local food sufficiency and more biological diversity, it strikes me that two things are going to occur. Number one, you're going to require more human labor in the production of food; and number two, you're going to have to reduce these massive food exports from the United States. Is that true?

Right now India is not importing much from the United States at all. In fact, for thirty years prior to last year, we had absolutely no food imports. But the World Trade Organization rules, which have been created by United States agribusiness, would like to see even more food imported. I don't think the world would be harmed if the United States stopped growing rice in California. I don't think the California desert was ever meant to be the bread basket of the world. It has better land uses and that's how it should be. It is not a loss to the world if the world is not dependent on United States companies for food production and food supply.

The most important issue, of course, is, yes, we will need more people in agriculture. But the measurement of productivity in agriculture as labor per unit was never more than a mechanism to get rid of labor in agriculture, to uproot the farmers, to leave less than one percent of the people on the land. We're reaching a stage globally where people being made dispensable, in my view, is the biggest social and economic crisis of our times—both because it's creating economic insecurity, but even more importantly, because it's creating people who don't have a dream of the future. They're not able to look hopefully into the future. I believe that biologically-diverse, intensive agriculture that makes room for people again is the biggest peace movement for society, creating societies that are at peace with themselves.

Last night I walked to the Oakland produce market, which is a few blocks from where I live. They start opening at about ten o'clock at night and these trucks pulling in are gigantic, vastly larger than they were thirty years ago. I saw one truck being unloaded and I looked at some tomatoes that came in from Sinaloa, Mexico. There was a whole bunch of produce stacked along the sidewalk there and I asked the driver, "Where did you come in from." He said, "I came in from Nogales." That's a long way from here.

I just have to think that such a huge truck—the driver said it cost about $150,000—certainly burned up a lot of oil, not to mention the tire dust being thrown out and we know that tire dust kills thousands each year in *the United States. That supply line, it strikes me, can't be a sustainable system.*

It's definitely not sustainable. India has just had a nine-day truckers' strike because of new taxes introduced on the trucking system. All the trucks went off the road. Nine days. If we had been living in a food system like the United States we would have had famine. We would have had riots. The reason nine days didn't hurt us is because in most places, people eat what is growing very close to their homes and therefore it doesn't matter if trucks aren't running.

A Danish Agricultural Minister gave me an interesting statistic. He said one kilogram of food shipped north, south, either way, either direction, contributes to ten kilograms of carbon dioxide. It reminds me of a wonderful statement by Gandhi. When someone said, "Don't you want India to be civilized and industrialized like the western world?" he answered, "One tiny island nation needed to enslave the entire planet to be able to run its industrial machine. Can you imagine how many planets an India imitating the British Isles would need?" And I think that is what we need to recognize—that the World Trade Organization is globalizing American agriculture. American agriculture is non-sustainable even for the United States. On a global level, it will just destroy societies. It will destroy the ecosystems and the biodiversity we have inherited.

Let me take up an issue that has to be at the center of this whole discussion. Many powerful people would treat this conversation as nonsense, and I believe the argument would go, "Well this sounds so primitive. This is another version of Rousseau and the noble savage." Gandhi himself didn't like railroads. Early in his career he rejected industrial textiles and mastered the spinning wheel. But I don't think we're going backwards to the way it was when there were a billion people on the plant, a hundred years ago, a hundred and fifty years ago. So where do we have progress, scientific utilization of knowledge, that is positive? In terms of survivability, in terms of elegance and power, where do science and technology fit in?

I was just reading *Time* magazine while coming over here, and it has this interesting two-page story about how everything that science taught about babies—putting them in a separate room and letting them cry to sleep, and so forth—all that is now being recognized as nonsense. Now, I never really believed it. I brought up my child exactly as my society has, with my baby sleeping next to me, feeding when he gets up in the night and everything worked fine. I think there are many similar areas where science and statistics are produced to prove things that, over time and with experience, are not true at all. It wasn't progress to shift from breast feeding to using baby food substitutes. It wasn't progress to bring up children the way we were told. It wasn't progress to make agriculture chemical-based and based on heavy energy subsidies. It was crude science. It was crude technology. We have paid a heavy price for it, and we should stop being foolish trying to perpetuate those models of sophistication. The power of your instruments is not the sophistication of your science. Sophistication of your science is how well you understand relationships within an ecosystem.

To me, the real progress in science, in food production, for instance, would be to understand fully the ecosystems in which you produce food, using their potential to the best while doing the least damage and, through that, maximizing output without wasting a lot of the resources.

I would use two yardsticks for general progress for human beings. The first is that people should be ecologically-oriented, enlightened in an ecological way, not reductionist, not fragmented, not blind to the relationships on which everything depends. And second, they should exercise democratic control. Technologies that are not under democratic control are made to look like improvements, but they are not so for people. Turning entire societies into automobile-dependent societies, for example, means that for the smallest need you have to get into a car and travel many miles, which means that society is, in fact, totally crippled. It's not a free society. It's a chained society.

In the same way, if people don't have flexibility in the way they grow food, and everything is controlled and timed in terms of where they will get chemical inputs and how they will use them, they can't use their freedom, they can't use their judgement. I basically see that as destructive. Democracy in the use of science and technology is a precondition to ensure that scientific changes actually protect nature and the interests of people.

Here in Washington, both the Republicans and Democrats are constantly singing the praises of NAFTA and the General Agreement on Trade and Tariffs. As for trade here in Oakland, we have a port with trains coming and going throughout day—130 cars at a time picking up containers that come off dozens of Chinese ships filled by people making thirty, maybe forty dollars a month. And this is this thing they call a global village with all these rules managing the flow of traffic. Now judging from everything we've been talking about, it sounds like your prescription is blow it all up! Get out of GATT! Let's get more local, reduce world trade, be more self-reliant.

I believe that the system will blow itself up. I don't think it can last. In fact you can see it blew up in Mexico with the collapse of the peso. It has blown up in place after place. The truckers' strike I was mentioning in India is a result of new international rules on the service sector that have crippled trade totally. And it's constantly feeding back negatively on itself. You get unstable governments. Right now I don't even know who is ruling India because the United Front Coalition has issued a withdrawal of confidence to the Congress Party. The global economic system creates unstable governments, it creates violence, and it also fosters fundamentalism. The rise of religious fundamentalism is intimately linked to the globalization of trade; as more and more people are dependent on fewer and fewer options, more and more people are made redundant. Redundant people, insecure people, turn to each other.

I'm thinking again of the truck driver I talked to at the produce market last night. He told me he was from Texas, and I said to him, "You know, very soon these trucks are going to be driven by cheaper workers from south of the border and you're going to be out of a job."

He understood that he was going to be hurt, eventually, by NAFTA. It hasn't happened yet, but it's pretty hard to stop the logic of that, isn't it? Why should a transport company pay somebody twelve or thirteen dollars an hour, when, by just going below the border a few miles. the business can save an enormous amount of money?

The world into which globalization was introduced was not a very equal world. We had tremendous north-south divisions. The divisions weren't always that deep, but over time affluence has grown in the northern countries, and poverty—which is closely linked to this growth of affluence—has increased in the countries of the Third World. Now instead of creating an adjustment so that the income gap is reduced, what globalization has done is maintain those inequalities and use them to the advantage of more affluent nations. This is a totally undemocratic way to deal with economic inequalities, between north and south, and between men and women.

More and more men in Third Word countries are now being put out of work because women can be hired at half the rate. More and more children are being drawn into the workforce for exactly the same reason. It takes twice the wage to hire the parents, so children are given the job. In India people are saying no to all of this in increasing numbers. The myth is that we're moving toward a free market system; the state wasn't efficient, so let's allow the market to work more efficiently. But it doesn't work! No! The free market is using the state—using it to deliver economic subsidies.

Intellectual property rights are one major subsidy, created by allowing corporations to make money out of what was free for people and came from the people in the first place. Another major subsidy in India that is being resisted and fought—and this movement is going to grow in the coming years—is that the state is asked by foreign companies to acquire land with state authority and force people off of it. The land is then handed over to these companies to build huge power plants and steel plants in the name of jobs, and growth and the free market. People are increasingly saying, "We will not move. We will not leave our homes. Why should we subsidize your profits with our product? Why should we be dispossessed?" People are saying that this is not freedom. Market freedom is not people's freedom. Our freedom is our ability to live where we belong; our ability to be engaged in fruitful ways and meaningful ways; to belong to cohesive and peaceful societies; to be able to look into the future and be linked to our past. And this movement of the people saying "No!" to globalization is, in fact, the face of India fifty years after gaining independence.

What is the role of the philosophy of Gandhi in this movement?

It is the most important philosophy in our times. Gandhi was not appreciated enough even in his own time except by the people who rose with him and were able to mobilize their energies to confront the armies of the British. But in my view there is no other philosophy that can get people out of our current crisis.

First of all, there is no other philosophy that empowers you and makes you fearless. And you need to be fearless in the face of authoritarianism. There is no other philosophy that enables people to carve out democratic spaces for action at a time when governments have been hijacked by lobbies of the corporate world; when governments no longer listen to people, but only listen to those who gave them kickbacks, to those to whom they owe a favor. And that is common to both the White House and in Delhi. There is no difference.

There is no other philosophy that makes us construct a good, satisfying, meaningful life with limited use of resources, without predatory behavior toward the environment and other people. In his writings Gandhi uses the word "enoughness." He says it very clearly. He says the world has enough for everyone's need, but not enough for even a few people's greed. I think Gandhi got it right. You need just one greedy person on this planet, just one. Just one corporation with a limitless appetite could tear this planet down.

A central element of Gandhi's philosophy is resistance and non-violent refusal to collaborate with unjust powers. Do you see direct action as part of the agenda for fundamental change?

Very, very much. I think there are three concepts in Gandhi's philosophy that are relevant, not just to India, but to every community that wants to reclaim democracy, wants to reclaim meaningful life. The first is self-rule; we should be governed by our own rules in our communities, then in our cities, then in our states, then federally, and then as a global village. You can't be a member of a global village if you have been denied membership in your own village. The second is a concept Gandhi popularized called *swadeshi,* to make the things you use and wear with your own skills, knowledge and local resources, and thus to minimize waste and increase the meaning and relevance of each person, so that each person has a place in society. The third was *satyagraha,* direct action in the form of non-violent resistance. In the struggles over intellectual property rights and patents on life, I believe not cooperating with this is the highest human duty of our time.

So you think people should disregard intellectual property restrictions, that the Chinese people should continue to make their Michael Jackson records, and not worry about it?

I am not worried about what happens to Michael Jackson's records. I wouldn't even make a commitment either way. I'm not committed to the right of the Chinese to copy, and I'm not committed to the right of the American company to prevent the Chinese from doing so. I am worried about what happens to biodiversity, to plants, to indigenous knowledge. I find it outrageous that human umbilical cord blood cells should have been patented, that cell lines of Panama and Papua New Guinea natives should have been patented, that neem should have been patented. These are not reflections of an evolved civilized society.

How about genetically-engineered tomatoes that are less subject to rot, and other genetic manipulations of food that we tend to associate with progress?

I believe that genetically-engineered food is totally unnecessary, both from a production standpoint and a consumption standpoint. First of all, the Monsanto tomatoes that were engineered to resist rot turned out to be a failure. And as far as the genetically-engineered soy bean that Monsanto is forcing upon Europe just now, I've been invited to many countries to help the fight against its proliferation—to Austria where there was a referendum against it earlier this month, to Sweden, to Finland, to Denmark. People do not want this food!

People do not treat the imposing of genetically-engineered food as an act of democracy. They believe they have a right to choose their own system of food production. Monsanto thinks it has a right to force genetic engineering upon unwilling consumers and to prevent people from knowing, through labeling, what they are eating. But the only way genetic engineering can be established as a dominant mode of food production is by ending democracy. The choice is really between genetic engineering and democracy. And I think people should decide. We must find avenues and ways to ensure that our choice is exercised in the means of food production.

The Politics of Friendship
Ivan Illich and Carl Mitcham

> "I believe that if something like a political life is to remain for us in this world of technology, then it begins with friendship. Therefore my task is to cultivate disciplined, self-denying, careful, tasteful friendships."

Although I have considered Ivan Illich a friend for many years, it continues to be a special privilege for me to talk with him, to learn about his latest projects and to share and test ideas. An opportunity to meet with Ivan and another friend, Carl Mitcham, came in the spring of 1996 in Los Angeles, shortly after the publication of the paperback edition of Illich's In the Vineyard of the Text: A Commentary to Hugh's Didascalicon.

I regard Ivan Illich, whose work offers insights into a wide range of social, political and philosophical issues, as one of the most important thinkers of the late twentieth century. He is the author of sixteen books, including Deschooling Society *and* Medical Nemesis, *two books that shook things up in the fields of education and medicine in the 1970s and early 1980s. Among his more recent writings are works on gender, spirituality, history and language. Carl Mitcham, who joined us for this conversation, is a Professor of Humanities at Pennsylvania State University, where Illich meets with fellow scholars for several months each year to explore and challenge accepted ideas. We did some of that here.*

Ivan, my first encounter with you was about twenty-five years ago, when I read Deschooling Society. *Can you reflect on what you were thinking about when you wrote it and how you might see that issue today? Because we're still struggling with schools; there's still a dependency on education*

professionals that seem to have control of how we learn or don't learn. I
wonder whether we have made any progress in creating a context where
people recognize that they are in charge of their own learning.

Illich: During the late 1960s, I gave a dozen different addresses to people
who were concerned with education and schooling, which I had looked
at as a historian. I posed the question, since when are people born needy?
In need, for instance, of education. Since when do we have to learn the
language we speak by being taught by somebody. I would stand in front
of a group and ask, "Who of you remembers who taught your child to
walk?" Among a hundred people, thirty would raise their hands, and I
would say, "I guarantee you are all graduates of education schools."

I wanted to find out where the idea came from, that in order to become educated, people have to be assembled in groups of not less than
fifteen, otherwise it's not a class, and not more than forty, otherwise
they are underprivileged; for not less than eight hundred hours per year,
otherwise they don't get enough, and not more than a 1,100 hours per
year, otherwise it's considered a prison; for successive four-year periods, supervised by somebody else who has undergone this same program for a longer time. How did it come about that such a crazy process
as schooling was considered necessary?

Then I realized that it was something like engineering people, that
our society doesn't only produce artifact objects, but it also produces
artifact people. And it doesn't do that by the content of the curriculum—by what we are taught—but rather by taking young people
through this ritual that makes them believe that learning happens as a
result of being taught; that learning can be measured and divided into
separate tasks; and that learning somehow increases a person's value.

The more expensive the schooling of a person, the more money he
or she will make in the course of life. This is in spite of the certainty,
from a social science point of view, that there's absolutely no relationship between curriculum content and what people actually do satisfac-
torily in life, for themselves or society. We have learned this from that

beautiful book by Ivar Berg, *Education and Jobs: The Great Training Robbery,* and at least thirty or forty other studies, all of which show the same thing. The curricular content has absolutely no effect on how people perform. The latent function of schooling—that is, the hidden curriculum which forms individuals into needy people who believe that schooling can satisfy their need for education—is much more important. That was the reason why I went into it.

So Deschooling Society *was based on the insight that the school industry teaches people to think that they have certain needs that the school itself alone can satisfy?*

Illich: It teaches people that they have needs. As a young man, not all people whom I knew had needs. We were hungry, for example, but we didn't translate our hunger into a need, a need for food. We were just hungry for a tortilla, for *comida*. The idea that people are inherently needy, that their needs can be translated into rights, and that these rights can be translated into entitlements—this is a development of the modern world. It's reasonable, it's acceptable, it's obvious only for people who have had their needs awakened or created by education, then satisfied, and who have then learned that they have less than others. In this way, schooling, which supposedly creates equal opportunities, has become a never-before-attempted way of dividing the society into classes. Everybody knows at what level of schooling he or she has dropped out, and, in addition, knows what price tag is attached to the education he or she has received. The development of this kind of education is a history of degrading the majority of people.

You take somebody who's poor, who doesn't have a lot of material goods, and you modernize their poverty by taking away the confidence and self-esteem that his parent or grandparent had.

Illich: And then we create a world for him in which he constantly needs help, a world in which people constantly must be taken by the hand and shown how to use a knife, or a coffee maker, or a word processor.

So basically we're getting a world that more and more makes people dependent, and the dependency isn't on nature or on friends, but on those who run the institutions.

Illich: I don't want to go that far in my paranoia. But I would say that, increasingly, people live surrounded by artifacts and become artifacts themselves, and feel satisfied insofar as they themselves have been manipulated to fit the artifacts around them. That is the reason why Carl and I, in our collaborations, concern ourselves with those things in the world today that function as determinants of the possibility of friendship, of people being really face-to-face with each other.

Usually the people who do the philosophy of artifacts, of technology, are concerned about what technology does to society. Inevitably modern technology has polarized society; it has polluted the environment; it has disabled very simple native abilities and made us dependent on objects.

Such as the automobile.

Illich: Yes. Which reduces the use value of your feet. An automobile makes much of the world inaccessible. It makes it unthinkable to use feet to get places. I recently said to somebody that I had walked down the spine of the Andes, which is true, and his response was, "You're a liar." Now, thousands of Spaniards in the sixteenth and seventeenth centuries did that. The idea that people could just walk! They can jog perhaps in the morning but they can't walk anywhere. The world has become inaccessible because we drive.

So the artifacts and institutions, such as a car or a school, change who we are.

Illich: Who you are and, even more deeply, they change the way your senses work. Traditionally, the gaze was conceived as a way of fingering, of touching. The ancient Greeks spoke about looking as a way of sending out the *psychopodia,* the soul's limbs, to touch another person's face and establish a relationship between two people. This relationship was called vision. After Galileo, at the time of Kepler, the idea developed that the eyes are receptors into which light comes from the outside, while people remain separate, even as they gaze at each other, even as they enjoy each other. People began to conceive of their eyes as some kind of *camera obscura.*

In our age, people conceive of their eyes, and actually use them, as if they were part of a machine. They speak about interface. Anybody who says to me, "I want to interface with you," I say, "Please go somewhere else, to a toilet or wherever you want, to a mirror." Anybody who says, "I want to communicate with you," I say, "Can't you talk? Can't you speak?"

Carl, were you going to jump in here?

Mitcham: The thing in Ivan's work that has been continually most challenging to me is the importance of artifacts, or objects, and how they influence the way we experience ourselves and relate to others. I've tried to reflect and think about the world in which I live, a world in which a hundred years ago, even fifty years ago when I was growing up, there was a predominance of natural objects around. Rocks, trees, animals, chickens. Even in the city there was a predominance of natural vegetation. That's all changed. We live in a world in which the artifice of our environment overwhelms the natural foundation or context of the past.

As Ivan has pointed out, that artifice is undergoing a fundamental transformation. We spend more time now in front of a screen of one kind or another than we used to spend face to face with other humans beings—either the screen of the television set, the screen of the computer, the screen of the little digital clock right here in front of us. When we're driving in a car the windshield becomes a kind of screen; the world becomes flattened to that screen.

Illich: It makes facing each other increasingly difficult because people can't detach themselves anymore from the idea that what we look at has been manipulated and programmed by somebody.

People have always been subject to domination in one form or another in society, but this seems to be an entirely new form of control.

Illich: Let's stop for a moment and consider that idea of domination. Until quite recently, in all cultures that we know of, what a person ought to do was determined by the idea that hierarchy is natural and inevitable. The human condition—whether in the tropics, or in a cold climate; in a highly sophisticated Greek *politea*, or in a twelfth-century monastery—was to suffer the obligations imposed by some kind of hierarchy which was unique to each place.

Now the two of us, Jerry, we haven't seen each other for a year now, and when we saw each other we bowed in front of each other. As I did so, I had this clear feeling of how deeply impressed I was by some of the things which I have recently read about you. You also had a similar bow, and perhaps you were feeling something similar. Consider the very idea of bowing. Bowing is impossible, or very difficult, for people who constantly see non-persons on a screen. I remember a child once telling me, "This evening I saw John Kennedy, and then President Bush, and then E.T." For goodness sake, I am nothing like what that child saw. I am somebody who wants to respect you, and perhaps to earn your respect in return. This has been deeply undermined. We are subject to a new kind of hierarchy, of manipulation.

Now in traditional society, where human was Adam and Eve, relationships between people were understood, like in music, as proportions. In music, you hear a quint, a fifth. You don't hear two sounds which combine to make a fifth, you hear a harmonious chord. This is what people all through history have enjoyed as beauty, as music, until Bach. And then from 1730 to 1890, modern music reflects a completely new view, which argues that you can make music out of separate tones which are artificially related, using logarithms. These tones are all slightly off proportion, but they provide the possibility of symphonic arrangements of international usage.

I'm really addicted to the horrible, impure noise which is modern music, but I know that it has nothing to do with traditional Gregorian or Greek music, where people didn't hear individual tones. They heard the relationship that lives between two sides of a chord. So translate this to friendship. The sense of proportionality, the sense that our friendship is not Jerry plus Ivan plus some interaction between us, as if we were two machines or two separate notes, but that it is a new reality which is beautiful in itself—that is the sense I would like to save. I can't do that in politics. I can't do that being manipulated at a screen. I can do that only when we get together over spaghetti and a glass of wine.

In your earlier period you were engaged in thinking and writing about medicine, education, tools, energy, transportation. Now you have stepped back to focus on friendship, on people around a table. Was it something that changed in you, or something that changed in the world that brought you to this new perspective?

Illich: I guess both. I am surrounded for the first time in my life by people older than twenty-five, who were born in the year, or shortly after the year, during which I experienced what they call in America a depression, lasting two weeks. I called it melancholia. I called it *acedia.*

One of the seven deadly sins. It's sometimes translated as sloth.

Illich: *Acedia* is the inactivity which results from a man seeing how enormously difficult it is to do the right thing. I had a very black period during which I learned what it means to have to move into a world of the technological shell, of which we spoke before.

Now I am surrounded by people born into that age. I can speak differently to these people than I could speak to people of the sixties. In 1968, when I made people aware of the horrors of sickening medicine, of stupefying education, of time-consuming acceleration of traffic, these were our main concerns. Today my main concern is to understand how technology has devastated the road from one person to another, which is friendship. I have not concluded that it is everyone's task to run out into the world to help others who are less privileged. Some people must do this, of course, but for me the real task is to remove from my own mind that screen which makes your face inaccessible to me, which removes the "thou" which you are. For without your gaze, your *pupilla*, my self is inaccessible to me.

Ivan, you called my attention to a letter written by Hugh of St. Victor, a monk who lived in the twelfth century who is the subject of the work you have just published, In the Vineyard of the Text. *I'd like to read it.*

> *"To my dear Brother Ranulph from Hugh, a sinner.*
> *Love never ends. When I first heard this I knew it was*
> *true. But now, Dearest Brother, I have the personal*
> *experience of fully knowing that love never ends. For I*
> *was a foreigner and met you in a strange land. But that*
> *land was not really strange for I found friends there."*

Illich: It's so beautiful.

> *"I don't know whether I first made friends or was made*
> *one. But I found love there and I loved it; and could not*
> *tire of it, for it was sweet to me, and I filled my heart*
> *with it, and was sad that my heart could hold so little. I*
> *could not take in all there was—but I took as much as I*
> *could. I filled up all the space I had, but I could not fit*

*in all I found. So I accepted what I could, and weighed
down with this precious gift, I did not feel any burden,
because my full heart sustained me. And now, having
made a long journey, I find my heart still warmed, and
none of the gift has been lost: for love never ends."*

Illich: Isn't that a marvelous little letter?

It's wonderful.

Illich: Today we would immediately say if a man wrote to a man like
that he must be gay. If he wrote to a woman, we would assume a marvelous sexual relationship. But do we need these alienating concepts? I want
to just go back to a great rabbinical and monastic Christian idea, which
developed out of what the Greeks, what Plato and Cicero, knew about
friendship. That it is the idea that from your eye, I find myself.

There's a little thing there, which I can see in your eye. They called
it *pupilla*, puppet. The black thing in your eye.

The pupil.

Illich: Pupil, puppet, person. It is not a mirror of me. It is you making
me the gift of that which Ivan is for you. That's the one who speaks when
I say, "I." I'm purposely not saying, that is my person, my ego. No. I'm
saying that is the one who answers you here, whom you have given to
him. This is how Hugh explains it. This is how the rabbinical tradition
explains it—that I cannot come to be fully human unless I have received
myself as a gift and accepted myself as a gift of somebody who has, well,
today we might say distorted me, in the way you distort me by loving
me.

Now, friendship in the Greek tradition, in the Roman tradition, in
the old tradition, was always viewed as the highest point that virtue can
reach—virtue meaning here the facility of doing the good thing—and

it was fostered by what the Greeks called *politea,* political life, community life. It was a political life in which I would not have liked to participate, with slavery, the exclusion of women, but they conceived of friendship as the supreme flowering of the interaction which happens in the *politea,* the good political society.

Today, I do not believe that friendship can flower out of political life. I believe that if something like a political life is to remain for us in this world of technology, then it begins with friendship. Therefore my task is to cultivate disciplined, self-denying, careful, tasteful friendships. Mutual friendships always—I and you and, I hope, a third person— out of which perhaps community can grow. Because perhaps here we can find what the good is.

To make it short, while once friendship in our western tradition was the supreme flower of politics, I think that if community life is to exist at all today, it is in some way the consequence of friendships cultivated by each of us. This is a challenge to the idea of democracy that goes beyond anything which people usually talk about.

So there was a time when the role of the democratic society was to create virtue and this virtue was the basis of friendship. Now it's reversed. Now we have to create friendship and in the context of friendship, we create virtue, which might lead to a community, and to a society which implements a whole other kind of politics.

Illich: Yes.

Would you say we understood each other?

Illich: We understood each other.

Mitcham: In some sense that's what you're trying to do, Jerry, at We The People. You've created a context in which what comes first is your friendship with people and the relations between the people in that community. Now out of that may grow some politics, but what visitors see and experience is primarily the hospitality of people there.

Illich: Here is the right word. Hospitality. This might be the starting point of politics: a practice of hospitality recovering the threshold, the door through which I can invite you, the table around which you can sit, and, when you get tired, the bed where you can sleep, and from there generating seedbeds for virtue and friendship on the one hand, and on the other, radiating out for the possible rebirth of community. But this is difficult because television, the Internet, newspapers—these have abolished the walls and the doorways, and therefore also friendship, the possibility of leading somebody through the door.

Let me ask you about the institutionalization of hospitality. You've written about the story of the good Samaritan, the good neighbor, which has been replaced by a world of needs, and rights, and institutions. Based on what we were just saying, can you say a little bit about what institutionalization does?

In my mind I identify it with this image of progress, which seems opposed to this reality that we're discussing of friendship, of love, of basing community on an immediate, unconstrained way of being together.

Illich: All right. Hospitality, that is, the readiness to accept somebody who is not from our hut, not from within our threshold, seems to be among the most universal characteristics that anthropologists can identify. But hospitality, wherever it has appeared, makes distinctions. For the Greeks, *xenia,* hospitality, distinguished between those who are Hellenes and those who are barbarians. *Xenia* primarily refers to Hellenes; it's a behavior which knows there is an outside and an inside. It is not for humans in general.

Then comes that most upsetting guy, Jesus of Nazareth, who, by speaking about something extraordinarily great and showing it by example, destroys something basic. When they ask him, "Who is my neighbor?" he tells a story about a Jew who has been beaten up in a robbery. First two Jews walk by the victim and don't notice him. Then a Palestinian walks by—a Samaritan is a Palestinian—sees the injured Jew, takes him into his own arms, and does what hospitality does not obligate him to. He treats him as a brother. This breaking of the limitations of hospitality, from a narrow group to the broadest possible group, might be taken as the key message of Christianity.

Then, in the fourth century, the Church was finally recognized. The bishops were made into something like magistrates. The first thing these new bishops do is create houses of hospitality, roofs and refuges for foreigners, institutionalizing what was given to each of us as a personal vocation by Jesus. Immediately, the great Christian thinkers of that time, John Chrysostom, for example, cry out, recognizing that if you institutionalize charity, if you make charity or hospitality into an act of a nonperson, of a community, Christians will cease to remain famous for always having an extra mattress, a crust of bread and a candle, for whoever might knock at their door.

For political reasons, the Church became, from that time on, a device for the state, enabling the state to prove it was Christian by paying the Church to care for, institutionally, a small fraction of those in need. The Church relieved the ordinary Christian of the most uncomfortable duty of having a door open for those who need help. This is what I speak about as the institutionalization of charity.

Now, I cannot imagine such a system being reformable, even though it might be your task, Jerry, and the task of others, to work at the reform of the service system and make the evils it carries with it as small as possible. What I have chosen, and Carl and other friends have chosen, as our task, is to awaken in people the sense of this Palestinian. I can choose. I have to choose. I have to decide who I will take into my arms, to whom I will lose myself, whom I will treat as that *vis-à-vis,* that face into which I will look and lovingly touch with my fingering gaze, from whom I will accept being who I am as a gift.

Mountains and Rivers Without End
Gary Snyder

"It may not be too late, in the city and in rural areas, for people to settle down and make cause with their own landscape and then make cause with their own neighbors, regardless of religion or color, because they share the land and the desire for reconstructing real society on North American land again."

Poet, political activist, teacher, naturalist and friend, Gary Snyder visited with me in December 1996, shortly after the publication of his collection of poems, Mountains and Rivers Without End. *The author of sixteen books of poetry and prose, his book* Turtle Island, *won the Pulitzer Prize for poetry in 1975. Gary served as Chairperson of the first California Arts Council, a position to which he was appointed during my term as Governor, and is now a Professor of English at the University of California at Davis.*

Gary, when I first met you I had just been elected Governor. It was 1975 and I remember it as a very exciting moment where the environmental movement was exploding. Here we are twenty-one years later. Are we making progress? Are we slipping back? I know we've added a lot of people to this planet.

When I think back on the range of ideas, the insights, the analyses, the body of facts that had been assembled in the environmental community at that time, I'm impressed by how extensive the movement was. The extent to which a picture of the future had formed in our imaginations, a lot of people's imaginations, and the range of issues that had been identified and blocked out—that is impressive. Various folks began to pick a territory and go to work. The other side of the story is that not a great deal has been accomplished, although I can talk about a few specific, small accomplishments, here and there.

In the early 1970s, you wrote a seminal piece called "The Four Changes," where you describe conditions and propose actions for population, pollution, consumption and transformation. What was the source of your inspiration? Was it from Rachel Carson, Buddhism, your own nature, direct contact, walking in the mountains?

I wrote "The Four Changes" in 1970 and it was first distributed in a kind of broadsheet that was passed out all over the United States. It also circulated through the underground press. Five years later, it was included in the back of my book, *Turtle Island.*

I had fallen into all of this from a very early age. I grew up working in the woods, working for the Forest Service seasonally, studying biology and botany in college, being an amateur naturalist from childhood on, and becoming a youthful conservationist starting at about seventeen. I joined the Wilderness Society and started writing letters to Congresspeople about logging issues in the Olympic National Forest and the North Cascades while I was living up in Puget Sound.

This came not from books, but from direct contact?

Yes, I grew up on a dairy farm near Puget Sound where huge, twelve-foot high stumps, overgrown with blackberry vines, were scattered through the woods. Eventually, I figured out that I was living in the remains of an old, ancient growth clearcut. I began to reconstruct environmental history in my mind and came to understand that only fifty years earlier there had been one of the world's largest forests where my father was dynamiting stumps and running cows. I was just beginning to put the picture together.

"The Four Changes" was about a different way of looking at the world—a departure from the model of nineteenth-century industrial progress, which was based on ideas such as expansion, growth and accumulation.

It was an attempt at laying out a program and drawing some meaning, some definitions as to modes of action, suggesting things that could be done, as of my poor little consciousness of 1969 and 1970.

The consciousness that runs the world, it seems, is still about unending growth. I saw a speech given by Alan Greenspan in which he commented that there might be a bit of overspeculation in the stock market. The market dropped about 140 points in the first hour of the following day. A stockbroker was asked about this and he said, "Well, Alan Greenspan is the Master of the Universe." I thought this was a rather ominous title, but it does reflect the central importance given to the money markets. These markets are all based on return on investment based on unending growth. Corporations, as an example, are premised on fifteen to twenty percent economic growth every year. Now that doesn't have a correlate in nature.

Absolutely not. The combination of our capitalist economy, the banking system and the way money is handled is, as you say, premised on ever expanding growth. Not to grow is, as they like to say, to stagnate, or to die. If you don't grow you die. That's a false ideology and one that, if pursued, will eventually destroy the biological wealth of the planet.

Now, is there a connection here between the biological perspective and the artistic perspective?

Art is the imagination, the imagination that plays with form, and the imagination is that part of consciousness which is wild. And so in its wilderness, that is to say, in its complexity, in its self-organizing and self-maintaining strength, its autonomy, the imagination shares the features of the wild, natural world. So yeah, art is wild.

DIALOGUES ≋ JERRY BROWN

Your essay "On The Path, Off The Trail" develops a few of these same ideas.

It plays with the first line of Lao-tzu's *Tao Te Ching:* "A path that can be followed is not the true path." There are many paths that we can follow. We can become accountants. We can become school teachers. We can become American citizens and stay on a path throughout our lives. The *Tao Te Ching* suggests that, although there's nothing wrong with these choices, the true path is a path that, to explore, you must move out of the ruts you're in. Staying on the conventional paths that you've become comfortable on, either as a human being, or an individual, or a whole society, will keep you going on the same track indefinitely.

Creativity and spirituality are learning to step aside, and when you get off the trail, what you get into is the rest of the world. You get the whole wild forest, which is rich and diverse and full of discoveries and actually not at all threatening.

I know that wilderness occupies a very special place in your sense of the world. I know that you have also spent many, many years in Japan. Isn't it the case that in Japan there isn't much wilderness left? What's been lost, what remains, and is there any comparison with our own country?

The Japanese economy and population have had an extraordinary impact on those islands. Up until a few centuries ago, they were remarkably complex and diverse with a rich array of mammals and fish, and thousands of bird species. It is still a remarkable and very beautiful place. Don't be mislead, however, by the term "wilderness." Wilderness is simply a place that has been left wild for a while, and has been self-organizing. It doesn't have to be pristine. It doesn't have to be virgin. Everything will become wilderness again, sooner or later. Nature's resilience and inevitability means that the universe is ultimately wild, just as we are surrounded by a vast wilderness called outer space.

And so what I look at is wild process at work—that which returns to wilderness. Japan, of course, is full of wild process. It's full of weeds. It's full of birds that manage to survive. And there are little patches of original hardwood forests, a few here and there. There are a few wild bears in the mountains north of Kyoto. There's lots of forested land in northern Japan—mostly conifers—which are part of the thriving timber economy. It's not pristine, it's not original forest. It's not even the original species. The conifers have replaced the original hardwoods. But it's still an extraordinary habitat. It's still quite beautiful, and eventually it will be wild, although they're doing a relatively intelligent, organized kind of small, mosaic clearcut logging on it constantly.

So with that in mind, how do you look at the fight to save the Headwaters—a spectacular 60,000 acres of ancient redwood groves in northern California—owned and logged by Pacific Lumber Company? How can citizens block any further incursion into these remaining groves, which provide a vital habitat for a number of threatened and endangered species?

In order to gain some perspective on the situation in North America, you have to spend some time traveling around Japan, China and India, as I have, with a naturalist's eye, to understand how thoroughly devastated the original ecology is. China was more or less completely deforested a thousand years ago, whereas Japan wasn't deforested until a century and a half ago, and Europe too. In the U.S. we still have some remarkable samples of these temperate jungles of huge conifers—Douglas firs, Sitka spruce, western hemlock, and small redwood patches—here on the west coast. The amount remaining is small. It's a treasure—a world-scale treasure. Why bother to log any more of it?

There are plenty of ways to get all the timber we need by intelligently, sustainably logging second growth, third growth, fourth growth, and on and on, for the next ten thousand years. We might as well keep our few remaining ancient growth forest stands.

So my heart goes out entirely to the defenders of the Headwaters, to the defenders of all the other ancient forest stands. There is no reason to take those trees except high-grading the profits because the profit margin in taking out a huge log is extraordinary. Pacific Lumber is just trying to maximize its profits, that's all they're looking at. Instead, they should be saying, "OK, we're going to have to scale down a little bit, but we'll make money in the long run anyway."

Does Pacific Lumber have a right to maximum profit, despite the irreparable ecological toll? After all, private property is relatively recent in terms of redwood history. What's at stake here, in principle, is much more than just redwood trees.

It's a tragic story how the Pacific Lumber Company's holdings fell into the hands of people like Charles Hurwitz. This particular case is so striking and so heartbreaking because the old Pacific Lumber Company had the makings of a long-range, family-operated, sustainable, redwood logging operation that could be a model for a careful, intelligent, but non-destructive redwood timber industry well into the future. The company fell into the hands of a guy who thinks like a barbarian and is willing to play his fantasies out in public. We can see the black and white of greed very clearly, and we can also see the Headwaters as a potential model fight for what is going on and will continue to go on in the tropical rain forests for the next fifty or sixty years, 'til they're gone.

When the Environmental Protection Agency recently suggested tighter air restrictions, their reasoning was based on the costs of associated health damage exceeding the cost of reducing toxic emissions. It's the same old paradigm, founded on a simplistic equation whereby the whole argument is expressed in quantitative economic terms. So when you look at the redwood trees, it's the underperforming asset that, when chopped up, starts to really perform. When we reframe this situation in the way that you're describing, we're really forced to reframe our whole outlook on life.

Well, you could even use economic arguments by making a cost-benefit analysis for the next two hundred years based on wealthy tourists coming to see the redwoods and paying for the amenities. Those redwoods would pay for themselves many times over.

Gary, on April 8, 1956 you started a book of poetry entitled Mountains and Rivers Without End, *which you completed forty years later. That's a long time. Could you describe the inspiration for this undertaking?*

My work as a seasonal lookout in the Forest Service took me up to mountain tops and kept me up there for weeks at a time. I encountered extraordinarily expansive space, marvelous mountain landscapes that I wouldn't have seen otherwise. In those days we didn't fly in planes all the time. So how do you get to see the world? You have to climb a mountain. And then I thought about the Chinese and Japanese brush paintings and how they too, in a way that occidental landscape painting never seemed to, caught the life of the mountains and the energy of water and mountains and clouds, the living energy of the landscapes, almost like a being.

With that in my mind and continuing to think about both nature and the Chinese painting tradition, I had this conversation with a marvelous Japanese painter, an abstract expressionist, Saburo Hasegawa. Alan Watts had invited Hasegawa to visit the United States. On April 8, 1956—the only reason I remember it was because it was the Buddha's birthday and I'm a passionately devotional Buddhist—Hasegawa told me, "Yes, you can do it, you can write a poem which does the same thing as a Chinese landscape scroll. Go ahead and try it." So, that day I said, "Mountains and rivers without end. I'll do it." I thought it would be done in five years, but found that it was going to take longer. I slowed down and relaxed and said, "However long it takes."

And on and off you've been working at it.

Averaged out about one poem a year for forty years.

Is there a poem from this book that you'd like to share?

Sure. One for the little known, but marvelously wild Tatshenshini River, one of the wildest rivers in the world. It comes out of the Yukon in Canada, goes through British Columbia, and cuts through the St. Elias mountain range, through the glaciers and ice fields, and then goes out into the Gulf of Alaska. It is the world of salmon, bear, ravens and glaciers. That was our world ten thousand years ago, at the end of the Ice Age. This is a poem about how we are all just little children of the Ice Age. Human beings, truly, are little ice age babies. We're just coming out of the Ice Age ourselves, still. Our bodies are shaped by it, shaped by that period of time.

RAVEN'S BEAK RIVER
AT THE END

Doab of the Tatshenshini River and the Alsek Lake, a long spit of gravel, one clear day after days on the river in the rain, the glowing sandy slopes of Castilleja blooms & little fox tracks in moose-print swales, & giant scoops of dirt took out by bears around the lupine roots, at early light a rim of snowy mountains and the ice fields slanting back for miles, I find my way

To the boulders
   on the gravel   in the flowers
At the end of the glacier
   two ravens
Sitting on a boulder
   carried by the glacier
Left on the gravel

resting in the flowers
At the end of the ice age
   show me the way
To a place to sit
   in a hollow on a boulder
Looking east, looking south
   ear in the river
Running just behind me
   nose in the grasses
Vetch roots scooped out
   by the bears in the gravels
Looking up the ice slopes
   ice planes, rock fall
Brush-line, dirt-sweeps
   on the ancient river
Blue queen floating in
   ice lake, ice throne, end of a glacier
Looking north
   up the dancing river
Where it turns into a glacier
   under stairsteps of ice falls
Green streaks of alder
   climb the mountain knuckles
Interlaced with snowfields
   foamy water falling
Salmon weaving river
   blue flower   blue sky singer
As the raven leaves her boulder
   flying over flowers
Raven-sitting high spot
   eyes on the snow peaks,
Nose on morning
   raindrops in the sunshine

Skin of sunlight
   skin of chilly gravel
Mind in mountains, mind of tumbling water,
   mind running rivers
Mind of sifting
   flowers in the gravels
At the end of the ice age
   we are the bears, we are the ravens,
We are the salmon
   in the gravel
At the end of an ice age
Growing on the gravels
   at the end of glacier
Flying off alone
   flying off alone
   flying off alone

Off alone

Thank you, that was wonderful. This experience that you have put to words is an experience not unfamiliar to people a thousand years ago?

Two hundred years ago.

In those two hundred years we have dramatically reinvented our world. A computer screen is not the world of a river and a bear and a gravel path.

But it need not be entirely in opposition either.

So how does someone respond to the world of television, cars, cellular phones and all the other contrived artifacts in our lives? Jean Baudrillard says that we have built a Disney World to conceal the fact that we are living in one. When the typical American family visits Disney World in Florida, or the Epcot Center, they think they have left reality behind, but Disney World is everywhere. The suburban world is clean, it's completely safe and totally predictable. It's a path that is absolutely crystalline in its limited clarity.

And so you step off that path. You meditate. When you just take a couple of deep breaths and turn towards your own consciousness, you find yourself in the wilderness area of the imagination.

You could do that on a space shuttle.

You could do that anywhere, but if you did that well enough, and regularly enough, you probably would not want to get into a space shuttle. It would seem too unimaginative.

That brings us to the whole question of where we are going as human beings. Where we're going is driven by something we've been calling progress and another thing called civilization. Now recently I read a book on the Holocaust that describes how progress and civilization actually alienate people from those aspects of a human being that constitute restraint, generosity and caring. According to the author, the Holocaust was not a product of civilization gone off the track; it was an extension of civilization, which, by definition, socializes individuals against their own state of nature, their true nature.

You could phrase this in a different way and say that civilization is the adversary of society. When civilizations concentrate power and wealth in the hands of a few, making the locus of power and wealth a metropolis, they marginalize everybody living on the land and working with their hands. These patterns of civilization alienate from the very beginning the conviviality, the autonomy, the natural democracy of small communities everywhere. And this is the history of history.

You once told me that archaeological excavations in China show a time when all dwellings in a community were equal, and then something changed, way back when, and you had one part of the excavated site showing a hierarchy and a movement towards civilization.

It's very clear in Chinese pre-history, during the Neolithic era—a long era, 9,000 years of relative affluence—that there were almost no tools or weapons for war, but only hunting weapons, and no signs of great class distinction. That was a convivial, creative society during the time when all of the technology on which civilization is based was developed—the domestication of animals, silk weaving, high-quality pottery, kilns and early iron work. This was a remarkably sophisticated period of stability without dominating classes.

Civilization seems to rise in China as a Mafioso-type protection racket in which taxes are extracted from the people and they are told they are being protected from some unknown enemy, and that is the beginning of the Chinese state.

One index of the civilization process is that in California, between 1980 and 1995, one new state college has been built while 8,000 teachers in higher education have lost their jobs. At the same time, fifteen new prisons have been constructed and 25,000 new guards have been hired. We are witnessing an incredible reallocation of commitments in California—and it's mirrored in most of the other states—toward greater coercive control as opposed to education and enlightenment. So are we kind of running downhill in this civilizing process?

You said it. It's appalling. But I have a frail little alternative vision, Jerry, which involves what I call bioregionalism and watershed consciousness. It's the idea that it may not be too late, both in the city and in rural areas, for people to start settling down and making cause with their own local landscape and then making cause with their own neighbors, regardless of religion or color, because they share the land and the desire for reconstructing real society on North American land again.

Could you explain that word "bioregionalism?"

It's just a way of talking about the jurisdictions in which we live, not as political entities, but as biological entities; to recognize that we live in a certain kind of plant zone, climate zone, in the watershed of a certain river system; that we share it not only with other people, but with fellow beings such as plants and animals. And then ask ourselves, "Can we make common cause within this jurisdiction in an intelligent way with our human and non-human neighbors?" By making an effort to stay put and be responsible to the place, rather than be quite so mobile as Americans generally are, we might begin to improve the quality of our civic life, our municipal life. We might even get more people turning out to vote because they have a stake in local elections as well as national elections.

It may be that you have to work hard in order to do this. I know in my own experience I do. You've got to make a choice to stay where you are, keep your kids in the school they're in, work with the neighbors that you've got, rather than take a job that will give you a jump in salary but move you to Houston. People have to make that choice sometimes. Make a choice for the place rather than for the career.

An enormous amount of effort and resources are used to reach beyond where we are. As a commonplace example, today I drove from Oakland to San Francisco to meet a friend. I drove a car made in the Midwest with parts from Japan. The gasoline probably came from Alaska or the Middle East. When I arived at his office there were three bottles of water that were shipped over from Italy. We're part of a web of stuff moving back and forth and people moving back and forth—this is modernity. Your mule along the road in Mexico is the opposite of where we're headed now.

I'm talking about postmodernity. Thoreau said, "I wanted to see what it was like to live deliberately so I moved to Walden." I know a whole lot of people around the United States who choose to live deliberately to some degree, not just for themselves, but for their families and for the sake of community. They might just be seen leading a mule alongside the road too, right here in California! And it may be that they have very nice water from their own spring or their own well so they don't have to buy it from Italy. And this is not a big deal.

What do you mean by the statement, "I want to live my life deliberately?"

The implication from Thoreau is that one wants to be aware of where the things that make life work come from. What is their cost—to you, to the world? To what degree can you eat vegetables and fruits grown by your neighbors instead of importing them over long distances? To what degree can you make your purchases from local merchants? And in so doing, encourage the fabric of a place and the fabric of a community. To do that in one community is to benefit other communities.

Now, is this a social idea, a spiritual idea, a political idea, an ecological idea, or all of these?

It's an ancient human idea. It's the way human beings live.

OK, but that was before we had fossil fuel.

Well, fossil fuel is a variety of slavery, that's all. How do you get extra energy to make things happen, things that you can't do with your own natural energy and that of your sons and daughters, friends and neighbors? How do you get extra energy? The old way to do it was to exploit people, oppress them or enslave them, and then you could build a pyramid. In the modern world, instead of using human energy slaves, we use fossil fuel as an energy slave to get more done than we could ordinarily get done. That's not necessarily bad, but it's out of proportion. And it's undeliberate in the sense that we lose track of understanding what our own natural powers are and what we can actually accomplish in our own existential beings.

So by giving up physical labor we lose something?

We lose our hands. We lose our biceps. We lose our eyes and ears.

Ivan Illich said that when the bishops condemned the condom, they missed the boat. They should have condemned the rubber on Mercedes Benz tires because tires frustrate the natural purpose of feet, which is to walk. But how do we distinguish between clarity and real human consciousness, on the one hand, and romance and nostalgia, simple harkening back to the good old days, on the other?

Let's not worry about that unnecessary and possibly false distinction. Let's explore it. Let's use the situation right in your own backyard. A few blocks away, the Port of Oakland and the City Council are preparing to sell a spectacular nine-acre waterfront plot to a developer.

Right now this land belongs to all the people. In that sense it is analogous to a wilderness area, to a grazing land, to a mushroom plot, to a berry field, to a salmon river, to a beautiful mountain that we all know, we all share, and that we all feel free to go to. Now what was it that destroyed the commons in England? It was the Enclosure Movement; the Enclosure Movement took away access to the natural wealth that had been built into English law from early times to favor the new industrialists and big land owners. Aren't we seeing that played out again right now, in Oakland and around the country?

The developer is going to buy the land for a ridiculously low price from the city and build a gated community with a moat. I saw an astounding phrase in the environmental impact report—"private open space." Right now, it's public open space but after the gate and the moat are set up, and the guards are hired, then it becomes private open space. It's an incredible transformation of the commons.

If you had enough people living here who felt comfortable and established, who had engaged with the place, who commonly walked over it, commonly went over to the estuary, and commonly looked at the weeds and the flowers and the birds, they would have a social and emotional and a community investment in that land. They would all be out fighting the city tomorrow. That's what happens when you get a bioregional, community watershed consciousness; people will fight because they live there and they know what they must protect.

So some things haven't changed, Gary, since we met in 1975. People still have the same opportunity, the same obligation to pick a territory and go to work.

Disconnection and the Death Penalty
Sister Helen Prejean

"I used to say, 'Oh, I don't want to get involved in politics.' It was just too complex for me. In my spiritual life I tried to hover above it, to pray for everybody without doing anything for anybody. I didn't make the connection between my faith and the love of God, and doing something to help people."

With the release of the film Dead Man Walking, *Sister Helen Prejean, the author of the book upon which it is based, emerged as an eloquent spokesperson for the inmates of Death Row in American prisons and those who have been impacted by them. A member of the Catholic order, Sisters of St. Joseph, Sister Helen works in the Louisiana state prison system, ministering not only to those awaiting execution, but also to their families and the families of their victims. The subjects of my conversation with her are crime, punishment, race, poverty, and how we as members of a society striving for justice form our ideas about the value of life and the delegation of power.*

Over the centuries, there has persisted the sense of an eye for an eye, and a tooth for a tooth, a belief in righteous vengeance, a primordial feeling that the killing of criminals will balance the scales of justice. Christian denominations have accepted capital punishment, and legislation expanding the death penalty to fifty additional criminal offenses has been enacted here in the U.S.. At the same time, Christian doctrine calls upon believers to forgive, to turn the other cheek, and in most European nations, the death penalty has been abolished.

We are faced with the question of the death penalty nearly every time we vote, either in specific crime-related measures, or by candidates promoting their stand for or against capital punishment. This question is noth-

ing less than a test of our humanity, of how we see ourselves and others, and how we define the role of the state.

Sister Helen, could describe for me the nature of your work. I've read Dead Man Walking *and seen the film, but perhaps what you actually do varies from that fictional account.*

My work is to accompany one person at a time on Death Row in Louisiana. I've been with three people who have been executed. I'm with a fifth person now who I've been visiting for six years. The fourth person that I accompanied got a life sentence. That's the only one I was with who came out of the death house alive. His sentence was overturned.

I also accompany the Death Row inmate's family. You know, that's a very important thing. There's an unseen victim's family in the death penalty, and that's the family of the one who's being executed. It's a terrible stigma to have someone on Death Row in your family, a terrible suffering. One time, the sister of a man on death row in Louisiana left the state. She went to work in Texas and wouldn't tell anybody that she had a brother on Death Row. So accompanying inmates and their families is an important part of what I do.

Then I work with murder victims' families. It's been interesting, since the film, *Dead Man Walking*, the number of victim's families that have contacted me. *Dead Man Walking* may be the first time that the dignity and suffering of murder victims' families were portrayed. Now the film, as you know, doesn't preach at you and it doesn't moralize at you and say, "If somebody in your family has been murdered you should oppose the death penalty." It just presents victims' families in two sets of characters—the Percy family and Delacroix's family. You see them dealing with terrible, terrible blows. Their loved one has been murdered.

In one of the families they're for vengeance; they can't wait to see the guy die. They see the guy die, and afterwards, they're glad they saw the guy die. They claim they got closure from it. In the other family, you see Delacroix and his wife split up. A lot of people go through divorce when they lose a child, especially by violence. People have different ways of dealing with grief. One wants to keep the child's clothes, one wants to give them away. It's just a terrible thing. So the vengeance just didn't cut it for Delacroix. He's trying to get out from under this rock; trying to find the healing; trying to find a way that the hatred really doesn't consume him. It's self-interest in a way. He just doesn't want hatred to eat him alive.

So I work with murder victims' families in a limited way. Probably what I do best is to help groups get started where those who have lost loved ones can help each other. For example there was a woman in New Orleans who lost her daughter two years ago—she was murdered. I'm supporting her and helping her to start a group of Parents of Murdered Children.

In a more general way, I do a lot of speaking. I'll probably have forty-five speaking engagements across the United States and a couple in Europe this year. I'm glad to do this because when I speak to groups, I don't lecture at them. I just say, "Look, let me tell you what happened to me. Let me tell you this story." It's the way I wrote the book. I tell people a story and bring them with me into an experience. Because after ten years of doing this, of talking to groups in church basements and universities all across this country, the one thing I know is that while people may have a lot of feelings about the death penalty, they actually have very little real information about the death penalty and how it works.

So when I go to talk to people, I tell them stories and I bring them over to both sides so that they can really see and weigh the moral questions. And then I tell them general information I know they don't know, such as how selective the death penalty is. You know, there are 20,000 people killed in this country every year, and less than one percent of those convicted of murder are going to be selected for death. How did we come to that? Is the death penalty really the punishment for people who commit murder, or is it a very selective process? And what's at work?

I've found audiences very moved. First of all, because they confront a Death Row inmate as a human being. You see, you can do anything to anybody if you first dehumanize them and say, "These are not human beings like us. These are monsters. They've done a terrible crime." If you can bring them close to people, it personalizes them, and they have to be respected as fellow human beings.

I imagine that among the people on Death Row, some are better people and others are worse. The same is true of homicides. Some seem almost understandable; others seem inconceivably horrible. As you get to know people who have done these acts, what do you find? Is killing something very ordinary to them? Do they change over time? What can you say about them?

Let me tell you a few stories, little short profiles of people I've met on Death Row, and then I'll tell you what they did. Here's a man who was a poet. He would go out for his hour in the prison yard and he would look at a little purple flower for an hour. He would write beautiful poetry. He was a beautiful human being. He was very handsome. Everybody liked him. I found out that he had killed an old couple. He robbed them, and he killed them in cold blood. Sometimes when he was alone in his cell, he would cut his wrist, or he would cut his arm, and he would watch the blood. And the other Death Row inmates would say, "Man, you're crazy! You're cutting yourself." And he would say, "There's this thing about blood."

Now, how do you begin to describe what is going on here in this human being? When he is incarcerated and he's put in a cell, he reads books, he gets along with everybody. He obviously was not violent to-ward other people—although he would cut himself—and everybody liked him. When it came time to execute him, everybody, including the guards, felt bad.

Here's another man on Death Row in Louisiana. He's an African-American man. He has the most gentle voice. You start talking to him—

he's very concerned about his grandmother. He writes to his grand-mother. He asks me sometimes, can I call her. He writes tender letters, feeling letters. He signs his name in parentheses. He seems to have no sense of his selfhood or his dignity. He regrets. He talks in every letter about what he did. It was such a crazy thing to do; he regrets it. He wishes he could go to the victims and apologize to them. He went into a conve-nience store with a gun, shot and killed one person, and tried to kill another. He was exploding with rage. He had had some kind of altera-tion with his girlfriend, and he went into this store and he blew off his rage. He killed people. They came in front of his gun site.

Another man I visit now has gotten a life sentence. He killed two teenage kids. The thing is he grew up very, very poor and he had this thing about dignity. If people ever tried to put him down, it would fill him with rage. He abducted these teenage kids. He had abducted other teenage kids but then let 'em go, kind of like it was a scary thing. He would rape girls or threaten girls for sex, but he had never killed any-body. But this particular night, with this particular teenage couple, the boy at one point said to him, "Put down that gun and I'll show you who's a man." It triggered all that had been in his past, all about being poor, all about not having dignity. When he himself described what he did, he said "I did a terrible thing. I killed them. The gun was in my hand." It was a volatile moment where the gun was in his hands and he killed two people.

I tell you these stories not to excuse people and say, "Oh, well, if you're really in a rage, or you had a poor childhood, or whatever, it's okay to take a gun and blow somebody away." I'm trying to say that violence gets triggered in people sometimes seemingly for the most trivial causes. And guns make it very easy.

But when people are in these cells, and you begin to meet them, my experience has always been that you find in them aspects of humanness that everybody has. They are more than this one deed that they did. And you try then to put that together with the unbelievable misery and sorrow they have plunged people into by the killing of a human being.

It's an impossible mystery to try to plumb. It's like climbing down a cliff and your foot starts swinging over the abyss. There is no way to plumb it; no way to understand it. Except the pattern has been that most often the people I've met on Death Row didn't seek to murder, they didn't premeditate and plan to go out and kill somebody. Almost always, they were in a situation where they lost control.

It seems that in the United States there are more and more people who lose control or develop homicidal patterns of behavior, far more than in Europe and other places that have a similar pattern of economic development. Something's going on here.

Violence is woven into the fabric of this country from its beginnings. Violence is part of who we are as American people; its the way that we settle things. There's a very interesting book called *Violence: Reflections on a National Epidemic.* It was written by James Gilligan, a psychiatrist who interviewed hundreds and hundreds of people in prison who had done terribly violent acts. So as a psychiatrist, he's trying to figure this out. He found sometimes that inmates had committed these acts over the most trivial things. "Man, he looked at me wrong." "Man, he shoved me." Or, as in the case that I just described, somebody said, "Put that gun down and I'll show you who's a man."

Gilligan concluded that it was shame, that people are ashamed, that they don't have dignity, and it erupts in violence because they don't have any other way, or feel they have any other way, to deal with the indignity that's heaped upon them. This book goes on to show how poverty kills people, how it kills many, many more people than guns and violence—the violence you can see. Poverty is the greatest epidemic. People die from lack of health care. People die all different kinds of ways because of poverty. But the trigger that he associated with violence was that people feel their dignity is assaulted and they explode.

Sister Helen, there's so much violence around the world, so much killing connected to governments, to our own government, that it seems like human nature tolerates it. It's as if the outrage we feel as a society at people being murdered is a very selective reaction.

It's very selective. What I've found is that people only get upset over certain murders. That's one of the reasons the death penalty can never be fair. The arbitrariness and capriciousness that the Supreme Court found in 1972 when they overturned it is just as true today as it was then. Twenty thousand homicides, but less than a hundred murderers are going to get the death penalty.

What's operative here? One of the things to start with is, who got killed? This is where the selectivity comes in. I found that—overwhelmingly—when white people get killed, the death penalty is sought far more often than when people of color are killed. And when people of "status" in the community are killed, a professor in a law school, for example, as opposed to some homeless person, the killer gets the death penalty. In talking to many, many people, I've found that they will feel rage over a death when it's somebody like themselves that gets killed. But when somebody gets killed that they can't identify with, they don't feel anything at all.

That brings us right into the D.A.'s offices. District Attorneys, as you know, have great discretion as to what charges they will file. So they will consider, is this one of those "status" murders, or is this just another one of those inner city kids shooting another kid? Should I plea bargain this, or maybe not even prosecute the case vigorously at all? But when a young kid gets killed in a suburb, the D.A. is on TV the next day saying they will seek the death penalty.

If you look just in recent times, for example, at Bosnia, where the Serbs killed many thousands of Moslem men without remorse; or at the Kurdish part of Iraq, where one faction is celebrating because Saddam Hussein has killed several hundred of the opposing faction's leadership; or at the U.S., who sent cruise missiles to kill a half dozen people to get back at Saddam—

how do you react to that? It seems pretty hard to just say, "Thou shalt not kill," even though that's what Moses brought down from the mountain.

What we have here is a whole woven fabric of all different kinds of violence of people toward each other. And God, I mean, I don't begin to know what to do about that. It's just so overwhelming, the violence in the world. Maybe we step back and say, "Okay, we can't do too much about what's happening with the Kurds, but we should try to do all that we can to create peace closer to home."

But then look at the way we treat people in this country! We have given the government our blessing to take people and put them in cells and torture and kill them. We endorse the use of violence on our own citizens in peace time, and let the government have control over human life. Now, we have to be pretty scared, in this age of taking power away from government, when we turn over to them the power of life and death, saying, "When it comes to the criminals, you can have all the power you want."

There are definite conditions that foster this violence, conditions that vary from place to place. The South has historically had a high murder rate, as have urban areas in almost all parts of the county.

One factor—I can't explain all of them—is people who live in poverty and have no way out and no hope of the great American Dream. They're living dead-end lives with no hope of being able to get in on the Dream, and as a result, they live on the edge. Work isn't even the way out of poverty for them. One out of five full-time working people making minimum wage are still living in poverty. Poverty with no way out and a dead-end life drives you to drugs and to violence. Drugs become a sub-economy, and then violence escalates.

In New Orleans, I go to Hope House in the St. Thomas projects every Monday to keep close to the people there. Everybody there has guns. Everybody! And on any given day in New Orleans, we have ten-to twenty-thousand truant kids from the public schools, which we have allowed to deteriorate. The community leaders send their kids to private schools, so public schools have been going to Hell in a handbasket for twenty-five years.

Do you think the people who are in leadership positions—the heads of the universities, the heads of the city government, the heads of churches, the heads of the newspapers, the bankers—do they really give a damn?

Not if it doesn't touch what they consider "people like us." Poor kids have been dying in New Orleans for years, not only kids shot with guns, but also kids who die from lack of health care. And you know what kills them, Jerry? It's separation. It's because we're not connected. Most people do not give a damn about those people. When they get connected with them, and meet them, and experience their sorrow and their entrapment, then they begin to give a damn. But we live in great isolation.

And then, of course, who feeds everybody the knowledge of what's going on in their city? We may have fifty million peaceful negotiations and transactions between people in the city of New Orleans on any given day. No matter. What are you going to get on the evening news? Who got raped. Who got mugged. Who got killed. And so it begins to grow in people's minds that the United States is a very, very violent place. It gets exaggerated in people's minds. And then people who live in the suburbs and are not in "the most dangerous parts of the city," even some of our own sisters, get scared to leave their own neighborhood.

They've done studies. The more people look at television, the more afraid they are. Now, real stuff's going on; violent things are happening. But television and media definitely play a part in exaggerating them in people's minds. And who most often is shown with handcuffs on? People of color. So people just get an outrageous fear of people of color, and when they go to the department store, they're afraid there's a black person lurking somewhere ready to shoot them and mug them and rape them and kill them.

Tell me something about Hope House. This is in a housing project?

Yes. St. Thomas is one of the housing projects in New Orleans, one of ten. Most of the residents there are mothers and kids.

When you say Hope House, what is the hope? Is there a vitality and a vibrancy there that we maybe don't appreciate, or is there despair?

First, I want to say that the only way you will find the answer to that question is by going to see for yourself. You can hear me talk about it, but I encourage everyone who is scared to death of poor people to find these places—a Hope House, a community center, a drop-in center for the homeless, a soup kitchen—and go there. That's what I did in 1981. It took me a long time to realize the connection between the social justice of the Gospel, and the Jesus I believed in and prayed to and tried to follow. It took me a long time to wake up.

Sister Lory Shaff began Hope House in 1969. She and another sister just went and started living among the people in the St. Thomas housing project. She didn't have a blueprint in her pocket. She didn't know how to bulldoze away poverty or crime. But she began to live with the people and accompany them. What came out of it is a literacy program. What came out of it is an adult learning center where people who have basic literacy can get their GED. What came out of it is transitional housing for the homeless. We have programs where families who've been on the street can have a home for six months, and get help with their budget and finding a job, so that they can get back on their feet and go back into the mainstream.

It's working. People are doing it. We have a lawyer from Harlem who got his law degree and came here. He's giving legal help to individuals and organizations in the neighborhood. Community organizations are getting stronger, tenant organizations have gotten stronger. They have a program of helping teenage girls and educating them about sex so that they don't get pregnant. They started a program to educate people about AIDS. All this is going on in the community among the people. We are there—sisters and brothers and people who care—but the people are doing it for themselves. People just trying to make it in Louisiana. A single mother with a child there only gets $128 a month.

So how can two people live on $128 and $130 worth of food stamps?

And you've got to make it for a month. So one of the things that Hope House does is provide a cushion for people. If they can't pay their electric light bill, for example, we'll help.

I came to Hope House right as Reagan took office, in 1981. You could see the changes happening. The mentality changed, as if all these poor people had too much. Instead of paying one quarter of the pitiful amount they got from AFDC for rent, Reagan said they needed to pay a third of it for rent. So you get that $128, you put forty or fifty of it into the rent.

So what do they do? It's impossible to live on that.

They help each other out. And sometimes, people go and get what they call a day job, cleaning somebody's house.

And they're able to keep that income without reporting it.

No, no, no! If they are caught doing that, they're welfare cheats. That twenty dollars is supposed to be subtracted from that $128.

So how do you feel when you watch these people on some of the national shows and among the political leadership debating welfare? What's your reaction?

I'm filled with both sadness and rage at the same time, and then I feel like what can I do? I've got to do more. I've got to help educate people

about this because they've been persuaded to believe that the big problems in our country are the welfare recipients and immigrants. My God,
I mean, how long is it going to take people to wake up? Corporate greed
and downsizing is what's eating us alive and taking away people's jobs.

*Do you see any evidence of stirrings at the grassroots level, of any kind of
new consciousness or shared perspective that might be the basis of a more
enlightened social-political movement?*

Yes, I really do. Look at the change in attitude that has happened in this
country across the board on the environment. We've got a long, long,
long way to go, but in general, people are more aware of the environment than ever before. I think people are also more aware today that
we've got other serious problems in this country that we have to deal
with. I see it at local levels. For the most part, churches are still asleep,
but I have seen in the Catholic faith a movement and a stirring of people
who have begun to get involved.

I'm an example of that. I used to say, "Oh, I don't want to get involved in politics." It was just too complex for me. In my spiritual life I
tried to hover above it, to pray for everybody without doing anything
for anybody. I didn't make the connection between my faith and the
love of God, and doing something to help people. But now in the Catholic Church, I see people who are becoming more politically conscious,
who realize that there's a connection between loving God and knowing
God, and the economics of poverty, and health care, and social justice,
and the death penalty.

*Well, we've got to fan those flames a bit. Now, Sister Helen, let's take a
look at incarceration. It wasn't long ago, maybe twenty years, that there
were a million fewer people behind bars in the U.S. than there are today.
With the increase in prison capacity that our leaders boast of, this country
is embarking upon an experiment in incarceration that has never been
tried outside a totalitarian regime. What are your thoughts on this?*

In the U.S., we incarcerate over 1.3 million people, more than any country in the world except Russia. One in every three African-American young men is part of our criminal justice system, either in jail, on parole, or on probation, and more are put in jail than go to college. If we heard of another country like that—that they had to lock up one third of the vital, powerful, masculine power of the tribe, the village, the society, the country—you'd have to say that they have a police state.

To have a percentage of a population reaching that level is staggering in its message of absolute oppression, disconnection. There's something so wrong and yet the response as far I can tell, is to do more of the same in some vain hope it's going to turn things around.

Just listen to the racism that permeates the political rhetoric. Welfare recipient is a code word for black person. Consider the fact that *The Bell Curve* could be published, and that people could seriously consider that black people, *per se,* are not as intelligent as white people, that people could even have a conversation about that.

I think of Martin Luther King, Jr. He wrote this book called *Where Do We Go From Here? From Chaos to Community.* And he said that when a group is oppressed, there's usually an economic reason—slavery, for example. Slaves were needed for the cotton industry. But to justify the economics, you find a transcendental reason. The next thing you know, you've got people quoting the Bible to show that black people are inferior. Then you find a scientific reason to justify the oppression, so books come out, such as *The Bell Curve,* that claim black people are deficient intellectually. You start to get scientific and religious explanations to justify what you're doing for economic reasons.

That's what is going on. And again, it's because people are not connected. How many white people have black friends, or have supper with black people, or know black people, or move socially with black people? The white suburbs are ninety-eight percent white people. There's very little interaction. Martin Luther King used to say that the most segregated hour of the week was Sunday morning, when people were in church.

So what you're saying is that ours is a profoundly divided society, and unless a new Martin Luther King, Jr. emerges, or somebody falls off their horse and is struck by God with a new illumination, all signals are go in the wrong direction.

And when the racial violence breaks out, who should be surprised? You can get really overwhelmed when you start having these discussions, and it looks so bleak and so despairing, you say "My God, what can we do?" We don't expect to get another Martin Luther King, Jr.

Give me some hope here, will you, Sister?

We can't wait for a Martin Luther King, Jr. We've got to each be Martin Luther King, Jr. in little ways. The English novelist E. M. Forester said, "Only connect." Only connect. So whoever asks me for hope, I tell them to think of the circle of people that they spend their life with—who they go to meals with, who they go to movies with, who they're engaged with. I ask them to build a bridge to people that they don't normally associate with, people who are of a different class, of a different color. Maybe through their church, maybe through educational institutions.

Maybe people can start to have a breakfast once a month where they pull together people from different backgrounds—gay and straight, black and white, poor and wealthy. If we could start having connecting breakfasts around this country, and people could get to know each other and meet each other, we would change the soil and the climate for what we need to plant and grow in this country.

And this has got to start where people are, where you are, where I am. It's not going to come from the top. It's going to come from the streets and neighborhoods, and one never knows what the spark is that moves great numbers of people to make things like this happen.

That's right. But we do know this: that when we're separated, when we're isolated, when our only images of each other come through the media and the politicians, it separates and divides us and makes us distrust. But when people come together, talk to each other, meet each other, and help each other, it can only be for the good.

The Myth of a Killing Instinct
Lieutenant Colonel Dave Grossman

"There is this natural safety mechanism—call it a
violence immune system—that is present in human
beings. The average human being is profoundly
uninterested in killing others, and the military has
had to confront this for millennia."

I first became aware of Lieutenant Colonel Dave Grossman when his book
On Killing: The Psychological Cost of Learning to Kill in War and Society, *was published in 1996. Colonel Grossman is a psychologist and former
soldier, whose work helps to fill in the blind spots we have about this whole
business of the taking of life—in war, in our media, on our streets—and it
does so in some surprising ways. What is behind this act of one human
being killing another? Is it natural? Why has the taking of life become so
common in our society? These are areas that Colonel Grossman can help
illuminate.*

*Currently teaching at Arkansas State University, he has served as an
army ranger and paratrooper, and was a Psychology Professor at the United
States Military Academy at West Point. Colonel Grossman's conclusions
are rooted in his own battle experience, in his interviews with veterans of
American wars since World War II, and in two decades of research into
the scholarship and literature exploring the taking of human life.*

Dave, what inspired you to address such a disturbing issue?

The root process was one of curiosity. If you're a virgin bride headed to
your wedding and need to understand sexuality, there are a hundred
books you can turn to for information. But if you're a young soldier like

I was, a young private wondering about killing—what it's going to be like, what's going to happen, how will it feel—and you try to look up the topic, there's nothing. It's this great taboo. It's a great void out there. So just as we've recently begun to explore the complexity of sexuality and the creation of life, my work is an effort to understand the process of its willful destruction.

In your book, you compare the repression of sexuality with the repression of death.

Absolutely. In the Victorian era in Europe, for the first time in Western civilization, we had a middle class with privacy. For thousands of years, human beings had generally slept around a common fire or in a common room; privacy was an unknown commodity for the vast majority of human beings. Then all of a sudden, in one very brief period of time, we created a middle class, and a widespread condition of individual privacy.

So, in other words, privacy is an invention.

That's right.

And the attitudes that derive from privacy are also social constructions.

Yes. See, for thousands of years, sex was something kind of noisy and funny that happened in the dark in the middle of the night. Animals were around engaging in it. Even children would get a fundamental grasp of sex as a process of life. Then all of a sudden, in the Victorian era, it became hidden away; we had this simultaneous repression and obsession with sex. We began to put skirts around the furniture because the legs were suggestive, while at the same time, child prostitution and pornography appeared on a vast scale.

Today, a similar process is occurring; we have hidden from our-

DIALOGUES ≋ JERRY BROWN

selves all aspects of death. There was a time when if you wanted to eat chicken, you had to go out and slaughter a chicken and gut it; that was the only way to do it. We no longer have that. The same is true for death in our families; mom and dad don't die in the back bedroom anymore. We ship them off to a nursing home and they die there or in hospitals, and we have mortuaries to care for the remains. All aspects of death and dying today are hidden and taboo.

At the same time we are exposed to death and violence in so many forms. Movies, television, video games. Even our President takes out television commercials to show how committed he is to killing criminals. You might say we have a stronger fascination with death than ever before.

Exactly. Now this, in a nutshell, is what my study is all about. Step one, there is this natural safety mechanism—call it a violence immune system—that is present in human beings. The average human being is profoundly uninterested in killing others, and the military has had to confront this for millennia. Step two, the military has learned how to turn it off. Since World War II, there have been tremendous technological and psychological innovations by which armed forces can take the safety catches off human beings. Step three, that's what we're doing to our children indiscriminately, we're shutting down their violence immune systems, primarily through interactive video games.

Now, video games can be a very positive thing. My son will watch a twenty-two minute television comedy showing all of life's problems, interlaced with commercials about what a slug he is if he doesn't ingest the right form of sugar and doesn't wear the right shoes. This is not a good thing.

It's a real bad thing.

Amen. I'd infinitely rather have him reading or playing outside, but far better than watching a sitcom would be to play Mario Brothers. You know, it takes days and days to get gratification. You memorize routes. You problem solve. You exchange ideas with other kids. You read books on it. But when a video game involves being rewarded for inflicting pain and punishment on other human beings, then we've crossed a line. In particular, when the video game builds in a conditioned response where you hold a weapon in your hand and point that weapon and kill another human being over and over and over again, this is not a good thing. This is exactly what the military does, and what police forces do, to take the safety catch off of their people.

The safety catch is the inherent inhibition we have as human beings about killing another person.

Sure. Every species has a safety catch. Animals with antlers and horns, when engaged in their territorial and mating battles, they fight one another, slamming head-to-head in the most harmless possible fashion. Against any other species, they go to the side and they gut and gore. Piranha fight one another with flicks of the tail, but they turn their teeth on anything and everyone else. Rattlesnakes wrestle one another, but they turn their fangs on anything else. Every species has this innate resistance to killing their own kind. Otherwise, their territorial and mating battles would destroy the species.

When human beings become frightened or angry, they stop thinking with the forebrain. They start thinking with the midbrain, which is a very primitive part of the brain. You know, you can't rationalize with a human when he's angry. You can't rationalize with a person when he's frightened. Anybody who's ever tried to do it understands that. Anybody who's ever tried to sell something to somebody who feels intimidated or threatened knows the first thing you've got to do is relax them and make them rational.

Well, on the battlefield, everybody is literally scared out of their wits. They're thinking with the midbrain, and in the midbrain exists this hard-wired, fundamental process that exists in every species. You look an-

other human being in the eyes and there is something right there that
stops you from killing. We can trace it all the way through history.

*You're saying that a majority of people in World War II didn't fire their
rifles?*

Yes. We've known that for a long time. Brigadier General S. L. A. Marshall
was the official historian of the European theater in World War II, and
he did the groundbreaking work on this. He asked soldiers immediately after combat, "Did you see the enemy. Did you fire?" Among the
individual riflemen who did not have a leader standing over their shoul-
der, only fifteen to twenty percent would fire at the enemy. And Marshall
concluded that many of them were posturing, firing over the enemy's
head trying to make a loud noise, trying to daunt the enemy just as two
cats or dogs would puff themselves up and make themselves as loud as
possible.

When Marshall released his data, we revolutionized military training. We know that the way to influence the midbrain is by very primitive processes—operant and classical conditioning basically—which we
have learned from psychologists such as B.F. Skinner and Pavlov. So
while in World War II our soldiers trained on bull's-eye targets, by the
Korean War, we had changed the technique a lot, and by Vietnam, we
had perfected it. In the Korean War, we had a fifty-five percent firing
rate, and in Vietnam, we had a ninety-five percent firing rate.

*Do you know anything about whether the Germans or the Japanese or the
Italians had similar killing ratios in World War II?*

The research on that confirms that around fifteen or twenty percent is a
universal human baseline. Some elite veteran units you'll see up to
twenty-five percent, but you very seldom see much more than that without the use of operant conditioning.

In the military today, when we teach a soldier to shoot, the conditioned stimulus we use is a man-shaped silhouette. It pops up. Stimulus-response. The soldier fills the view of the gunsite. He has a split second to engage the stimulus. Stimulus-response. He fires. If he hits the target it drops, and there are rewards for a hit and punishments for a miss. This forms a powerful habit that will work even when he is frightened.

We do it with children in fire drills. A couple of times a year, the fire bell goes off. The children are taught to stand up and walk out calmly. We do that a couple of times a year, and then, one day, the school is on fire. Everybody's screaming. There's smoke. They're scared out of their minds. But the bell goes off, and it's stimulus-response. The children do what they have been conditioned to do, and they save their lives.

That's what we've done to our soldiers. We've conditioned them to respond to a stimulus, a man-shaped form popping up. As a reflex they fill the view and kill the form. By this kind of training we took the safety catch off and we enabled killing in Vietnam in a way that's never happened before in human history. We had a force that kicked tail. They did a magnificent job; they were never defeated in a small-unit ground engagement.

But when this happens it creates a problem. All your life, you're told, "Don't kill anybody. Don't kill anybody." We reserve the ultimate punishment for people who kill people. And then they put a gun in your hand and they tell you to go kill these people—this is what we call cognitive dissonance in the field of psychology—and so you do. You go. You participate. Maybe you don't personally kill, but you're part of the process. In the back of your mind, there's this little voice that says "I've been bad. I've done something very bad. I'm going to be in trouble."

When you come back, you desperately need a purification ritual. Every warrior tribe has a purification ritual. In America, after the war in Vietnam, instead of a purification ritual, we mistook the warrior for the war and there was a widespread process of condemning the returning veteran.

So you would argue that post-traumatic stress disorder is a result of the absence of purification.

Oh, absolutely. There are dozens of studies that indicate that even more than the nature of the trauma that individuals endure, the nature of the support structure afterwards is responsible for PTSD. And that's why, incidentally, the other major cause of PTSD is rape. Rape is a close-range interpersonal trauma. But then the social support network almost always breaks down for the victim. The males around the victim spin out of control and fail to provide the victim the support they need. Even our law system encourages blaming the victim. So this combination of trauma and condemnation is just guaranteed to result in this horrendous degree of psychological suffering.

Is there more of this post-traumatic stress disorder after Vietnam than after Korea or World War II?

Absolutely. People are horrified by what was done. But consider this: the military has a Draconian discipline that is ground into the individual during training. This helps to insure that the returning veteran represents no threat to his own society. But if we're concerned about what we've done to our soldiers, how much more concerned should we be about doing the same thing indiscriminately to our children without the discipline process? For example, you've seen the movie *Clockwork Orange?*

I have.

Well remember in *Clockwork Orange*, they take a sociopath, a mass murderer, and strap him into a chair and have him watch vivid depictions of human suffering and violence. Unbeknownst to him, a drug's been injected into him that makes him nauseous. After months and months of sitting and watching this violence while he gags and wretches, he begins to associate violence with nausea. This is very doable. But we're doing a reverse *Clockwork Orange* to our children. They watch vivid depictions of human suffering on the screen, and what do they associate it with? Their favorite soft drink. Their favorite candy bar. Their arm around their girlfriend.

So you come down on the side of those who say that the violence in the media translates to violence on the street, or violence in people's family.

The American Medical Association has said, "the debate is over." There is no question about it. The American Psychiatric Association also has issued unequivocal statements on the media and violence.

During the Gulf War, we saw green missile flashes broadcast on CNN. We didn't see Iraqi people, human beings, young boys—many of them Christians—buried alive by vehicles driven by American GIs. If we'd gotten that picture, we might have had a very different reaction to this very popular war. Television plays what it chooses to play, and there we are. We're taught to accept violence, because it doesn't feel like violence.

The issues get very complex. Now I hold the view—take it for what it's worth—that pure pacifism is as morally bankrupt as pure militarism. There are times and places where a nation needs to fight. In World War II, to liberate the concentration camps, in the American Civil War, to free the slaves—these were times and places when war was appropriate, maybe. You know, I'm proud to be an American, Jerry. I'm proud to be an American soldier. In all of history, in all the world, there's nobody that does a better job of the nasty, vile, vicious business of war in such a manner that you can live with yourself, and the nation can live with itself, when it's over. But that doesn't mean that it's always right. It doesn't mean that we're always right. And these are the kind of questions we need to ask.

The question I'd ask is, as we have more and more powerful weapons, and as we're conditioning people to take off the safety catch, how in the world do we stop the human race from wiping itself out? That's the question. War has been part of human civilization for as long as we know, as far back as the Homeric epics and before. But now we have biological weapons. We have nuclear weapons that can be made in a garage, if you've got the plutonium, that can be miniaturized to fit in a bowling bag. So we're entering into an entirely new brave world, and unless we can shift our sensibility and get that safety catch back on, it's a very questionable assumption that we can keep going.

Absolutely, and this release of the safety catch is not only an American phenomenon. Take a look at the rates of violent crime in America. Don't look at the murder rate; medical technology is holding down the murder rate. If we had kept medical technology stable at 1940 levels, the murder level would be ten times higher than it is. What you've got to look at is the aggravated assault rate. In America, since 1957, the aggravated assault rate has gone up from sixty per 100,000 to 440 per 100,000.

That's more than a sevenfold increase in how many years?

Since 1957, just forty years, and it's an international phenomenon. I just got back from the Interpol offices in Washington, D.C. Their data shows that in Norway, between 1978 and 1993, the attempted murder rate increased fivefold. That's just in fifteen years. It's the same in Sweden, Finland, all across Scandinavia, England, Scotland, Wales, Australia, New Zealand; there has been a steady increase every single year, year after year, in the violence rate in every nation that has accepted human suffering as entertainment.

You think it's primarily the entertainment industry that causes these numbers to go up?

LT. COL. DAVE GROSSMAN

That's not the whole picture. Here's a way to think about it. AIDS is a good analogy. AIDS doesn't kill you. AIDS shuts down the immune system and makes you vulnerable to dying from other things. If you have AIDS, a cold can kill you. In the same way, there is this violence immune system, and everywhere in the industrialized world, to varying degrees, it is being turned off. As a result, things that previously would not have resulted in killing are now doing so.

We have a thousand things that will lead a person to take up a weapon and a thousand social forces that produce the conditions for confrontation. Poverty, drugs and alcohol, racism, ignorance, abuse—all these things must be fought. But when you're frightened to death and it comes to pulling that trigger, there's only one thing that will enable you to actually do it. That is a conditioning process that teaches you to associate violence with pleasure and to act reflexively.

And that kind of conditioning is fed through our system at an unprecedented level of intensity.

Absolutely. Unprecedented at any time in human history because the technology was never there before.

I'd like to make a point about the Gulf War and the media. When the troops returned, we started having all these parades and celebrations. I never heard this described as a purification process. To some people, it seemed that the media was in collusion with the politicians and the military to glorify killing in a very obvious way.

What you're saying is right. But when we *didn't* hold parades, which are a kind of modern day purification ritual, for our Vietnam veterans, the result was anywhere from a half a million to one-and-a-half million cases of post-traumatic stress disorder that our society, and these men, are still paying the price for. The bottom line is, you don't do these things lightly. You don't train people to kill lightly. You don't kill people lightly.

You don't take killing as entertainment lightly.

So what one or two things would you suggest to reduce this killing sensibility?

The most important thing is what I call censure and not censor. We need to turn around and look at people who are offering human suffering as entertainment and tell them, "You are sick." And we need to inform those who watch the high body count movies, or let their children watch them, or who produce and play these reflex-action videos that reward killing, that they are establishing the psychological conditions for violence and destruction. Let's do that first.

The Remnants of War
Donovan Webster

"When we went into Kuwait and when we went into
Iraq—it was a television show for the guys who went
in. The first Apache helicopter crews in there, they
flipped down these night vision goggles and watched
what was happening on a screen within a screen that
magnifies everything, so that from four miles out you
can see what you're shooting at. It's all virtual
reality."

*The horror of war does not cease with the agony of those who have been
laid low by the bullets, the knives, the shrapnel and the gas. It goes on and
on and on. To explore what happens after the blood has soaked into the
ground and after the spending of the Pentagon is finished, I spoke with
Donovan Webster, the author of* Aftermath: The Remnants of War, *and
a contributor to such publications as* The New Yorker, The Smithsonian,
and National Geographic.

*Webster has studied the nature of modern war from Napoleonic times
to the much ballyhooed technological conflict in Kuwait, and has traveled
to Europe, Southeast Asia and the Middle East, documenting the lasting
effects of war, effects that are perhaps too disturbing to enter into most of
our debates about the righteousness of military action.*

*Donovan, the horror of war is such a disturbing picture. What inspired
you to take up this issue?*

I'd just finished a long story for *The New Yorker* on crop dusting, and I
took my wife to France just to get away. Sitting in a flower market in the

town of Vence one day, I was reading a French newspaper. The French are very cryptic—they will plant little items in the middle of their newspapers and not really give you any context. And I saw one of these little announcements that said that, while digging the new rail bed for the Channel Tunnel to London, the Interior Ministry had collected six tons of unexploded artillery shells from World War I. That's all it said.

I thought this was really unusual, so I did a literature search and found that someone had written a small piece for *The New York Times* on the subject. I called him, and he wasn't giving up any facts, so I began to hammer at the French Interior Ministry until they let me in. It turns out that I was the first person they ever let look into the *Deminage,* which is a group of about 125 men across France whose job it is to clean up the remnants of World War I, which are everywhere. They make two million stops at residences each year, just cleaning up artillery shells that are in gardens and places like that and have popped up after seventy-five years underground. They were duds. Somebody might hit them with a shovel and bang, they go off.

The only recent year the French collected numbers for is 1991—ninety people in France were killed or injured by these shells that year. It's pretty amazing. In fact, on average, eighteen *deminers* die each year. So *The New Yorker* sent me over to do the story and then decided not to publish it, and it eventually appeared in *Smithsonian* magazine.

That's an interesting sidebar right there. Is this kind of indictment of war no longer of interest to editors at magazines like The New Yorker?

I don't have any idea. I choose not to think about it, frankly.

Well, what certainly is interesting to a lot of editors is the martial fervor that gets called up every time the U.S. launches any kind of military offensive. We recently fired missiles on Iraq and killed some people there; the pundits were all agog about what the President's poll numbers might do. It's all part of a cultural cover-up, not only of the fact that human beings are killed—most of them noncombatants—but of the enormous cost of the war.

You add up all the casualties of war and the expenses of war, and then you look at the polls that show that close to half the American people believe that we shouldn't cut military spending. You realize how powerful the propaganda and distortion is about the nature of this business called defense, called sending a message, called flexing our muscles, putting force behind foreign policy.

Yes. I find it fascinating that George Bush was riding as high as any President ever has just before the Gulf War. He pulled most of the country together, and whether you disagreed with him or not, at least you thought he was a bully guy.

That's because it's all kind of unreal. For most people, these are stories made for television. It's dots.

When we went into Kuwait and when we went into Iraq—it was a television show for the guys who went in too. The first Apache helicopter crews in there, they flipped down these night vision goggles and watched what was happening on a screen within a screen that magnifies everything, so that from four miles out you can see what you're shooting at. It's all virtual reality—a TV show—for them, too. Which is a far cry from what it was in World War I, when guys were launching themselves at one another from the trenches.

The discussion of Alfred Nobel that opens your book gives a good perspective on the violence of modern war. Do you want to talk a little bit about that?

Sure, I think it's important. In his obituary, which Nobel himself happened to read because of a journalist's mistake, Nobel was vilified as the man responsible for the escalation of war at the end of last century.

He was called "the Merchant of Death," because he invented dynamite, smokeless gun powder, blasting gelatin, cordite—basically, if it blows up in this century, Nobel had a hand in it, even nuclear weapons. He invented the first blasting cap, and nuclear weapons are two-stage explosions which use blasting cap mechanisms; also the first nuclear weapon, our Hiroshima bomb, used cordite as its primary trigger.

When Napoleon was marching across Europe, there was a lot of suffering, a lot of blood, and a lot of bodies. Was Nobel's gunpowder really a ratcheting upward in the quantity of killing and suffering?

Certainly Napoleon's march back from Moscow to Paris was horrible, but it was all bullets and bayonets. It was Nobel's invention of smokeless gunpowder that suddenly made the battlefield visible. Instead of soldiers wearing diagonal white stripes across red uniforms or blue uniforms and brass buttons so everybody could see, suddenly they were all wearing camouflage. You could see the field a lot better and kill a lot more effectively. That's just the effects of smokeless powder. Then dynamite. Just the idea that an explosion can take out dozens of men, whereas a bullet takes out one at a time, changed everything.

Also, with these kinds of explosives, things could be fired farther. You didn't have to actually see the people you killed. René Teller, the technical head of explosives and testing and things like that in France, said that when men learned that they didn't have to see another army in order to kill them, everything changed. He said that men learned that God could abandon them, and thus a religion without God came into existence.

Wasn't it Nobel that called war "the horror of all horrors and the greatest of all crimes?"

That's Nobel, yes. But he firmly believed that if he could invent something that assured mutual destruction, all fighting would stop. He was exactly 180 degrees wrong. In this century, just in the large-scale wars, a hundred million people have died. That's just wars. That's not street violence; that's not domestic violence; that's just real declared wars. That's not civil wars, insurrections, and things like that. Fifty million people died in World War II alone.

Now let's look at the war in Kuwait. I still don't know how many casualties there were in that war. I read about the disease and chemical agents that veterans say they were exposed to; and then there was this business about the oil wells being burned and that's going to cause an ecological disaster. Children are starving in Iraq. Can you enlighten us as to the facts in that celebration of the New World Order that George Bush organized?

I can try, although when it comes to the facts, you have to triangulate them because you generally get two or three versions of the same fact. It's done that way partly on purpose and partly because all the details are hard to control. I have no idea in terms of casualties how many there were and I'm not sure you can know. The Iraqis conscripted Kuwaitis and other non-Iraqi nationals who were in Kuwait. They took them at gun point and said, "You will sit in this foxhole and you will defend what is now our land or you will be shot."

So, Kuwait is fascinating, in part, because it's impossible to get a straight story about what happened there. You can get rough estimates on how many land mines were left in the ground, but casualties are an impossibility. Even the guys who were there cleaning up after the war, there were places—like the highway leading out of Kuwait City toward Iraq—that they just wouldn't go near. The Americans just wiped out everything that moved on that highway using every piece of high tech weaponry we had. The road was choked with vehicles, mostly with plunder in them and things like that, and American helicopters hid behind the brow of a hill. The vehicles came up a grade, and when they got to where they couldn't escape, the helicopters just popped up over the top of the hill and blew 'em to pieces. It was amazing.

We were playing for keeps in that war, there's no question about it. I think what we were doing, frankly, on a larger political scale, was saying to the rest of the world, don't mess with us.

So you can't tell me how many people were actually injured and killed?

I can't. And I'm not certain I would trust the Pentagon's number either; they would lowball it. When I went to Kuwait, I was there to learn about the land mine crisis.

Is that the big aftermath in the Kuwait-Iraq theater—land mines?

To me it is, and it's indicative of something that's going on all around the world. The United Nations says there are 110 million, and the International Red Cross says there as many as 300 million land mines in the ground right now.

Land mines cost three dollars a piece, or even less. In small scale conflicts where they don't have a lot of soldiers and they don't have a lot of money, land mines can ring a population and keep them in check. They're incredibly effective. They're not like soldiers—they don't need to eat, they don't need to sleep. They've just proliferated and the U.S. has sold millions.

Do you know how many land mines were put into Kuwait or Iraq?

Seven million. We put a good deal of them there, our coalition of allies put in some, and most were probably put in by Iraq.

Donovan, I'm looking at one of the pages in your book, Aftermath, *and you have this to say:*

> *"Cluster bombs were exploded above a landscape,*
> *spitting hundred-loads of submunition bomblets across*

*an area the size of twelve football fields before the
smaller bombs exploded in unison. The fire from these
submunition explosions, it was said, was like that of a
nuclear blast: burning all the area's available air, the
explosions created a vacuum so ferocious that lung
tissue was storied to be pulled from soldiers' chests and
out through their mouths. And, of course, there was
still the garden variety low-tech bombs and artillery
shells, the "steel" as they were now known, which—just
as in Vietnam—were dropped by the ton from the
bellies of B-52s and fired from American M-1 tanks,
Bradley Fighting Vehicles, and gunboats in the Persian
Gulf.*

    *Three years after the war, though, it's not the five
weeks of high-tech pounding—which ultimately spread
fifteen times more explosives than were used by all sides
in World War II—that's proved the long-term problem
in Kuwait. Instead, it's a far older technology: land
mines."*

*Now, before you tell me about the land mines, is that true? Fifteen times
more explosives were used in that incident over there in Kuwait than in
World War II?*

That's the accepted number.

*Is there any moral calculus that can be applied here in terms of what was
at stake and what was the human toll compared to what our purpose was—
taking the monarchy back, protecting the oil, showing who's toughest, flexing muscles, whatever it was? I have never seen an article that said this is
the number of casualties, this is what they suffered, and this is what the
justification was.*

You quickly get into a morass. It's usually just summarized that Saddam Hussein is the worst dictator since Hitler. That is the phrase that keeps coming up again and again and again.

But my mind is just boggled at this. You just told me that fifty million people were killed in World War II, and now you're telling me fifteen times as much weaponry was dropped in the war in Kuwait.

It's amazing. What we wanted, by my lights anyway, is this: American interests had funneled arms to Saddam during the Iran-Iraq war—legally or supposedly illegally—and we knew he had an outmoded stockpile. Now we go back five years later and use our highest technology. We wanted to get in and get out of that war, and we wanted to make a statement about what kind of technology we had and what we could use against other upstart nations. It's hard. I'm not a priest or anything like that. It's a very complex issue.

It sounds pretty simple to me.

It does?

Yes. It's an unspeakable evil. Sometimes, in self-defense, you have to do a lot. But here there was no issue of self-defense. The greater the magnitude of harm you inflict on other people, the greater the justification ought to be. And here, there's no proportionality whatsoever. By any standard of ethical or moral judgment, by any tradition I know of, there's culpability.

I can guarantee what the generals would say—that it's better to go in and stun them quickly and get out than it is to enter another Vietnam, where 58,000 of our own died.

I want to just interject another thought. Perhaps the real message of the Gulf War—to China, India, Pakistan, Libya, and every other nation—

was that whatever weapons they have now, they've got to get better ones. Kuwait was a demonstration case, a message to other countries, that technological innovation in the weaponry of death must be pursued with a vengeance and with renewed commitment. So really, the Gulf War was not about making the world safer, it was about making the future far more dangerous, for the United States and everyone else.

I'm glad you said that because that kind of statement is very difficult to make as a journalist. My role is to document what I see. I just leave a big hole there and people are free to drop in the appropriate morality. What I can't say is one of the difficult things about my writing. I'm not a priest, that's not my agenda. I'm there to see what's going on and let people do the algebra themselves.

Well it goes beyond algebra here; there's a geometric progression. There's an emulatory factor that's very, very powerful. While the generals and the conservatives keep saying how much they're defending America, the absolute reverse is true—true in the sense that as America demonstrates the sheer war value of technological advantage, other countries that have the money and the brain power must copy them. If you take a country like China with 1.2 billion people, they certainly have physicists and chemists that will, in our lifetime, develop a sophistication as great or greater than ours, and therefore make sure, by an almost absolute certitude, that the world that's coming is incredibly less secure than the one that we live in now.

U.S. foreign policy, the Germans and French and British, none of them are doing anything to break this chain of escalating military technology. Every weapon that has ever been created has proliferated to other countries. So every weapon we create, at some time in the future, will come back against ourselves. That's a very depressing thought, but I think it's a true thought.

It's very dark and we might regret that we live at this end of the century.

DIALOGUES ≋ JERRY BROWN

As horrible as World War I was, you now, there wasn't this kind of col-lateral damage. Eighty percent of the people killed by land mines are women and children—noncombatants.

Now there were seven million land mines in the ground in Kuwait and parts of Iraq. Where did the Iraqis get their land mines?

China, Russia, Italy.

All buddy nations of ours. And still there's not a concerted effort by the so-called civilized leaders to say, "Hey wait a minute, this thing is so horrible that we're not going to facilitate it." Not among ourselves, not in China, not in Russia, not in Italy, not in any of these places. Have you ever heard a statement like that?

Well, what they've come up with—in fact, the United States was the leader on it—is a moratorium that has now been extended to three years. What it means is that sales and shipments of land mines out of our coun-try are not allowed. It isn't a ban on use. If we went into a war right now, we would use them because they're so effective. That's the problem. They're very efficient. They're very effective, and you know there's a world full of maimed people to attest to that.

Okay, so you're saying that there's a moratorium in peace time, but we will use them when we need them—in the next war. That's good isn't it? Now, as we talk, is anyone making land mines in the United States?

Yes, but they can't sell them outside of our boundaries. They can sell them to the Pentagon and the Pentagon puts them in a big warehouse and waits for the next war.

That doesn't give me any comfort.

Nor me either. In fact, when the President decided he wanted to revisit the land mine issue, I got a call from the Pentagon. They wanted to meet me and have a talk, because I'd done a story for *The New York Times Magazine* about it, and written my book. I sit down with this guy, and he says, "What about this?" And I said, "Well, I think you should just throw them all out, get rid of them." And he says, "We really can't do that. Our enemies have them." I said, "What's your option?"

I went away and came back about two weeks later. They had come up with this new idea that they were calling "shaving," where you lure enemy armies out, then drop land mines behind them. Not just a few land mines, tens of thousands, tens of millions of them, so they can't retreat; if they do, they're going to get blown up. Here are people, effectively trapped on an island, facing the American war machine bearing down on them. I can't think of anything worse, and I pray to God that the President decides to outlaw all use of them.

Many of the smartest people on the planet are working on ways to kill the greatest number of people at the cheapest price. That is a major policy issue and there's nothing that any American President has said that seriously deals with that.

You probably know the story of Ted Taylor, a bomb designer in the 'fifties and 'sixties at Los Alamos. He's an amazing guy, who now opposes these weapons for obvious reasons. He was one of those encouraged to make as many bombs as he could. He was working with the best and the brightest at Los Alamos, and even if he was against it, as he became, it was also fascinating to him.

Ted Taylor once told me he never used cocaine, but he imagined that the thrill of seeing one of the weapons he designed go off at the Nevada testing grounds was equivalent to a cocaine high. It was a rush. It was the most exciting thing in his life.

It's easy to get addicted, and that's the environment we're talking about.

So you've got the greed going, the martial fervor, the cocaine high—and you have no leader, none of the power guys, saying anything about this. I can't think of any greater argument for the total illegitimacy of consti- tuted government in the contemporary world.

I completely agree.

So how about getting some of those mines out? When can you feel confi- dent, if you're a Kuwaiti seven-year-old or a young Iraqi, that there won't be any land mines to run into?

Right after the war, Kuwait came up with one billion dollars and offered it to all the countries that liberated them; they could sign contracts and come in to clean up the mines. The Americans and the French and the British got the biggest segments of land. The British took the oil dis- trict, and they were in there first. It was nasty; not only did they have flaming oil wells and oil everywhere, but they had land mines beneath them. The oil would harden and they would have to pry the oil up and, by doing so, they'd often blow up land mines. People got hurt constantly.

It seems that area may now be cleaned up. The Kuwait Ministry of Defense has pretty much gone through that entire desert, which is the size of northern New Jersey, with a fine-toothed comb. The contracts stated that all sectors had to pass their approval, and if they found a gun, if they found a piece of steel out there in the sand, the contractor had to go back and clean it up. So it's pretty clean now. Still, I wouldn't want to go walking around out there. Land mines were just everywhere. I mean, they were like beads in New Orleans at Mardi Gras.

Donovan, describe some of what you saw over there in Kuwait.

The group I was with was a private company with a contract to clean up land mines. We were staying in this high-rise tower right on the Persian Gulf, which is a beautiful, deep blue. I would wake up in the morning and see the sun rising, and it was remarkably beautiful. Kuwait City is set up like Los Angeles or Dallas or something—the buildings are separated by quite a bit of land. There were buildings that were just destroyed, with huge gaping holes in their sides and what's left of balconies drooping down. The Iraqis had taken over the buildings and put in cinder blocks where the balconies were in order to make bunkers out of them. They were really dug in.

As we drove out of town, we'd go past the really nice oasis-type houses that the sheiks have and out into the land of the Bedouin, where there were camels and dead goats and big piles of war refuse everywhere. We went to the Kuwaiti airfield that was suspected of housing Iraqi aircraft. All the hangars, which the Americans had built with poured concrete and rebar, every one of these buildings had a hole in exactly the same spot in the roof. Obviously we'd gotten satellite photos and the coordinates of where these things were and then boom, just dropped weapons on them. Among the rebar, there were these big piles of rubble on the floor and the rebar would just be draped down sort of like ropes. You'd think it wasn't even made of steel; you'd think it was made of nylon rope or something like that. It was that torn up.

The whole airfield was rubble. They'd used Hellfire missiles, which are supersonic missiles fired off Apache helicopters that go in and break things up, and Hydra rockets, which are also fired off Apaches, that dispatch these finned darts that, when they explode, spatter all over the place and if you're in the way, you're not going to be alive terribly long. It's really horrific. And then we went on to the mine fields where these guys were doing a Sisyphian task. The sand stretches as far as you can see in every direction, and beneath it are land mines, and you've got to move one inch at a time using a metal detector trying to find them.

Now do you have any sense of how many land mines are left there?

DIALOGUES ≊ JERRY BROWN

I've got to say it's been pretty cleaned up, but it cost a billion dollars to do the job. It's going to cost $300 billion to clean up those that are in the ground all over the world.

And where are most of these others?

Most African nations where there has been civil war in the last ten years have a land mine problem—Angola, Zaire, Burundi, the highlands of Mozambique. Much of the civil unrest of these countries has become land mine warfare; it's very simple and inexpensive. Then there's Afghanistan, where the Russians put in twelve million land mines.

Now how does that work? The Russians were defending their puppet regime in Kabul and dropping twelve million land mines? How do you protect your own people when you're playing with something as indiscriminate as a land mine?

You have to distribute maps and tell people that you've mined an area and to not to go in there.

So you're strategic. You find an area where your enemy is and you land mine around it. But then don't the soldiers just clear a little path and get out?

Yes. That, in fact, has been the problem for fifty years. All they do is cut a little path by blowing up enough to get through and then everyone follows that path. It's the people who move back in afterward who have to deal with the problem. And the way they deal with it, like in Vietnam, is often bloody.

So let's talk a little about the aftermath of some of these other wars—Vietnam, the two World Wars.

One of my most powerful memories is of a hospital in old Saigon, now called Ho Chi Minh City. It was a maternity hospital and this guy took me into a room that was full of deformed babies, all of whom were the children of mothers who were born during the Agent Orange spraying years. The incidence of birth defects here, compared to say, baseline figures in any U.S. area, is astronomical.

I mentioned before some of the problems France is having with explosives from World War I, and the effects I've witnessed from World War II are mind blowing. In December of 1995, I went to Volgograd, which used to be called Stalingrad, right as the snow started to fall. I went out to this little town called Peschanka; I was told that during the war the Russians had beaten the Germans pretty much right there. They had surrounded them with a million soldiers and let them freeze and starve to death. Hitler abandoned them. The Germans couldn't get aircraft in to them. Well, there are still somewhere between a 160,000 and 225,000 men lying out there, in their uniforms a lot of them, just lying there. The Russians never cleaned them up. No one goes out there. The Germans were not even allowed to mourn these men until 1995.

People ought to know about this, Donovan, since their tax dollars pay for it. Very human, very important. It certainly tells you something about where we are in the modern world.

The Practice of Peace
Thich Nhat Hanh

"There are people who are equipped not with anger,
but with other kinds of energies, such as compassion
and loving-kindness, and they have been able to
succeed in the fight for justice and independence and
freedom."

*In September 1995, Thich Nhat Hanh accepted an invitation to my home
in Oakland. Thich Nhat Hanh is a Zen Buddhist monk from Vietnam,
now living in southwestern France at Plum Village, a religious community of the Order of Interbeing. Thich Nhat Hanh took his monastic vows
over fifty years ago as a young man in Vietnam, where he joined many of
his Buddhist brothers and sisters in opposition to the war. After emigrat-
ing to the West, he continued his peacemaking efforts, always right at the
center of the creative energy here in this country and throughout the world,
fighting that horrible tragedy.*

*The author of more than thirty books on spiritual practice, social
change and poetry, including* Living Buddha, Living Christ, *Thich Nhat
Hanh has taught, through his writings and way of life, a politically-en-
gaged spirituality that has deeply influenced many western thinkers and
activists.*

*You may be aware that I have been involved with a grassroots movement
based on "We," a movement committed to pushing forward some cultural
shifts, which we call We The People. It is a result of seeing that change
from the top down doesn't work. But what really will work in terms of
shifting our emphasis from hatred, ignorance and greed? That's where I
think you may have something you can share with us.*

We are the people, and you are the people. When we are able to see that, and that we all "inter-be" with everyone else, and that we are all made of elements that are not ourselves, then we begin to see our true nature. It is like a flower—it is made of non-flower elements; like America—it is made of non-American elements. The moment we see ourselves in this deeper way, we begin to realize that we "inter-are" with other people, and the feeling of distinction, the feeling of discrimination in us, vanishes. Then we begin to have peace, and we begin to communicate better with so-called other people, and with other living beings.

When you say, "inter-be," do I understand by that that there is no such thing as an individual, separate and apart, but that the basic reality is "inter" or between? If so, then we are not truly separate. We are all connected, and our striving and competition and subordination of one another miss the point of what we truly are.

This is correct. We may like to use the word "self," but if we are aware that self is always made of non-self elements, we are safe. When we are able to see that our peace, our joy, our happiness depend on the peace, the joy, the happiness of others, we will not be angry anymore. Instead of trying to get happiness for ourselves, we will try at the same time to get the happiness of others. When others feel content, we, too, will feel content.

So if someone were to say that we can't save the spotted owl, which lives in redwood trees, and at the same time preserve the livelihood of people who cut down redwood trees, you would say there is a misunderstanding. Because it is not a question of one or the other, it's the interbeing of both together.

Right. In the light of interbeing, well-being is not an individual matter. If we care only for our own well-being, our own happiness, we may not get it. But if we care for the well-being and happiness of others, then it will come back to us. Even if we don't try to grasp it, well-being and happiness always come back to us very naturally.

Let's look at this on another level, the level of states and governments. It appears that governments are based on the idea of vital interests, the interests of the state. They call that realpolitik, pragmatism—*we have to make sure that the interests of France are protected, or the interests of the United States, or Japan or Vietnam. That seems precisely opposite to what you are saying. And it follows that if the arrangement of power in the world is by states, and states are based on not caring about, or taking into account, the interests of other states, then we are doomed to exactly what we are getting.*

Exactly. Because of that way of looking at things, we have got ourselves into difficulties. In the Order of Interbeing, there is a precept that addresses the ending of war, but not in the spirit of partisan politics. We have to practice the spirit of equanimity; then we see that within our nation, there are weaknesses as well as strengths, and within the other nation the same thing is true. If we can keep that insight alive, we will not be caught in anger. We will be able to preserve peace and loving-kindness for ourselves and others. We are humans. We suffer. The other people, they are also humans. They also suffer. And so the politician, the activist, will work for the peace and well-being of all.

The Vietnam War is almost twenty-five years behind us. Do you see that the United States, or that the people and leadership in Vietnam, understand that war better now?

I think the Vietnamese and Americans learned something from the war in Vietnam, but not enough. I am afraid that if we are not able to learn more from our mistakes and suffering, we are going to repeat the same thing.

Some years ago, I first read Noam Chomsky's comment that the United States had invaded Vietnam, and my initial reaction was that this view was mistaken. But then I began to study the history of Vietnam and the origins of the conflict there—Vietnam's importance as a colony and its role in World War II, the arrival of the French, and then the English, and then the return of the French, and all the covert money the U.S. spent there. I realized that I had never heard—certainly not from our political leaders—the true history of the war and all its causes.

I feel that if we don't focus attention on learning what has happened, we can't very well come to the truth. So I wonder, how do you see the value of knowing what has happened—for example, the true history of the Vietnam War? Is there something to learn in these histories, or in your work are you telling people, "Practice where you are. Deal with the here and now, and leave those other issues to somebody else?"

The war in Vietnam started because of one idea, perhaps because of the good will of some people, the desire to save, to protect. But people are subject to wrong perceptions. Even if you have good will you can create suffering for the people you love. That is why it is very important to be still, to look deeply, in order to understand what is there in the heart of reality.

During the war in Vietnam, we suffered so much, but as a monk I continued to practice in order not to lose track of reality. In the situation of war one might be carried away by despair or anger. But if you are caught by despair or anger, you lose the insight you need to bring people out of danger. I was living very deeply each moment of my life, and the life of my people, and I was capable of seeing that the war created suffering not only for the Vietnamese people, but also for the American people. I was able to see that the young Americans who went there in order to kill, they were also victims of the war, victims of a notion, a policy. And I had compassion to offer to them, because I was able to see them as victims of the war. They suffered just as much as the Vietnamese.

When you are able to see things like that, you are not carried away by your anger. You are able to see where the roots of war really are. They may be in the good will of people who conduct the war, and that good will may just be based on a wrong notion of the situation. If you do not have enough peace, enough practice of deep looking—namely, meditation—you cannot discover the kind of truth that avoids such suffering, so much suffering for two nations.

Is this practice of looking deeply only available to monks and nuns in isolated communities? Or should those who represent the state, national governments, also follow this path and be able to understand their affairs from that very wise perspective?

The insight of interbeing is not only for monks and nuns but for everyone, including politicians. That is why I believe firmly that activists and politicians have to practice looking deeply in order to regain their strength, their calm, their capacity for peace, the capacity of resistance against despair and anger. If they can do that, many people will benefit. If they are carried away only by action and willingness to act, we will not profit the maximum from their effort.

Each activist has to be something like a monk at the same time. I believe everyone, man or woman, has a baby monk or a baby nun within his or her heart. We have to allow that baby monk or baby nun to get stronger. And when the monk is there solid in you, you have endless peace inside, to serve as the foundation of your action. Otherwise even with your very active life, even if you have good will, you may cause suffering to the people you want to protect. It's very important. The monk in us has to be as strong as the activist in order for us to be true servants of humanity, of God. That is what we call engaged Buddhism, engaged Christianity, if you like.

Now, practically speaking, how do we do that?

Everyone needs time to pause, to stop, in order to preserve himself or herself. Many people do so by the practice of sitting meditation or walking meditation. Many friends of mine do so every day, sometimes by concentrating quietly on their breath, like this: "Breathing in, I calm myself. Breathing out, I smile."

There are people who practice breathing in and out every time the telephone rings. We call this telephone meditation. It is an opportunity to practice going back to yourself, using the telephone ring as a reminder to become calm. When the telephone rings, it makes you a little nervous. You wonder who is calling; is it good news or bad news? So your peace is not perfect. If the other person has something important to tell you, he or she will not hang up after the first ring. So you are able to meditate on breathing during the second ring. And when the telephone rings for the third time, you pick it up and now you are smiling, you are calm, and that is not only good for you but also good for the person who is calling.

Even this small action is the practice of peace. In our daily life we can do many things like this to bring more tranquillity into ourselves. You can practice breathing and smiling as you drive a car, or as you walk from your office to the bus stop. This is what we call walking meditation, not thinking of anything at all, but just enjoying breathing and walking on this beautiful planet. If you walk like that for three minutes, you recover yourself. You bring back the peace, the serenity, into yourself. This is the practice of meditation in our daily life.

So breathing is at the essence of your peacemaking.

Breathing is a very wonderful way of uniting body and mind. In daily life, very often your mind and body are separated and you are not your best. You are your best only when they are together. We call it "the oneness of body and mind." What can link these two things together is mindful breathing. The moment you hold to mindful breathing, your mind and body come together, and you are concentrated. You are really there. This can bring the fruit of practice right away. You don't have to practice five years in order to arrive at that.

I understand that you speak from a Buddhist point of view. Does it in any way limit the power of what you are saying if someone is Christian, or Jewish or has no religion?

In the Buddhist tradition, we speak about the practice of mindfulness, but we can find the equivalent in other traditions such as Christianity, Judaism, and so on. Mindfulness is the capacity of being there, in the here and now, so that you live each moment of your daily life more deeply. Mindfulness helps us witness what is happening in the present moment. Mindfulness helps us to touch deeply what is there, to look deeply at what is there, so that we can understand. And when we understand, we are able to accept and to love.

The same kind of energy is found in Christianity. It might be called the Holy Spirit. All of us are able to identify the presence of the Holy Spirit, the energy sent by God, when it is there. If the Holy Spirit is there, then there is true understanding, there is true love. You and I and all other people—every time the Holy Spirit is there, we love. If understanding is not there, if love is not there, we know; and if understanding is there, love is there, we know. To practice our beliefs in such a way that the Holy Spirit is there in our church, in our family, in our community—we all have this experience. We may speak in different terms, but we speak of the same thing, and we all practice in order to make the Holy Spirit present in our daily life.

So as a Christian you live your daily life as if love is always there. You do everything in the presence of love. You have the impression that God is ever present and whatever you say, whatever you do, is seen by God. That practice of doing everything in the presence of God is very much like the Buddhist practice of mindfulness. And this is also the practice in the Jewish tradition.

I'm reminded of your book, The Raft Is Not the Shore, *which you did with Daniel Berrigan. There you described how Catholicism, Buddhism, Judaism, how they are a raft that can take you somewhere, but the shore is what is real, and is different than the path or the pointer.*

I was taught, growing up Catholic, that there were certain essential rituals. You had to be baptized, there was holy water, and seven sacraments. It was all part of a mechanism of salvation, and if you don't have that mechanism, then you can't get it. There were even diagrams in our catechism that showed how if you went to mass you received a certain amount of grace. It was like going to a gas station to get gasoline for your car, and the only gas stations were run by the Church.

But you're not talking about any particular religious dogma, but rather an experience, a reality that, without any words or any particular mechanism, is immediate and direct—the awareness of what you call interbeing.

Yes. Everyone feels the need of peace; everyone feels that there must be stability within their body and mind; everyone feels that they need freedom. That is the shore, where we all want to come. Not only those of us who have a spiritual tradition feel the need of peace, stability and freedom, but everyone. In order to have these things, we should know how to live. The Buddhists describe that way to live as the practice of mindfulness. We can describe it in different terms, but all of us have to know a way, in order to feed ourselves with the peace we are so hungry for.

But we should not be caught up in the forms. When I drink a cup of tea mindfully, I am real and the cup of tea is real, and during that moment I live deeply that moment of my life. So my way of drinking tea is like a ritual. It is like something very sacred, because I am really there, very deep. But if you only value such actions only as a form, as a ritual of drinking tea, then you miss the point. The point is to be very alive, very aware and happy in that moment of drinking tea. So when you receive the bread and the wine in the performance of the Eucharist, if only the act is performed, only the ritual is performed, but you don't get life, you don't get peace, stability, and freedom, you are missing everything.

There is only a raft but there is no shore at all.

The Holy Spirit is what you want to get, and not just tea or wine or bread. When I drink tea deeply, not only do I get tea, but I get life. The bread offered by Jesus to his disciples contained life. If his disciples only got bread, that is not enough. The purpose is to eat bread deeply, looking at the bread as the flesh and the blood of life, and then, I think, they get true life. If they are satisfied only with performing a ritual, they miss the whole thing. And that is why we say, "The raft is different from the shore."

There are others here who would like to participate in this conversation. Robert, do you have a question?

Robert: This all sounds so nice. The voice of the pacifier. The escape from a world of illusions. Renounce violence. Leave the monopoly of violence to the state. But isn't this just a beautiful way to disarm the people? The revolutionaries are saying, "It is okay to be angry. It is okay to fight the system. It's okay to fight." Why did Marx say that religion is the opiate of the masses? It's precisely because it works to maintain the status quo.

This is a perennial question: that religion is a distraction, encouraging people to accept the status quo rather than to revolt, to assert their independence and their freedom.

Robert, I think that people who follow a religion, yet who do not embody the spirit of religion, have given that impression. It is a notion that many people have because they have not seen the enactment of laws that embody the spirit of religion.

We have to fight injustice, and we can fight it in many ways. The best way is the way that can bring justice, not create more injustice. You may use anger as energy in order to fight, but there is danger in it. When you are angry, you are not calm enough, you are not lucid enough, to understand the situation. It is better to be calm and to be strong. Because if you are calm and you get the right vision, you are going to succeed in bringing change into society.

But one aspect of Robert's comment is that if we're going to walk around peaceful and calm while forces of injustice have the guns, the media, the economic control over people's lives, we may just be dooming people to their suffering. If we mobilize our anger and our frustration, can't we actually move some kind of positive change?

There are people who are equipped not with anger but with other kinds of energies, such as compassion and loving-kindness, and they have been able to succeed in the fight for justice and independence and freedom. Martin Luther King, Jr. had compassion within him. We cannot say that Martin Luther King, Jr. was not active enough. He was active his whole life. Mahatma Gandhi, you cannot say he was not active, that he was not fighting for his people, the people who suffer.

During the Vietnam War, Buddhist monks fought very hard against the war and injustice with compassion in their hearts. They burned themselves alive in order to serve the cause. When a Buddhist monk such as Thich Quang Duc burned himself alive, that did not mean that he was angry. He was caught between two big powers of war, and his people had no means to express themselves. They were victims of injustice, not only from one side but from both sides. Sometimes injustice is imposed not only by one side but by all sides. And you have no guns, no mass media, no way to cry out, to express your suffering.

The Buddhist monks who burned themselves alive were motivated by compassion, by the desire to make the suffering of their people known. They left behind very moving letters full of compassion, calling for understanding, calling for efforts to stop the war and injustice. They acted out of their compassion and not out of anger. When you are guided by compassion and loving-kindness, you are able to look deeply into the heart of reality and to see the truth. If you are angry you may not understand and you may make mistakes during the time of action. Serenity helps. We have to learn that. Calm helps. To be serene, to be calm, does not mean to be inactive. You can be very active and calm at the same time.

Rita, do you have a question?

Rita: I have a question about cultivating the seeds of compassion and mindfulness. What does one do, both at a state and personal level, when another party is resistant and does not wish to participate in the process? For example, if politicians in one country take the time to understand themselves and cultivate compassion, how is this going to help when another state is eager for war, or doesn't accept the same mindful world view.

Rita, I think if an individual is at war with someone else, or if a nation is at war with another nation, it is partly because communication has been impossible. We have to communicate with the other person or nation in order to avoid war and conflict. If you practice compassion and peace, and if it does not inspire the other party to do the same, it is because we have not done well enough. We have to do that. We have to show that our compassion, understanding and loving-kindness are real and not just talking.

If you are able to radiate that kind of energy around you, you can talk to people very easily. But you have to do the work of education, so that people will see the beauty, the effectiveness, the pleasure of that kind of energy. When people see that, they will begin to support you, to congratulate you, and they will try to do the same thing you have done.

If, during a peace talk, your nation proves to have the good will of reconciling, and if your nation is being supported by many nations in the world, the other nation will have to look bad. They will be isolated. Therefore the answer to your question is that we have to practice deeper and we have to practice with many friends. We have to practice *mahayana,* the way of the masses.

When you observe conditions in this country, and other countries as well, where you have separation based on race, separation based on material wealth, violence and isolation, biological and chemical weapons, do you have despair or do you have optimism? Or neither one?

I see that many who believe they are running after happiness may be going in a direction of suffering. Many of us think happiness means to be able to consume at least as much as others. But the person who consumes a lot is not necessarily a happy person. You can live a simple life and be very happy at the same time.

We have to make our lives a demonstration of that fact. We should live our daily life in such a way that the future is possible for our children and our grandchildren, and at the same time be at peace with ourselves and with others in the world. When we do this as individuals, we have the power to inspire the community, the nation, many nations, to change their way of pursuing happiness.

Globalization and the Destruction of Culture
Helena Norberg-Hodge

"It is very important to keep this fact in mind: that
roughly half of the human population still lives in
rural villages. When you bring that up to people in
the West, immediately they call you a romantic,
unrealistic ... In fact, it is we in the West who have
become unrealistic, because we ignore the reality of
what's going on in the world."

I met Helena Norberg-Hodge many years ago during my tenure as Governor of California, when the state's Natural Resources Department was soliciting the input of environmentalists around the world. At that time, she was living and working in Tibet, witnessing the slow destruction of that traditional culture by Western economic forces. Ms. Norberg-Hodge is the author or co-author of several published works, including Ancient Futures: Learning from Ladakh, *and* From the Ground Up: Rethinking Industrial Agriculture, *and contributed two essays to* The Case Against the Global Economy, *edited by Jerry Mander. She is also a founding member of The International Forum on Globalization.*

The subject of my conversation with Helena is globalization. It's about the homogenization, Disney-fication and McDonald-ization of the planet, this incredible phenomenon that is eliminating the world's social, linguistic, and biological diversity, and, in turn, replacing local self-sufficiency with dependence and poverty.

Helena, the last time I saw you, you were showing slides and speaking about a sustainable society very different from anything in the West. It was Ladakh, wasn't it?

Yes. That was Ladakh, a part of Tibet that belongs, politically, to India. I had the amazing experience of ending up there twenty-one years ago when it had just opened up to the outside world, and I learned to speak the language fluently and got to know the culture from the inside. In retrospect, the most important thing was that I experienced the psychological impact of the western global economy coming in to a place that hadn't been effected by it.

Ladakh was very special in that regard. When people travel today to India, to Africa, to many parts of the world, they think that they're looking at tradition—that they're looking at Indian culture, African culture. But actually, most of the villages they observe were very dramatically transformed by colonialism. Colonialism wrought enormous changes. It redrew boundaries, changed identities, and above all, created slave economies. But twenty-one years ago Ladakh hadn't been effected by colonialism. And I think what was so striking was that I came to see that, at a deep psychological level, the people hadn't been enslaved. They were respectful of themselves. They were deeply at ease with who they were.

I remember from that presentation that Ladakh was sustainable, in part, because it had not experienced population growth. And I remember too that they practiced polyandry there, women had more than one husband. Could you elaborate on these two issues? Maybe they're connected.

They're certainly connected. Polyandry, where a woman has several husbands, tends to be common in areas of the world with scarce resources. And Ladakh—central Tibet—is a high altitude desert with very scarce resources. Villages there were almost like islands with very clear limits. You can only feed so many people, and so they practiced polyandry, usually fraternal polyandry. Several brothers would have one wife. This went hand in hand with a very strong respect for the religious tradition, for Buddhism, so you had monasteries where a lot of celibate men lived, and there were also quite a few nuns. This combination—a large section of the population remaining celibate, and polyandry—helped to maintain a stable population.

What has happened there recently?

As everywhere else in the world, the new model is the nuclear family. It's everyone to himself and herself, splitting off, and because there aren't very strict measures in terms of contraception, the population is exploding very rapidly. I've also witnessed the breakdown of people's connection to the land. In other words, people are being pulled away from the rural village economy into the city and to paid employment. There, very soon, they get the impression that the only thing that matters is money, that as long as they have more money, there are no limits.

So with all this money, do people buy things made in Ladakh, or made somewhere else?

Oh, it's made outside.

So it's a way of disconnecting people from the place where they are.

Absolutely. And that disconnection leads very quickly to the sense that there are no limits. You can hear the older generation saying, "Oh, my God, what's going to happen? The population is exploding; where is the food going to come from?" But the young, urban, monoculturized minds—the newly educated—don't see that. They're thinking just in terms of making more money.

Does this so-called progress have a certain fatal attraction in Ladakh? I'm thinking, for example, of colonial Latin America and California—the way the Spanish built things, the way they had the stirrup, the horse, the sword, the steel helmet, the arch. The Spanish met resistance, but they also held a certain attraction. Western wealth and technology seem to be a very per-

suasive religion that has enrolled more believers than Buddhism, Christianity, Islam, Judaism, and Hinduism all put together. I don't want to overstate its power, but it definitely has a lot of juice.

What I've experienced in many different places—not just in Ladakh, but in Ladakh it was most dramatic—is that the seductive power of Western technology is most influential over children. And I am absolutely convinced from my experience in rural Spain, in Greece, and in many less untouched areas than Ladakh, that if there were no children, this imported economy would not succeed.

What I see specifically is that the gadgetry of Western technology is very intimidating and, at the same time, very attractive to boys and young men. These tools seem very powerful and exciting; they allow you to ride through the countryside very fast on a motorbike, they allow you to use a tractor instead of a horse and to work faster. These things are very attractive to young men. But what they do almost immediately is to create a sense of inferiority, so that the real mechanism is one of making people feel inferior if they're not part of the club, making people feel that they're left behind. It also makes people feel that if they don't join that club, they are going to be overpowered. So I think there's a sense of intimidation, a sense of shame. That, I would say, is the single most important factor in the attraction you refer to.

On top of that, you have to keep in mind that this operates systematically to undermine cultures. It comes in with great hooks that, on the surface, appear very attractive, very neutral. For instance, education is presented to you as knowledge about the world, as if there were some neutral sort of knowledge that will edify you, that will make you stronger and wiser. Many people immediately have no reason to question that. It's only afterwards that it becomes apparent that it's killed off your own language, your local knowledge, and that it's actually trained you into urban consumer culture.

Schooling is certainly not something that evolved slowly out of Himalayan experience. We think of school as an almost universal idea. In the first grade, you learn a primary level of knowledge, and then a second, and then a third, and you advance through a progressive revelation of reality. But in fact, it's a carefully constructed artifact that has a historicity, a particular origin and location that is very specific to the people of a particular place and time.

It's very specific, and the European empire has spread in this way around the world and continues to grow and to spread. Everywhere you find that the so-called educated speak one of a few European languages, and that the so-called illiterate speak a local vernacular.

It's important also to keep in mind that education changes dramatically one's economic relationship to place. Today in the Third World—what many people refer to now as the South—roughly fifty percent of the population is still rooted in a more or less local rural economy, where there are small scale fishermen, farmers, nomads. But this whole process of education is pulling people out of rural areas. Young people in these rural schools learn nothing about economic survival from their local resources. They essentially learn how to survive in New York, Rio or Mexico City, which is, of course, a monocultural, cement-based environment. And so it lifts the young out of the knowledge and the skills that would allow them to survive from the biological diversity of their native place.

It is very important to keep this fact in mind: that roughly half of the human population still lives in rural villages. When you bring that up to people in the West, immediately they call you a romantic, unrealistic—unrealistic, when you start talking about rural villages in the Third World! In fact, it is we in the West who have become unrealistic, because we ignore the reality of what's going on in the world. We speak as though human nature has evolved to some sort of urban industrial existence.

If we could just stop doing that, if we could constantly keep in mind that the other half of the world lives differently, I think we would find that we have far more opportunities, far greater space and potential for the future.

What about the work of organizations like the Grameen Bank in Bangladesh who loan very small sums of money to the poor? Is that good or bad?

Well, it's not all that great.

I recently heard Muhammad Yunus, the Founder and Managing Director of the Grameen Bank, speak at the State of the World Forum in San Francisco; he got a very rousing applause. He said they had started off with forty-seven dollars and now they have a billion; ninety-eight percent is lent to women and they pay it back; and in another generation, if they keep doing this, there will be far less poverty and need in one of the poorest parts of the world. I want to know your thoughts on that, and there's another point I want to add.

When I was in Calcutta, where I spent some time with Mother Teresa, and when I've been in villages in Mexico, I have seen terrible problems of poverty and disease. Couldn't somebody say that it's our obligation to bring the civilizing of manners, of equality, of respect and nonviolence to these areas? And I ask that somewhat hypothetically, recognizing that there's been more killing in the twentieth century in the interests of so-called civilization than ever before.

In many of those villages, you certainly don't find paradise. In many of those villages, women's status is too low; there is poverty; the water is dirty, but we need to look at how that happened. We need to look at the history of colonialism. European powers came in and persuaded people to stop producing for themselves and to start producing for Europe. Force was involved, murder, and, of course, slavery—carrying people to the other side of the world to produce for the industrial powers.

Now that history has continued, and today, in the name of

globalization, there is even greater pressure on people of the South to produce for other parts of the world. Specialize for export—that's the essence of the modern economy. To me it's sad that many well-intentioned organizations, including the Grameen Bank, support this as the way to help people. Even companies like The Body Shop, that go into rural areas of the so-called Third World and employ people to produce sweet-smelling herbal products for the North, they may not be doing very much good. It is absolutely vital that we look instead at how we can help people everywhere regain greater power over their lives by diversifying their local economic activity by focusing on basic needs— starting with food. We all need food three times a day, every day.

The Nation magazine recently had a report out of Juarez, Mexico, where a large number of women work in the maquilladoras, producing shoes and T-shirts and windshields for the U.S. market. The maquilladoras, according to this report, have brought women a perverse sort of liberation, a sense of freedom from rural traditions, but they have also brought a new form of servitude, which has reached extremes of murder and abuse. So in this global economy, women may believe they have advanced, but it's a complete trap, because of the pay they get, the way they're treated, and the demoraling of their community through a way of life that is totally at variance with very old traditions.

Many Westerners have accepted these stories about how women in traditional societies are not equals and need to be empowered. Not long ago in England, they televised a program about women in Bangladesh who were working in the fashion industry making textile clothes for the North. And they were interviewed, saying "Yes, this is wonderful. I'm earning my own money. I probably won't get married." The BBC analysis was that this was a great way to solve global problems because it could help reduce the population explosion.

This is a very tragic con job. The situation in the village may not be ideal, and certainly to the extent that we can, we could—perhaps—try to help. I don't quite know how, we'd have to be very modest about intervening. But the tragedy is that even programs like the Grameen Bank, which goes in and imports debt into rural areas where there's never been debt before, are creating dependence on a global market. Those women may no longer be dependent on their husbands, but who are they dependent on now? Some man who sits on Wall Street and plays in the global gambling casino. A man they'll never see. Someone they can't even talk to. They become victims to forces over which they have no control. At least they can speak to their husbands. At least they can talk to their brothers and sisters and people in a living community where you have a voice and you're able to see your oppressor.

So let me repeat that roughly fifty percent of the population of the world is not dependent on this very vast and unaccountable global economy. And there are very, very successful projects now whereby people in the North and the South are taking back control over their lives—recreating the fabric of a more participatory, more democratic and alive way of being—by delinking from the global economy. We should realize that the number one thing that we can do is inform people about the seductive and overpowering nature of global market forces, and help people strengthen their local economies, particularly in food.

For example, in the industrialized world, there is an inspiring grassroots movement of reconnecting to the sources of our food and strengthening the local economy through agriculture. In every industrialized country, the growth rate of these grassroots initiatives is astronomical. And everywhere you look at it—I know of almost no exceptions—it raises the prices to the farmer, it lowers the cost of food to the consumer, and it helps farmers start to diversify. It kindles a sense of connection and community. And in many cases, children have the chance to go out and work on a farm and actually have contact with animals and the living fabric of nature. It's amazing. So I really think it's vitally important that people know that potential solutions are right under their nose. They just need to understand why they're so important and get involved.

I want to highlight this notion of development; it's so powerful. Harry Truman announced "The Development Decade" in 1949, and it has since become an overwhelming obsession. To challenge it is almost obscene. It's almost like taking your clothes off in public. It is taboo to challenge the notion of development. Now, I came across a statement by Wolfgang Sachs in The Case Against the Global Economy *that I find haunting. He says, "Development without hegemony is like a race without a direction." Hegemony means control, domination—the opposite of democracy, participation, equality; all the things we say we believe in. So why do we accept development as an unquestioned good?*

Development is a race, and the rules of the race are made by influential people as part of a system that dramatically expands the gap between the rich and the poor everywhere in the world. This logic of development is rarely—if ever—challenged by The New York Times, *the White House, the G-7 summit, at major party conventions, in the mass media, or even in the schools.*

The issues of development, progress and globalization are essentially flip sides of the same coin. In the industrialized world we talk about progress, which we tend to view as something evolutionary, something that happens of its own accord. In the South, on the other hand, we talk about development, and we have a sense that there's a certain amount of planning and funding involved. In fact, progress in the industrialized world and development in the South are now both carefully planned and funded, and the model for this is globalization. In other words, we're all now—North and South—in a centrally-managed global economy led by the World Trade Organization, very much accelerated by trade treaties, such as NAFTA and GATT.

I've been questioning this and opposing it for twenty years. I felt very lonely as recently as five years ago, but I've been instrumental in putting together the IFG, the International Forum on Globalization, who produced the book you just quoted from. What I find now is that there's much more understanding of the issue because the globalizing process is marginalizing the majority of people on the planet. It is creating mass unemployment and job insecurity everywhere, so that even the heads of the biggest corporations feel their jobs are at risk.

Let's talk a little about the IFG, the International Forum on Globalization.

It's a group of about sixty thinkers and activists from around the world, and we've been meeting for the last three years. As we sit around the table, we find that in every culture the problems are the same. And the problems are coming from a centrally-managed global economy. So we have literally one World Bank, one World Trade Organization, one International Monetary Fund, dictating policy to every government. And the manifestations of the problems that arise as a consequence of this centralized planning are always a little different in each country, but essentially, they're the same.

It's an absurd situation that there has been such a strong voice of criticism from the West about Communism and centralized planning, but until very recently, there has been almost nothing in the mainstream media about the centralized nature of the global capitalist economy. But it's beginning to come and as the IFG has come together, I think we've helped to highlight this issue. Awareness is also bubbling up everywhere as people wake up to job insecurity and unemployment, and as government leaders wake up to the fact that enormous global monopolies have been allowed to grow more and more powerful.

Not only have they've been allowed to grow, but in fact, government has been subsidizing them. And these very heavy subsidies are what lies behind so-called efficiencies of scale. Subsidized transport infrastructure means that almost everywhere you go in the world today, milk from thousands of miles away costs less than local milk. There's this complete perversity. The consequence is the breakdown of healthy production, the breakdown of small producers and of small businesses globally.

And the loss of human dignity and power over one's life.

Of course, and what we're getting is old food from very far away—irradiated, packaged, and treated to prevent spoiling. Of every food dollar in America, we pay roughly three cents to the farmer. In the meanwhile we're paying for advertising, irradiation, refrigeration, preservatives, packaging, transport, all these things we didn't ask for. So it becomes very, very clear how insane it is to have food from, in many cases, ten thousand miles away. New Zealand butter in England costs less than English butter. In Mongolia, where they have 25 million milk producing animals, you can't find Mongolian butter in the cities; you find German butter. In Kenya, Dutch butter costs half as much as Kenyan butter. America exports roughly as much corn as it imports. England imports roughly as much wheat as they export, and on and on it goes. And endemic to this economy are these enormous subsidies for export, for trade.

Today in The New York Times, *retiring Labor Secretary Robert Reich put out a kind of valedictory; he had a bar chart and some nice words for President Clinton. He happened to mention that the wealthiest twenty percent—all the people who do things in this society that get any visibility—that their income has increased thirty percent, while the bottom twenty percent had sunk significantly. The story also says that our President has been told specifically not to talk about these class issues.*

Now Reich might have said, "This is a horrible thing. It's a scandal. The President's doing nothing; the Congress is doing nothing. I quit." Instead, he explains that the President is on the right track and he'd be doing even better if Gingrich wasn't in the way. But it's there if you read it. The shameful growth of inequality in America is continuing. So, in some ways, what's happening in Ladakh is happening right here in Oakland, and all the other cities of this country. The global economy is creating dependent populations.

It's happening in Sweden as well. And in Sweden, just as in the U.S., there are deep cuts to the social welfare budget while taxes for corporations signing on to the neo-liberal corporate agenda are being sharply reduced. It's very frightening what's happening right now at the level of government policy. Not long ago in England there was a serious suggestion that corporations should pay off the debts of African countries and essentially own the countries. So we are now even getting publicly voiced support for having the world run by corporations.

It has become urgently important that we tell people that there are solutions, beginning with efforts to localize economic relationships. One of the most wonderful things I have seen is people who have been told in school that they have failed, that they don't know anything useful in the global marketplace, begin to recognize that they have all sorts of skills relevant to a local economy. They can do a whole range of things. There are projects where people are rebuilding local economies, constructing houses, growing things, making things, baby-sitting for each other.

We're really talking about understanding how human beings live, and how we ought to live.

I've lived in cultures that are polar opposites on the global spectrum. I've lived in America for long periods, many years, and I've also lived on the Tibetan plateau. These two countries represent the least developed and the most developed. In between, I grew up in Socialist Sweden, and I've studied and lived in Germany, England, France, Spain, Austria, and I've also spent long periods in Mexico. This broad cultural experience has convinced me that in order to understand how to live, we need to understand how profoundly we are shaped by the culture in which we are placed. I've seen myself change in different cultural contexts, and I've discovered that things like speed, for instance, dramatically change my relationship to nature, to my friends, to my family, to other people. I've discovered that time is very much a product of technological change, and that's just one of the many variables that change with what we call progress, with what we call development and modernization.

As we speed around, can we even imagine a world where the fastest speed is provided by a horse?

Well, not only can I imagine that, but I have been living it. For the last twenty-one years, I've lived for part of the year in a place where I ride a horse or walk to get where I need to get. A lot of people don't understand that, in many places in the world, everything one needs is within walking or riding distance. Decentralized structures enable one to get everything one needs at that pace. Now, of course, choices are limited. And in Tibet, I don't have access to Hagen Daz ice cream or Mcdonald's burgers. I have a fairly limited diet, but it is fresh, and I don't miss these things.

I was in Chiapas, Mexico, in 1983, near San Cristobal, and during that time I would observe that people native to the area would walk sometimes eight, ten miles a day from one village to the next, walking in silence. I'm afraid that if I had to walk that far, I could feel myself getting restless, my mind jumping around a lot looking for distraction. I wonder whether the pace that we live at, our acclimation to continuing novelty, sets us in a very different world-view from the indigenous cultures we're talking about.

Well, this is a very tricky issue. One of the things I discovered in Tibetan culture was that the daily experience there was more enriched with diversity than the daily experience in a typical modern context. What I mean by that is that because people there were so closely interacting with nature, and because each individual had grown up in much more secure circumstances and had been able to develop their own characteristics in a much richer way, there was actually a greater degree of individuality. So daily experience, everything you did, was far more attractive, far more enjoyable, precisely because it was more, if you like, diverse. The irony is that our lust for so-called novelty is part of a world that is becoming more and more homogenized and monoculturized. It's no wonder that we seek to escape, because the world we've created has become so deadened, so completely devoid of the spontaneity and diversity of life. We're surrounded by dead objects, and we are increasingly surrounded by dead people.

So if I'm in my car, driving from Oakland to San Francisco, I'm going to be in a hurry to get there. I've got the radio going. The traffic is highly frustrating. I'm surrounded by dead objects—dead cement, dead cars, dead equipment. I'm traveling in a dead zone, a dead point between where I was and where I want to go. Now if that's the case, I'm spending a lot of dead time moving from point A to point B, and so is everybody else. But in a world where you don't have all those machines, and where nature is fully alive, getting from place to place might be fully active, fully engaged. Perhaps in the village, you are wherever you are, and dead space may not even exist at all.

A good example of this that I reflect on a lot is when I found myself, within just a matter of days, in two very different situations. One of them was in a traditional context. I was working with a monk doing a dictionary of his language into English. He lived on top of a mountain on the other side of the village, and it's quite a hike up there. Now he didn't have a telephone. I didn't have a telephone. I had a prearranged appointment. I walked through the little town, climbed the mountain all the way to the top, and he wasn't there. Now you'd think that was a very frustrating experience, but actually, the entire process was pleasant. I'd been walking through the most magnificently beautiful landscape—snow-capped peaks and beautiful architecture everywhere. There was almost nothing ugly in my view. My eyes were just sort of drinking in the beauty of the architecture, the landscape, and as I walked through the village, I continually met friends, people I knew, stopping to chat

DIALOGUES ≋ JERRY BROWN

because everything was happening at a relaxed pace.

A few days later, I found myself in New York City trying to reach someone by telephone to arrange an appointment. Here I had all this wonderful technology, but the whole experience was thoroughly unpleasant. I'm trying to get through a phone mail system that is very frustrating and the phone I am using has call waiting. So there I am, very out of touch with this, and this call waiting thing is going on, and it's about to give me a nervous breakdown. This is torture. So the frustration of not reaching someone on the phone was far greater than walking across the whole village up to the top of the mountain and finding that my monk friend wasn't there.

I can make the same point by contrasting other kinds of experience here in the West. I have found that when I give lectures, there's great variation in different cultures in the length of time people are willing to participate, even between Spain, England, Scandinavia, and America. If I give a lecture in Spain, people show a great deal of patience; they are willing to sit for a long time, and they listen and discuss deeply. If I go to England, it's speeded up very dramatically, so that people can only tolerate roughly an hour and a half. If I go to Scandinavia, it speeds up another notch; the most they tolerate is about an hour. I come to America, and I find that there's a palpable difference in terms of time availability between the East Cost and the West Coast. And the fastest place on earth is New York where nowadays you really can't speak for more than forty-five minutes. So you can imagine with my complex message, it can be very frustrating trying to get out my complex message in such a short amount of time.

Wolfgang Sachs, whom I quoted earlier, edited The Development Dictionary, *and in this book, he criticizes the environmental management rhetoric and rationale. He suggests that in the name of sustainability and environmental management, we are being programmed to give power to a management elite that will demand even greater control over our lives so that efficiency and productivity can be achieved in order to minimize pollution. But at the same time, the market system, the destruction, extraction and mass consumption, won't really be affected.*

The jargon and the rhetoric of sustainability has been essentially set by corporate interests. The summit meeting on the environment in Rio de Janeiro in 1992 essentially followed a corporate agenda. The whole discussion was framed by corporations. They prepared for years in advance—many of them, perhaps, well-intentioned people, but completely blinded by the notion that economic growth has to continue at any cost.

After they leave that issue aside, and leave aside corporate monopolistic control of the global economy, all that remains is to talk about treating symptoms. How do we rescue biodiversity? How do we rescue forests? How do we treat symptoms? This is the corporate agenda. And what's even more insidious is that now—for the last ten years or so—what cannot be questioned is trade, so-called "free trade." So in these ways, environmental movements have been steered away from looking at the essential problem, which, I believe, is the internationalization of corporate monopolies.

I want to dig a little deeper into this issue of environmentalism. There are a lot of good people running around—The Natural Resource Defense Council, The Environmental Defense Fund, The World Wildlife Fund, Audubon—and there are a lot of corporations talking about sustainability and pollution in their annual reports. And yet, there seems to be a danger in this kind of environmental ideology in that it obscures the need for attitudinal change, for a shift in our relationship to the land, for a spiritual connection to place. The environmental discussion is not only about whether we can make a more efficient car and then recycle all the parts, because if we add millions, or hundreds of millions, of drivers to the planet and don't change the attitude, which emphasizes having rather than being, we will not forestall catastrophe.

I don't totally agree with that. There's a certain danger in overemphasizing the attitudinal change. It's vital and it's very important, but there's also the more pragmatic approach which has to do with looking at what is actually efficiency. It involves exposing the enormous hidden subsidies for transport, and for petroleum generally, as well as the enormous tax breaks given to supposedly competing corporations.

What we've been taught about efficiencies of scale is a myth. As you move around, you see that in each and every locale, food from thousands of miles away costs less than locally produced food. Whether it's garlic or butter, this is true wherever you go. There is a very definite pattern that what is subsidized is what you can afford to buy.

I would still argue that the environmental movement needs to address attitudes as well as efficiencies. The polluting effects of a car may be reduced from one hundred to ten, but if the population is increasing and if new forms of pollution are created by the system used to manufacture the car, then we're just postponing the day of reckoning. We have to change an attitude, a collective attitude, and that has to be politically represented by national policy. That challenges the automobile. It challenges the design of cities. It challenges international trade. It challenges all the things you're saying. But at heart, it's a shift of philosophy, values, from having to being. And that is a much bigger agenda than the Sierra Club is talking about.

This is a much longer term agenda. I would say that, first, we need to shift our understanding. A lot of people who have been promoting the ideas of development have genuine faith in them. They sincerely believe that superhighways and genetic engineering are good for the economy. But individuals, local communities and nation states can now see that these projects are not good for the economy. So we now have the most wonderful opportunity to get environmentalists and people who are concerned about economic survival to join hands, in order to protect their environment, their spirituality, and their jobs. Now is a moment in history that is quite unique because the current economic trends are marginalizing virtually everybody.

I understand where we have to go. I understand, in part, because in my Jesuit training many years ago, we had a saying that referred to spiritual life that I have found applies to economic life as well, and that is, in Latin, Tantum quantum. *So much as needed; that's how to much do or take. It's a principle of harmony, balance or enlightened happy asceticism. These are good principles. They're preached by Buddha, by Jesus Christ, by St. Francis of Assisi, by lots of other enlightened people. But here we are in the world of cars, television, and computers. Helena, where do we start in the transformation?*

We start by rethinking the things you just listed. And I would like to add that I am not advocating asceticism. I'm advocating wealth, richness, joy, culture. I've seen dramatic changes not only in the Himalayas, but also in Europe. I've seen cities and towns die over the last twenty years. Even in Paris, where I was living twenty years ago, the culture was so much more alive. Every section of Paris had community, had color, had music. People made their own music—danced, sang. They had more leisure. They had more time to enjoy life. The food wasn't prepackaged, didn't come from thousands of miles away. The food was alive! There was a wonderful culture around cooking and eating together, drinking delicious wine together, and as I say, literally singing and dancing.

When you walked in nature, you didn't have high tension wires everywhere. You didn't have airplanes and cars humming in your ears everywhere you went. I really think that if people could just remember that, or if they could just taste what that means—to have more time for friends, for nature, and for enjoying yourself—they would realize that we need to step back and look at how impoverished we've been, how dead we've become, how meaningless our work now is.

When we sit in front of our computers all day, alone, and when we get on the telephone and we don't even get another human voice at the other end, our lives are being diminished and they're being diminished very, very rapidly. In addition, many of these jobs that are supposedly so important, they're miserable jobs—sitting all day in an office and traffic jams for hours of the day and then rushing to a supermarket full of neon lights with everything designed to draw your eye to the products that are the most profitable, not the most nutritious or delicious.

And the worst of it is that even that unfulfilling life is threatened. The forces of globalization that gave you a miserable job are the same forces that will take it away. They are economic dynamite that we still don't have a proper understanding of because we're too caught up in a paradigm that was formulated a hundred years ago.

The alternative is not to shift towards keeping our jobs, but to shift towards more meaningful work, to shift towards more time and more nature, more natural production. That does not mean that we tell people living in urban shanty towns that they should stay happily where they are. We're talking about making a few shifts in policy. If we make these shifts, if we stop subsidizing corporations and stop subsidizing trade, what will happen is that local businesses will flourish. The local becomes much more competitive than the global when you stop subsidizing the global. And suddenly, you have a proliferation of smaller businesses, many more mom and pop shops, many more small farmers, smaller producers of all kinds, much more actively engaged, much more stimulated to produce in a healthy way, and having fun doing it, in flourishing communities.

The Evolution of the City
Paolo Soleri

"If we eliminate all the cities from this continent,
what remains is not much. Even though we Americans tend to be very skeptical about the city, we must
recognize that the city is still the place where things
are happening in scale and in quality."

*A native of Turin, Italy, Paolo Soleri came to the United States shortly
after the Second World War to study with Frank Lloyd Wright. An archi-
tect, author and pioneer of new human spaces, Soleri founded the urban
research laboratory, the Cosanti Foundation, in Scottsdale, Arizona, and,
in 1970, began construction of Arcosanti, an experimental community in
the high desert outside Cordes Junction, Arizona. Covering twenty-five
acres in the center of a 4,000 acre land preserve and designed to accom-
modate 7,000 residents, Arcosanti embodies the principles of "Arcology,"
a combination of architecture and ecology, that Soleri has continued to
develop throughout his life.*

Soleri is the author of ten books, including Arcosanti: An Urban Laboratory, Arcology: The City in the Image of Man, *and* The Omega Seed:
An Eschatological Hypothesis. *I first met him many years ago when he
visited California, and later traveled to Arcosanti to spend time with him.
In this conversation, which took place in December 1995, Paolo articulated many of the factors that have shaped the design of Arcosanti, and
can help to shape livable cities of the future.*

*Paolo, let's start with some of the ideas which inspired the building of
Arcosanti.*

We have been attempting for the last thirty years to introduce society to an old idea, the idea of overseeing the gathering of humanity into towns, cities and metropolitan systems. It is a very old story, in fact the Latin word for city, *civis*, is the root of the word, civilization. The term itself indicates that there's no separation between the appearance of cities and the development of civilization.

So the city creates civilization. And yet there seems to be a destructive element along with it. It seems like the city, at least in modern times, in so many places, is very hostile to civilization, if by civilization we mean something that's elegant and creative and beautiful and pleasurable.

Well, that has somehow become the pathology of the city. But every phenomenon has some pathologies, so we should be careful to discriminate between what the city can offer and has offered for millennia, and what we are now making the city into, which is, as you are saying, an environment which is not very conducive to good society. The fact is that if we eliminate all the cities from this continent, what remains is not much. Even though we Americans tend to be very skeptical about the city, we must recognize that the city is still the place where things are happening in scale and in quality.

It's interesting that things are happening there in scale and quality, and yet cities receive such a low estimation, not only by people in government, but by people who are moving away from cities, and have been doing so for almost thirty years.

That's a horrendous mistake. Let me give you a glimpse of why. We know that the population of the globe is doubling from five billion people a few years ago to ten billion by the year 2050. Whatever stress we put upon the planet now will double by the doubling of the population. So we will need the equivalent of two planets by the year 2050.

Then, we Americans have the American Dream to implement. Well, if we implement the American Dream and then make the American Dream a planetary dream—which would be very much in tune with the notion of democracy, justice, equality, and so on—then we must multiply the number of planets we need. Americans consume twenty times more than the average person on the planet. So if the American Dream becomes the Planetary Dream, and we double the population, we will be in need of forty planets by the year 2050.

So we as Americans are modeling a way of life that will either require forty planets, or we will need to reduce our standard of living by forty.

This is the sore point. Unless we moderate, unless we re-invent the American Dream, then it's not going to be a dream. It's going to be doomsday. Because the planet, for the first time in the history of mankind, appears as one of the main actors in the play. Its limitations are now becoming evident and we cannot ignore the very clear and very substantial fact that we cannot demand from the planet whatever we please. So we need to take the American Dream and frugalize it, to make it into something that instead of being geared to the ends of a materialistic Eden, becomes more oriented toward the inner life of individuals and societies. You might need less of the physical in order to produce more of the mental and the spiritual.

We have to recognize that current patterns of affluent living, in America and the rest of the developed world, if not corrected, pose a real threat to the continuation of civilization.

It seems to be really so.

I think it's important just to pause a moment with that. The way we are, the way I drive my car, the way I live along with the other 265 million Americans—as we puff ourselves up as number one, we're validating a way of life that, when generalized in accordance with our own principles

DIALOGUES ≋ JERRY BROWN

of democracy and equality, will result in the devastation of the planet. Or, to look at it another way, we as Americans will require increasing numbers of people, billions of people, to live like serfs so that the planet can support our way of life.

That's right. A privileged class of Americans and Europeans and whoever adopts their way of life would have to control resources and to, let's say, limit the fulfillment of the majority of the population of the globe. Think what's going to happen when China, India and Africa accept this cycle of hyperconsumption that we are championing. Things are going to precipitate very rapidly, and all that we are slowly developing is going to be catastrophic.

All it takes is for China, India and Africa to copy middle-class American ways of being, and it's going to be a war for the dwindling resources available to sustain that hyperconsumerism.

Another difficulty is that now many countries, even China and India, have nuclear weapons and transcontinental missiles. Someone in India might say, "Wait a minute, we don't want to live on two hundred kilograms of grain a year. We want to live on four times that amount like you do. We have some nuclear missiles here, and either you start sending us grain or else. And let Vishnu take care of the rest."

Yes, in a very short, concise statement that's a possibility. But now let me take this a little step further and bring in the aspect of planning and architecture. Why? Because of all the activities of mankind, the bulkiest, the most expensive, the most demanding, and the most necessary is sheltering. We have to shelter ourselves, our families, our society, and the institutions that society needs. So sheltering is really an immense imposition, an immense transformation of nature. Now, the most consuming, the most wasteful, the most polluted, the most segregating kind of shelter we can devise is the suburban home. So we are presented with a problem—we like the notion of expanding into suburban development, even though it's the most pernicious way of going about generating the future for our children.

Okay, so that's another important point. It invalidates totally the discussion in the United States and Europe about expanding economic growth to bring suburban reality to many more billions of people. This is a distortion of what the human spirit is capable of.

That sounds very, very harsh, but I'm afraid we have to read it for what it is. Since shelter is the most imposing activity in which we are involved, if our choice of habitat is the wrong choice, we are in for catastrophe.

Are the suburbs wrong because they're spread out? Because they cover the soil? Because they kill other species? Are they wrong because they create shelters that have to be filled up with stuff that must be imported over great distances, and then someday disposed of, filling up even more space.

All these reasons. Consider the single family home. The more financial power people have, the bigger their shelter, and the more they have to purchase in order to fill it. So we begin this process of building larger and larger units, isolating them into what you call the suburban sprawl, and then connecting each of them to the resources and the utilities and the retrieval systems like sewage and garbage and so on.

Those boxes are the epitome of consumption. So we have set up a cycle where we say happiness is consumption, therefore we have to consume more, which means we have to produce more, which means we have to transform more of the planet into what is connected to our own fulfillment, what is consumable. Orienting ourselves to that kind of materialism is going to kill us—number one, because of the limitations of the planet; number two, because it's an indication that instead of transcending toward mental and social excellence, we are embracing hedonism.

Not to mention what being isolated and entertained in that box called the suburban house does to the spirit.

Yes, because the more we surround ourselves with gadgetry that we feel we need—and some of the gadgetry we do need—the more we tend to generate a condition where mental processes are not very interesting, not very necessary, and what becomes more necessary is to take pleasure in playing with gadgets and in other activities that are, in the end, not very fulfilling.

And the less fulfilling they are, the more consumption we have to engage in to cover up the emptiness. It's almost like we've been cursed, so that our greatest skill is our ability to create the need for stuff that our second greatest skill, technology, can produce. And by reducing intimacy and friendship, we are forced to satisfy more and more inhuman and artificial needs.

That's really what the consequences are. If a child is told from the moment he gets out of bed to the moment he gets into bed that the purchasing of an object is part of his or her own right and happiness, that child is going to be very faithful to this dogma. And so we end up having this notion that unless we partake in the market cycle, we aren't good Americans. The politicians tell us that; the corporate community tells us that; the theologians tell us that; academia tells us that. So we are really leading some kind of a utopian dream that is very dangerous.

That's very interesting—even the religions. Christianity defines distributive justice as Thomas Aquinas talked about it five hundred years ago, but now it is being applied to a totally different world. We are surrounded by all these physical elements—these toys, these gadgets, the stuff—and if it isn't divided around equally, that's morally wrong. So the theologian argues for an equal distribution of stuff that's not needed, and which, when obtained, will destroy the basis for human community and religion.

If you will think for a moment about what a shopping center presents us with, really try to penetrate the superficial impressions, and then consider the response to this of an Indian or a Chinese person for whom it is an incredible place of fantasy, then you begin to wonder where we are wandering with our minds.

I remember when I was growing up. I was born in 1938, and I was probably six or seven when I went to a department store in downtown San Francisco for the first time. It was around Christmas time, and the top floor of the Emporium was a toy land. It was so exciting! I mean, I can't describe the rush that I had going there. But it was just a toy land during Christmas. Now it's Christmas every day!

Yes, the exception makes for excitement, and now it's becoming almost boring. The little child with a mother that cannot afford even to make a living—the child goes into the department store, into the shopping center, and he asks the mother to buy this, and this, and this, and the mother has to say, "Yes, I will do my best in order to satisfy you." If she cannot satisfy the child, the child is a second-class citizen, evidently not worthy of the American Dream.

Now, you have been grappling with this for a long, long time.

I am seventy-six, but it doesn't take many decades to see that we are presented with a population explosion and with this demand for material fulfillment, and thus with a very limited future, and possibly a very bloody one.

This is the dark side. What's the other side? What's the vision of the city that doesn't fall into this abyss, but starts things on a different basis? It was human evolution that brought us to where we are, but the purpose of the creation of the human mind can't be to fall into this trap. I don't think God would have put this kind of a hex on us.

We can write a future history that shows other ways of fulfillment, and this might be a history of cities. They might tend to be very large, because through numbers we are able to afford things that are otherwise too expensive. At the same time the city presents an environment that is more frugal. Think again to the houses. Instead of having a large suburban house, I might have a very small urban unit, and I cannot fill that unit with as many things as I can fill the big house. So we have to see if we can adjust our mindset in such a way that we recognize that excellence and worthiness are not measured by ownership.

I recall my first visit to Japan, in 1960. My room was very small with a futon that rolled up. I would use the same room for eating, or reading, or sleeping, or whatever. Now we've taught Japan that they are doing something wrong. They're exporting stuff rather than creating domestic demand, and actually, in trade discussions between the United States and Japan, the assertion is made that the Japanese are hurting world trade because they're not consuming enough. So what you've just described as a virtue has already been defined as a vice in the western economic system.

That indicates a kind of utopian economic thinking. It means doomsday because of the limitations of the planet. What in the past could have been promoted as pleasure is now a real menace because of this contest between the number of people, the consumption that we feel is imperative, and the planet's inability to deliver. And then overlaying that are the values and virtues of the human species, which might, in fact, be far more profound than materialism, hedonism, and so on.

Since the human species can't go down the same road it's on, then there must be built into our structure some other vision, some other way of being. It can't be that what we need is what destroys us.

I think this other way of being is interiorization, to make reality more and more an inner reality, where ideas are filtered by our minds and made very, very fulfilling. I will try to put it in more plain words.

Whenever we are in the presence of life, at any level, from the bacterial to the human, we are in the presence of a process that interiorizes matter and transforms it into life, and then eventually into consciousness, and then superconsciousness. This is what any biological system is driven to by its own interior motivation. Any technological system, on the other hand, has to be ruled and regulated by external drives.

So life has some sort of inner principle that pushes it in certain directions, while technologies have to be pushed by outside purposes and plans.

That's right. Life moves by an interior drive, which you might also call genetic or instinctual knowledge. With the appearance of the human mind, it also becomes cultural, which means this inner motivation is driven not only by the biological aspect of the individual human system, but also by the cultural aspect of the human community; but it is always coming mentally, from a decision from inside the organism. It's not coming from outside.

So if what's driving us is coming from within, then what is without shouldn't be able to determine our way of being.

What is without evidently is the reality in which we are immersed, so we cannot ignore it, but we might be able to guide it. And the best guidance is not to say, "Well, I'm going to gulp more and more matter in order to find my own fulfillment." We are now called upon to transform the exterior world in ways which are going to give more fulfillment in terms of our inner drives, ways which encourage our movement toward values which are generating from within us.

It's almost as though our suburban materialistic expansion is like the paganism of the ancient world, which was overthrown by a new interior religion called Christianity. But the paganism here is so predominant that

even religious groups are caught up in it and have adopted the material-
ism that they profess to be overcoming.

And it's becoming more critical because now, as you were saying, we can arm ourselves with weapons which are really catastrophic. Our power to impose our wills is becoming greater and greater, and that which before was the ability of the despot to impose upon society, now is transferred to everybody. We are each in a way despots and want to impose what we feel is our right, ignoring that the right should always come with duty and responsibility. So by generating the conditions where we say we are free agents and we do what we please, we are trans-forming the singularity of a despot into a majority which says, "Yes, I was conceived, I was born, and now I do what I like to do. Period."

Do you think the custodians of today's paganism, today's materialism, will treat those who oppose them any more kindly than the Romans treated the Christians in the Coliseum?

Well, when things get very tight and the options become very limited, then the violence that we carry within ourselves could explode. I do not believe in the goodness of reality, in a benevolent cosmos. I try to gear my ideas to the notion that hardness and cruelty and suffering are very attractive and are ready to take over anytime. That is why I think that the future could be very bleak. Once the resources are limited, if our mental and moral resources become shallower and shallower, that's when something horrendous might be triggered.

I spoke recently with Gar Alperovitz, the author of The Decision to Use the Atomic Bomb. *And I'm thinking here that if democracies can drop a bomb with such insensitivity, and, even fifty years later, can't acknowl-edge the inhumanity of the act, what would the so-called bad people, the tyrants, do?*

It might help to try to understand where we come from. And I don't mean that in terms of just your own experience, but the human experience. We come from three and a half billion years of exercising the life drive, and this exercise up to now has been opportunistic. Any kind of species works at being able to survive and to multiply, and in order to do that, the driving force is to find the most opportune ways of doing things. It has always been a question of opportunism in terms of population and species.

We have transferred a portion of this opportunism from the population or the species to the individual. We have invented something that we now carry in our blood and in our bones. It's a glorious invention. It's love, compassion, generosity, and so on. So we have to try to combine the opportunistic drive, the ego-center mode that increased our species, with this new invention, which is the loving, the generous, the compassionate. The kind of social Darwinism that seems to impregnate capitalism needs to be injected with a compassion imperative. And if we are not able to do this, I am afraid that we are in for terrible troubles.

And there you have a problem—that the organisms of capitalism, corporations, reduce human beings to units of that one variable called "return on investment," denying their opportunism and their compassion.

Perhaps I am more optimistic than you seem to be in this. I really believe that we are beginning to realize that this pure drive that says, "I'm the most intelligent, the most cunning, the most able, so I'm going to dominate," this drive is now seen as in need of an added dimension—the loving dimension. We should recognize that greed is ingrained, it's part of our make-up, because of this opportunistic drive that we have. But we have the ability to re-orient our greed, to make it into a desire which relates to the family of man, and to the family of all life.

Greed has to be collectivized, has to be communalized.

Yes. We have to transcend our individualism. Life is a transcending process. That is how we evolved from the bacterial into the human.

Let's focus now on the city of the future. Having talked about all this, I get a sense of the criteria for the new city. It certainly doesn't look like Oakland or Manhattan or Los Angeles.

Perhaps it is not too different from the old examples of successful cities. There have been periods in European history, for instance, when cities were successful. They gave us the Renaissance and then developments from the Renaissance up to the present day. The fact that we are gregarious, we are political, we need each other, indicates that eventually, the city is going to be, as it has been in the past, the container of community.

Now, Phoenix, Arizona is a structure of about six hundred square miles. So it's gigantic, and like so many cities, it doesn't work very well. It's sluggish by necessity, because it's gigantic. It depends on logistical systems which are colossal, in fact futile. So just in physical terms, in terms of gravity and thermodynamics, Phoenix negates what Phoenix would like to be, which is lively, intense, joyful and so on. What we need is to take Phoenix, and in a way, fold it over upon itself, make it three-dimensional, so that we miniaturize its landscape, and by doing that we eliminate all the problems of the gigantic. This is pure physics; this has nothing to do with metaphysics. This is the fact that time and space are very precious and we should use them in the best way we can.

Okay, now as you fold Phoenix into a three-dimensional city, what's it going to look like?

Well, perhaps we would subdivide Phoenix into, let's say, ten sections, and then begin to build properties that are no longer one or two floors, but that are many, many floors, maybe up to fifty, maybe more. This is very efficient, it's where frugality comes in, producing less pollution and less waste. Depending upon the population, each section might be a quarter of a mile square, that depends on the number of people and the technology you want to put in.

Would everything people do be done within that building?

I would tend to say, yes, if you want to achieve a great efficiency, but we don't have experience with that kind of architecture. That's why we need laboratories to investigate what that implies and slowly generate the logistics, the transportation, the necessary functions, that are going to be the answer to this problem of the gigantic and the wasteful.

And the city would husband resources and create far less waste.

Yes. And the resident is going to be a city and a country person, because he or she can walk out of their home and be in the heart of the city or in the presence of nature, which is now impossible in the cities we have developed. At one side of the doorstep there will be culture, and, at the other, nature, the condition of nature in the area.

Okay, you have study, you have sleeping, you have intimacy, you have working and production, learning and play, celebration, ritual. Now it sounds like people are going to be living a lot closer together than they are now.

This goes back to the European experience. For instance, my personal experience was in Italy. I was living in what you might call an apartment; it wasn't the best apartment because we were not wealthy. But our living room was the city. I could walk down four or five stories and be in the middle of the city, which offered to me all the resources a city provides, including the theater, the library, the university, the hospital, the playground, and so on. And that was available to me as a pedestrian, not as a person who has to enter this magic machine, which is the automobile, and then drive myself to those places further and further away.

What about the concern that this is like a bee hive? How is this city made to be elegant, and not monotonous.

That brings in the skills, the intuition, the vision of the planner, or the planners. That is why we need urban laboratories. In chemistry, in physics, in technology, we have laboratories. The laboratory is where you develop an experiment, and then you take the experiment to the breaking point so that through this failure, you learn about the subject. Well, we should do the same thing with those urban problems which are the most complex, the most demanding.

Is it your feeling that if we are ten billion human beings and in need of forty planets, that through appropriate urban design, human beings could evolve in a way that would allow us to keep transcending in the way you described earlier?

You're asking me to be knowledgeable, to be wise, in everything, and I'm not. But I believe so, because the future city must be frugal and frugality is ultimately interiorization. To be frugal does not mean to find happiness without ideas and without the aesthetic. You do not renounce when you become frugal. You open yourself to the interior values that are fundamental to the human animal. So to be frugal is not a necessity only, it's a necessity which almost automatically becomes a virtue.

Paolo, I want to talk a little bit about your idea of the omega seed.

Maybe we should start with the semantic. Why omega? Omega is the last letter of the Greek alphabet, so it suggests some kind of a conclusion, an ultimate condition toward which we are developing. It's a sense that many theologians talk about—they talk about a conclusion. That's why the term omega. And why seed? Because any kind of seed, including the human seed, is a blueprint for what an organism is going to become through its internal direction of development.

Now one could imagine that there is a seed that has a universal scope, what you might call a universal seed, a cosmic entity which contains all the information about reality. This seed contains the information about everything that happens in the process of becoming, from the very beginning to the very end. There really isn't very much of the metaphysical in this idea, but there is a notion that information generates knowledge, and knowledge, ultimately, is self knowledge. This implies that the omega seed points at the end of things, and at self-revelation, with reality becoming more and more conscious of itself from the very beginning to the very end.

Now, I tend to believe that at the beginning, at the Big Bang, there wasn't a written law or creational act by a divinity, but there was a choice between existence and non-existence. It just happened that existence came about, and when existence came about, it began to change. So that's the movement from being into becoming, and the evolution of things into becoming reality. That becoming at the beginning had rules that were co-natural to the nature of being; these are what we call natural laws.

Now, when life comes about, there is a new entity, a new agency that comes about. We add a new layer of reality, a higher level of reality, which is the layer of mind. Here we have animals; animals are intelligent and opportunistic. And we have humans; humans are intelligent and opportunistic, and they are also mindful, which means that we move into the realm of consciousness and superconsciousness, where we develop new laws by way of invention. We add new levels of reality, and it becomes very evident that opportunity is no longer sufficient. We need something that goes beyond opportunity, and we call it compassion, we call it love, we call it generosity, we call it altruism. That's what characterizes man among the animals, the animal kingdom.

So, you are saying that love and compassion are the next essential evolving structures that have to be brought into being by humanity.

And it exists now. But it's fragmentary, it's weak, it's fragile, because we are still driven by the opportunistic frame of reference, and naturally we depend on the physical, the deterministic. We come from eons of development, so within ourselves there are these forces which are very powerful, and the most powerful of them all is opportunism.

That is incredible, if love is what we are evolving toward. So do you think that love and friendship might evolve through the design of habitat?

Yes. But we cannot go from zero to a hundred in one short week. We start from zero, one, two, three, and so on. A hundred years from now, we will not exist as we do now. We will be very different, so we must start now to realize the importance of cutting into the gigantic systems that we have been building. We must invest in laboratory work in urban questions, just as we do in other fields, such as medicine. We use ourselves as guinea pigs in order to carry medicine forward, and should do the same thing with the urban condition.

In order to get to that point we need to persuade our politicians and people in power that as things are developing now there is no way we can succeed. And more important than just the politicians, we are going to have to get this idea into our own minds and really deepen it and share it. And as we begin to understand it, it can become part of the philosophical base of where our country, and every country, might go.

Absolute Trust in Nature
Alice Walker

"Kindness is possibly the best indication of wisdom."

Novelist, poet and activist, Alice Walker, is one of the important literary figures of our time. The child of Georgia sharecroppers, her education included not only her experiences at Spelman and Sarah Lawrence Colleges, but also her deep involvement in the southern civil rights movement of the early 1960s, and her subsequent travels among people throughout the world. A former teacher at Jackson State University, and Wellesley and Tougaloo Colleges, she is the author of many books of poetry, fiction and essays, including The Color Purple, *for which she won a Pulitzer Prize,* The Temple of My Familiar, *and* The Same River Twice.

I spoke with Walker in June 1997, shortly after the publication of her collection of essays, Anything We Love Can Be Saved: A Writer's Activism.

Alice, in your book, Anything We Love Can Be Saved, *you make the statement, "The Earth on which we live is the body of God. All people and living things are the body and soul of God. We serve God not by making the Earth and its people suffer, but by making the Earth and its people whole." Now, when you look at America, where do you draw your optimism in light of the gadget-richness and loss of "Godness" that you also refer to?*

The sense of Godness for me is in nature itself and it has not yet been defeated. And until it is defeated, I am not defeated.

So the world, the created world as you encounter it, gives you optimism?

Every bloom that I see, every spring, every blade of grass, every tree, every river that's not horribly killed already, gives me hope.

In light of your experiences in the civil rights movement, in your travels to Cuba and Africa, and in your own growing up, what gives you this hope?

I grew up in the South and we were farmers, so from the beginning, I had a very deep appreciation for what the Earth does. It never was to me anything other than very alive and very sustaining. My mother was a kind of Earth goddess. She could grow anything—other people's flowers would grow to two feet, hers would grow to six feet. She was this being who radiated intense liveliness and goodness. I grew up actually knowing what vibrancy is, what being alive is—what it looks like, and also knowing what goodness can be. I saw that and I saw her as part of just what is—what we are given.

It's always very amazing to me that people have a desire to destroy the Earth—that they put heavy things on it, like some of the buildings, for instance. They're really entirely too big and too heavy and they should never have been built. I would never have done it that way, but that is what we're up against. What you're left with is this sense that the cathedral of the future will be nature, because finally, it will be so contained that you will actually go to these little bits of nature and that will be your connection. You'll finally realize that that is the body of God, that the gift that we are given automatically by being born here is what is natural.

People who want to leave, like the people who wanted to attach themselves to the comet, I find this so difficult to even grasp. No matter what madness man is doing—and usually it is man—the Earth itself is doing something so marvelous and so enchanting and so beautiful that my heart is lifted. As often as my heart is cast down, it is lifted, and it can be lifted by the smallest thing, because each small thing has all the magic of the big things. A turtle is just as amazing as an elephant. A bee is just as amazing as a bluebird. So these things are just there, they're just in your life. I've often said that as long as the Earth can make a spring—and it has never failed in my lifetime—so can I. And we will go down together—Earth and I.

So do you see this as a cyclical reality—the spring follows the winter—as opposed to an ascent upward, a trajectory forward of progress and increasing sophistication?

I'm a cyclical person. I'm not a linear person at all. I don't believe in this progress that people keep telling us we have. It's a straight line that seems to lead to destruction. That's where it logically will take us, and that's probably why people are trying to get off the planet. They can see the logical end of where we're headed and they want to be among the people who escape. My feeling is that life is cyclical, that nature has a way—has always had a way—of going in a circle, not straight up, not straight down, and not in a straight line. Sometimes I think that people who have that linear view are really recent. They've never noticed that things do move in a circle, and I wonder, why?

Do you feel your own life moves in a circle or that you're getting wiser or deeper?

I'm probably getting more humble as I get older. I was brought up to go to school and to think that if I just stayed in this straight line I would end up somewhere special. I have had to slow way down and really be in the moment I'm in. That is a kind of lesson in being humble—to know that that moment is a gift and to just rest there; to not be so concerned about the future and not be all that aggrieved about the past; to make of the moment that you have the very best moment that it can be with the person, the thing, the flower, the tree that is right in front of your face.

Schooling is pretty much the opposite of that.

Schooling is designed to erase a lot of that, to substitute other people's knowledge for your own. What I love about Buddhism, which I've been studying the last couple of years, is that they tell you up front that the whole point is to reacquaint you with your native wisdom, with what you already have. This is true; you have it. When I was writing my fourth novel, *The Temple of My Familiar,* it became so apparent to me that everything I was writing was my own knowledge, but I had no idea how I got it. In some way, I accessed that part of myself that knew so much that school had distorted. I had to go down to another level of myself in order to write the things that I was writing, and I knew they were true.

Many people are proposing education as the answer. They say it's the answer to poverty; it's the answer to other problems. And yet, in many respects, education is a deeper embedding of alienation. It obscures the fact that we have, as our original nature, all this knowledge you talk about.

But that's because of where we are. We have to be educated now. I'm not saying that we should be ignorant of what's happening in the world and not know anything. We have to be educated as well as we can possibly be. Everybody in this country and the world should be educated. But at some point, if you are educated, you see that you've actually been educated away from this other self. That's when you really are able, if you're lucky, to reconnect with that self, and bring the two into some kind of balance.

I retain all the things that I loved, and none that I didn't love, at Sarah Lawrence, and Spelman, and wherever I went to school. But now I also have a greater trust in my own innate knowledge about life and about experience. And again, I can see that my mother had this. My mother only went through fourth grade, and yet she was one of the wisest people I have ever known, partly because she was so kind.

Kindness is possibly the best indication of wisdom. This is the kind of person that I saw on a daily basis and it made quite an impact. Even though my mother's speech was "Ebonic speech," and my teachers spoke standard English, I could always hear her wisdom better than I could hear theirs. Their wisdom came to me through all the rote learning that they had to go through, and their brains often seemed to be a step behind what they were actually saying.

Tell me about the patterns of speech that you picked up from your mother and the patterns of language that are uniquely African-American. If education stamps that out, what's lost in the process and what's gained?

My parents, and especially my grandparents, spoke the way everybody in their community spoke. They had this very colorful, vibrant, direct way of speaking. That is what *The Color Purple* is written in. Half of *The Color Purple* is written in black folk speech that I deliberately copied from the way the ancestors talked. I wanted to show that even though it's not standard English, it is just as resilient and vibrant and colorful and beautiful and strong as English—which I like. It's a very good language. The second half of *The Color Purple* is written in standard English. There you get to see what standard English can do, and it can do a lot. But at the same time, some of that color is lost. Some of that immediate, vibrant expressiveness of black folk talking among themselves is lost—it really is. But at least you should be able to see the good in both.

The teachers in Oakland who are trying to help black students who speak in an urban black folk English, they realize that you cannot teach them standard English by making them ashamed of the language of their parents, the language they learned at home. You have to tell them, "Okay, this is fine, this is how you talk. You are okay. But when you get out here with all these other people from all these other countries, and they're all speaking standard English, you will be much more comfortable and happier if you can also speak like that."

Now, do you think the teaching of black English, Ebonics, is misunderstood?

I think some people are frightened of it. Some people think it's just a ploy to get money from the government. But because I come from an environment where people speak black folk English, and I can do it myself when I want to, I understand these teachers. I understand what they're trying to do. Wherever I go, I talk to people about how necessary it is for children not to be ashamed of how their parents sound. They mustn't have shame anywhere in their education about who they are. It's fatal to being educated.

What is necessary here is that we respect the teacher, and try to remember what he or she is up against. The students aren't speaking standard English; their families and the rappers aren't speaking standard English. They're speaking an urban black language. What the teacher is trying to do is to prepare students to understand not only what the rappers are saying—on all levels, with the sexism and all of that—but also to prepare them to learn standard English. The teacher sees the hold that this language has on the children; they know every word of the songs they hear. So the teacher can't say the language is wrong, it's ungrammatical, it's bad, you're bad. She has to recognize that the students are smart enough to understand both of these languages, and teach them how to speak and write the standard one while not making them ashamed of the one they feel comfortable with already.

So I think as adults—and you know in Cherokee tradition, and my great-great-grandmother was Cherokee, you become an adult when you're fifty-two—we are called upon to use our best thought in approaching these very crucial problems in the world. And that is where I say to myself, well, I have never been to Oakland. I don't know a thing about these schools. Maybe they're terrible. But I bet that these women—and most of them are women and some are men—I bet they're giving this all they have and they have really thought about this, and they really are in there trying to teach these children. Now that's the faith. That's the faith that I have.

They say today there are about 5,000 languages in the world. The regions where the fewest number of languages are spoken, such as Europe, are also the wealthiest. The prediction is that in not too many years—perhaps a generation or two—that 5,000 is going to drop to maybe a hundred languages. So just as species are being extinguished, linguistic variation, which represents a species of human artistry, is being extinguished. When I heard about this Ebonics controversy, it dawned on me this is a form of expression that belongs to the structure of a community. Therefore, to stamp it out is to cause the destruction, in a very fundamental sense, of a part of a community. In that sense, would you reflect a little more on this whole issue?

That's one reason why *The Color Purple* is written half in a language that is on its way to extinction. It was such a joy to write in the language of my grandparents because it made them live. The reason for the life of that book is that the people are constructed out of their own language. Many people read it and say they're making grammatical errors and this is a mistake and so on, but that's because they're coming from a world of standard English. But even these readers use dialects. Thomas Hardy, when he's writing in dialect, I see his people. I see them because of the way he writes. That is what happens when you read *The Color Purple*. You see these ancestral black people speaking this very alive, funny language and seeming to leave out verbs or whatever, but actually they're getting right to the point.

So often I have seen people who are very straight—white students for instance, at Wellesley—finding themselves so overwhelmed with happiness when they read this and they get it. They didn't think they could. It's not what they're used to. But, of course, you can get other people's language. I struggle now to learn Spanish. I've been studying it for five years. I do it with tapes, and a tutor, and it's very hard for me—it's so hard. It's such a beautiful language and yet, I know that until I actually get fairly good in it, there's no way I can get closer to these people that I like so much. So I'm willing to work to make that connection, because I want to be able to say to them, however haltingly, some of what I feel when I'm in their culture and in their communities. Language is about respect and kindness, and being able to extend yourself as a human being. It grieves me that we're losing languages just as we're losing cultures. We're losing dances. We're losing songs. There are sounds that people have been making on this Earth for so many years that are disappearing—they will never be heard again.

It's often pointed out that schools in America are failing the African-American community. If you look at grades and test scores and retention rates, they're low in comparison to other groups. Children show up in the world with desire and exuberance, so if there is widespread failure, what does that say about the context in which those children are growing up?

I was just glancing at the paper the other day, and two things struck me. One was that they're now thinking of sentencing thirteen-year-olds to prison as if they were adults. The other was that several billion dollars that Clinton had proposed to repair inner city schools have now been taken back. These crumbling schools will just continue to crumble.

Although I grew up living in shacks—they were really horrible— my mother, being this Goddess woman, planted all these flowers around them so I was always just aware of beauty. In my life I have found that beauty is a completely necessary and wonderful thing. Many of these children never, ever experience it. When you drive through some neighborhoods, it's no mystery why people don't learn more, why they're not more energetic. They're living in places that are quite ugly and noisy. There's very little feeling of being loved and being cared for by a community, and on top of everything else, there's so much violence.

Let's make a comparison to Cuba. You've been to Cuba a few times, looking at schools and neighborhoods. There is certainly as much poverty, or more poverty, in Cuba than there is in many inner cities in America.

No, I don't think so. Even with the embargo and with the people beginning to be malnourished, that assumption is wrong. The life expectancy for black people in Cuba is much higher than it is for black people in Harlem.

What if you compare the poorest people in Cuba to the poorest people in the United States? My hunch is that in Cuba, the literacy rates look a lot better.

Absolutely, but that's because the whole society gives the best of whatever it has to the children, and the children know this. They grow up thinking if there is a quart of milk, they're going to get it. If there is meat, they're going to get it. That's how they grow up. They are expected to do well. Nobody assumes, as they do here in this country, that black people are somehow not going to do well. They assume that everybody is going to do well. If you spend time with children, if you teach them, they will learn. This was true when I was growing up. I had all black teachers, all black schools. It's not about that. It's about being in a situation where you are scared to death, you are probably hungry, you're worried about your parents, and you're going to a crumbling school. Then you read in the paper that the President, who said he was going to repair your school and keep it from leaking and turn on the heat, has just decided that the Pentagon needs heat more than you do.

You grew up as an activist. You were in the civil rights movement in the South. You lived in Mississippi for several years during that time. As you look over the urban landscape now, you don't see a lot of activism, at least not with that spirit of the late 'sixties.

Spirit has to manifest itself as it is. It can't just hearken back to some high point, although I think that period in the 'sixties was very fine. I really learned a lot. I also find a lot of people now who are doing things, who are active in their own way, sometimes in seemingly very modest ways. I think that a lot of people are almost ashamed that their activism is not more glorified and glorious. In *Anything We Love Can Be Saved* I'm saying that even if you're a small misshapen stone in this building that we're building, you should just bring it and add it to all the rest of us. This building has to be a building of hope. There is no way of emulating or trying to be these people who are so gigantic in our minds, many of whom, unfortunately, were assassinated—which is another blow to the spirit.

Now, when the civil rights movement flared up, and even before, there was a great deal of racial violence in the South. Churches were burned, children were killed. When the status quo is truly threatened, violence seems to become the response of those in power. On the other hand, when the status quo appears to be well protected, there seems to be much less direct violence. My question is this: is the absence of violence a result of the opposition being so ineffective? Is whatever is left of civil rights, liberalism, activism, whatever, is it now so domesticated, that violence and repression aren't needed?

Well, many of the people who have been most vocal are now in prison. I was just visiting Mumia Abu-Jamal last month. It's very clear that there was a plan for him from the time he was fifteen and a member of the Black Panthers. The FBI had him under surveillance and they plotted and planned to eventually put him away. I think that he's only one of many, many, many, many such people.

Those who aren't in prison then, can we suspect, by that fact, that they are relatively ineffective?

I don't see it that way because I think that there are many ways to be active. My feeling is that the first step toward activism is quiet and meditation and a centering of the self. Then you go out to make an impact on the world and on the lives of people with focus. If you do it this way, you don't have to reflect very much on the view that you suggest, which I would find so depressing. I wouldn't be able to do any of the work that I do if I saw it that way—that they have just won.

I'm not saying they have won, but I wanted to reflect on the possibility that they're way ahead.

No, they're not, because they are wrong; and when you're wrong, you're not ahead.

Now, I'd like to return to another subject in your book, Anything We Love, *that I found very surprising; that was when you talked about your hair and dreadlocks. You said that you didn't understand the nature of your own hair for a good part of your life, and that you were alienated from that part of yourself.*

Right. Well, let me just give you an analogy—circumcision. Anyone who is circumcised is alienated from part of the natural self. I say that because I think that black people's shame about their natural hair is similar. This is how I also talk to black people about female genital mutilation; they find it so awful and so horrible and they can't understand why anyone would do this.

I remind them that, generally speaking, from the time we are tiny, our parents have straightened our hair. In the old days, they did it with a hot iron which, literally, hurt like hell. It was painful, but you had to endure it, because your own hair was kinky and curly. It's really wonderful, but it was considered to be awful because it was not like white people's hair. White people's hair was the norm.

White skin, also, was the skin of choice. By now not so many people bleach their skins, especially with the ozone layer getting thinner and people understanding that you actually need to be brown, but they still straighten their hair. In my twenties, thirties, forties, maybe, I didn't know what would happen to my hair if I just left it alone.

It was Bob Marley who reintroduced to us this way of wearing our

hair long and still natural. So dreadlocking is basically what happens to
our hair. The roots of it come from the Mumbista and Mau Mau cultures, where black people took to the hills so that they could fight against
their oppressors. They forgot about their hair. In the process of fighting
for their freedom—I love this, it's so wonderful—in the process of fighting for their freedom, they forgot about their hair and, of course, that's
the way it should be. Why worry about your hair if you're fighting to be
free? To make a long story short, when I understood that if I left my hair
alone it would just start to curl into these long, long locks, it was so amazing and so incredibly wonderful. It's another reason why I have absolute trust in nature.

*Okay, so here you have an example where the most personal thing about
yourself, your own hair on top of your head is something that is—*

—a mystery.

It's alienated, it's taken away from you.

Absolutely.

Now, that's power!

Isn't it?

*I know you have been involved with trying to stop the practice of female
genital mutilation in parts of Africa. What about this, and similar cultural
practices where mouths are distorted, the body is scarred, or the feet are
bound. Many cultures have traditionally manipulated the body in some
way.*

Absolutely, and especially women's bodies, and for control. Last April
I went to Bolgatanga, in northern Ghana, to this incredible meeting of

Africans who want to abolish female genital mutilation. The Amnesty International official there had been scarred facially as a boy. It was so moving to talk to him about what that had been like. I was used to hearing a lot about women, but now I was hearing about men. He told me that he had been taken by his grandfather to his grandfather's house, and while he was there, these people had done it and he had been scared to death. Who wouldn't be?

People do these things to children, generally speaking. And these children need the help of adults who believe that nature was correct when she gave girls genitals and boys smooth faces, adults who will stand forward and say, "This is not right. Leave the child alone until the child can decide." Maybe at eighteen years of age, the young woman will say, "I would like to have all this removed." Or the boy will say, like they do here, "I would like to have a nose ring or a pierced lip." They can choose to do that and that's fine. I have no problem with it.

Do you see that as a positive statement or just another aspect of culture?

I would never do it to myself. I even regret the holes I had put in my ears when I was a teenager, because again, I really love the natural body. I think it's fine just the way it is. But for those people who choose it, that's fine. They're old enough to know what they want through their nose.

Leaving nature to her own devices out of a sense of reverence suggests that we might return to a more primitive state. So I have to wonder, how are we going to reverence nature, and, at the same time, give full vent to our creativity in fabricating different kinds of structures and things?

People have opposing Earth views and that's a real serious problem; the people who are destroying it are winning. Nature in its naturalness is the most elegant thing. I see it as the most sophisticated, most refined expression of life—much more elegant and refined and sophisticated than a BMW for example. This is something that Earth people—I consider myself an Earth person—feel to be our responsibility. Our task is to try to remind people, or to acquaint them for the first time, with this elegance, so that they don't think they are slipping back into something they have already struggled to leave behind. I think that Euro-Americans and Europeans, unfortunately, keep this memory, maybe genetically, of the Ice Age—a feeling of being severed from the warmth and glory of nature that is always benign. People who are more southern and who had less experience with this kind of icing, just don't feel some of the ways Europeans seem to.

I was describing to someone last week the moment when I first understood that things were out of balance with the races in the South. Some white people appeared in our yard and my parents did turn to ice. They changed. It was as if the climate changed. This was because the whites controlled everything. They owned the land that we were standing on, the house that we lived in, everything that you could see. They came in with the voice of authority—looking the way that they looked, and being the way that they were—as if that was correct and that we were somehow wrong in every possible way, even though without our labor they could not eat.

Is race still the fundamental issue in this country?

Not for me. Constantly I am thinking about issues like understanding and forgiveness, compassion and love, freedom.

Things that have no racial divide to them?

The things that seem to be innate in all of us. We're all trying to get to deeper levels of understanding in ourselves, and deeper places of connection with other people. We're trying to learn how not to throw stones.

What I love about Tibetan Buddhism is that it helps give you the discipline to understand that what you see out there that you don't like is often what is inside you that you don't like. This happens when you haven't examined yourself, when you haven't made friends with those parts. When you do make friends with those parts, and you see them outside of yourself, they're much more tolerable. You still may not like them, but you don't automatically want to erase a person who's carrying traits that you have in you that you don't like.

So as you look at the world, it's not so much as an activist whose first impulse is to change it. Your first impulse is to understand who you are, and learn from nature, learn from your own being. At that level, race and gender tend to slip away. They're there, but there's something underneath that is the link.

Right, because we do have a similar heart. We have a similar spirit. The deeper you go, the more you connect with that. Race is still there, but you tend to see it as the beauty of nature. You see that it's wonderful, whatever your color is, or how your hair is, or your eyes.

The world is increasingly cemented and manufactured and made of plastic and standardized. We are medicalized, starting with Ritalin if we're too active and ending with Coumadin if our heart doesn't pump right. From Ritalin to Coumadin, there has been a massive reinvention of the person. This reinvention effort seems very unhooked from natural processes, and very opposite to the Buddhist concept, to the spiritual traditions and wisdom traditions, which deal with the patterns that human beings don't create, but by which they are constituted.

I am a natural person. I prefer it that way. I like to encourage other people to be that way also and to disconnect from whatever takes them away from themselves, because being your true self while you're here is the highest form of worship. If you are not your true self, you are missing the entire experience of being here.

Schools of Alienation
John Taylor Gatto

> "I know this sounds fantastic to many people, but the truth is that you and I could spend hours talking and not come to the end of people who have accidentally stumbled on the great dirty secret of American schooling—it does not teach the way children learn, nor can it be allowed to."

John Taylor Gatto, an English teacher in New York City public schools for thirty years, was named New York City Teacher of the Year in 1989, 1990 and 1991, and New York State Teacher of the Year in 1991. Shortly after receiving this last award, he resigned from teaching, protesting what he saw as fundamental flaws in our ways of educating children.

Gatto is the subject of the documentary film, Classrooms of the Heart, *and the author of two books that critique American education,* The Exhausted School, *and* Dumbing Us Down: The Hidden Curriculum of Compulsory Schooling. *I had the opportunity to speak with him in the spring of 1997 about the state of American education from the perspective of someone "in the trenches," and about his proposed "guerrilla" curriculum, an alternative way of teaching that involves seminar-style classes and working apprenticeships that, in his experience, open children's minds to discover meaning and purpose in their lives.*

John, you've been teaching in the public schools of New York City for almost three decades, so can you state here what the problem is? People in America are just wringing their hands over the state of education in this country, and it doesn't seem like anything is going to get better if we stick to the path we're on.

Well, there are a lot of problems, Jerry. But I think they boil down to this: we don't teach the way children learn, and because education has become a central part of the American economy, you're really not allowed to teach the way children learn. You have the perfect example of this out your way. In a school near Los Angeles, Jaime Escalante, an elderly Peruvian immigrant, in less than four years, helped his students to achieve some of the country's best scores on the Advanced Placement calculus test. Working with a group of kids with no mathematical tradition and very little literary tradition, he made Garfield High School the third ranking school in the U.S. on Advanced Placement calculus. Mr. Escalante's fate is just fascinating—he was harassed and hounded out of the school. They made it intolerable for him to stay.

The same thing in Chicago. A teacher named Marva Collins, working with black kids from the ghetto, many of them from broken homes, found out what I did later on—that these children have no resistance at all to very high level work and ideation. If you set the idiom aside, they will produce work of a caliber that we associate with adults. I know this sounds fantastic to many people, but the truth is that you and I could spend hours talking and not come to the end of people who have accidentally stumbled on the great dirty secret of American schooling—it does not teach the way children learn, nor can it be allowed to.

Maybe that's just momentum and not design, but we're dealing with a $700 billion a year industry, which is a gatekeeper for all of the rest of the jobs. We couldn't turn out an excess of competent people without really doing damage to this economy. Now if this sounds like I'm playing a conspiratorial string on my violin, consider this: The President of Columbia Teachers' College, Dean Russell, in a keynote speech at the 1908 NEA convention, said that there was a tremendous danger that our schools might produce too many leaders, and it would cause a collapse in the system.

I'm looking at a quote that you use in one of your books, a quote from Edward Ross, the author of Social Control, *written in 1906. He warns that, "Plans are on the way to replace community, family and church with propaganda, education and mass media. People are only little plastic lumps of human dough." Now for you, does that encapsulate the underlying spirit of education in America?*

This is probably the most trenchant reflection of the prevailing attitude towards children, that they're little plastic lumps of dough. Edward Ross, who fought for this view, was one of the two or three people who created the discipline of sociology. And you also have, a few years later, the chairman of the psychology department at Princeton, who warned that standardized testing would function as a dunce cap, making people aware of their inferiority, making them reluctant to compete and, perhaps, even to reproduce themselves. After all who were they? There's a powerful central current of this kind of thinking right before the First World War that reaches a tremendous visible crescendo right after the Second World War. And then it disintegrates, almost as if it became a duty to avoid controversy and not talk about it.

I stumbled upon all of this as I was trying to figure out why on earth so many people appeared to have a vested interest in stopping me from doing what I knew worked in a school setting. When I talked to these people individually, they'd admit, "It's stupid, but I have to do it because—" And then they'd refer me to the next highest person up the administrative ladder. Eventually, when I got to the State Education Department and talked to the people there, they referred me to certain politicians. And when I spoke to some of the politicians' assistants, a few were honest enough to refer me to non-profit corporations, foundations, think tanks, which, I inferred, were running this particular politician, although this was hardly said.

What we have done, I discovered, is displace authority over the lives of children into so many different hands—many of those hands quite invisible—that to approach this with a problem solving frame of mind is really to frustrate yourself to death. We're dealing with a system that's working exactly the way it's supposed to work. Now there are ways around that. You can sabotage it like I did for many years, and that works sometimes, locally, until you're caught. You can sidestep it by sending your kids to private schools, although most private schools function the same way, except that they're more cosmetic. You can homeschool your children. There is a variety of ways around it, but none of these tackles the problem.

You said that anytime you did what you knew was right, you were blocked. Could you give me one example of this?

I'll give you the actual example that triggered my resignation and the op-ed piece I wrote for *The Wall Street Journal*. My school system, as I continued to succeed—in the sense that my kids were succeeding, including the kids that weren't supposed to—continued to move me into worse and worse school settings. Finally, I ended my teaching career at the school that, among its other distinctions, produced seven of the nine Central Park jogger rapists. There I used essentially the same teaching methods I always had, and gradually—it took longer because I was an older man and had slowed down a bit—the kids began to lose their "kid" quality and began to become people. They began to take an interest in developing their minds and spirits and characters as far as they could. Whenever I saw this kind of heartening response, my method was to offer more and more challenges and, at some point, the next challenge to a kid is navigating in the adult world of reality that they dimly see around them.

I had arranged with the President of one of the major corporations in New York to have my kids take a tour one of their locations. This is the kind of thing I had been doing for fifteen to twenty years. At the same moment that an executive from the company arrived at the school to pick up the kids, our principal raced to the door, confronted me, and said, "These kids can't go out. You haven't filed the proper papers." I said, "Sure I did, Jules. I dropped those in your box forty-eight hours ago." He said, "The policies have changed. It has to be done two weeks in advance. It has to be sent to the district, and approved." And I said, "OK, Jules, the next time," and he said "No!" In front of some Vice President of the company, with the kids all assembled together.

At that point I realized that this was not an independent decision by the principal, but rather a frantic blocking maneuver by the school district, which happens to be on the Upper West Side of Manhattan. They were disturbed by the continued success of children who happened to be under my direction. The truth is, they could have been under anyone's direction who followed the sort of teaching system dirt farmers would have followed 150 years ago.

Now what did you do with the kids that triggered this kind of retaliatory response?

I operated on a couple of really simple assumptions. First of all, that the bizarre and disturbing behavior that kids in New York were producing—not only poor kids, but really prosperous kids—was a direct result of their lives being stripped of significant experiences, confined in these abstract cells for all of their natural youth, and fed a diet of low-level abstraction. They were not even being offered the level of materials or texts that you would have found in a fourth or fifth grade class in the middle of the nineteenth century. I mean, the stuff that is reserved for the "gifted" or "talented" high school students, it's sixth or seventh grade work by the standards of a century ago.

So you deviated from the standard curriculum that the administration wanted.

I wrote what I call a "guerrilla" curriculum, Jerry, which was composed of stuffing them with primary experiences—as much as I could—on an ad hoc basis. I would read the paper in the morning or the night before, and the kids would be dispatched to investigate, with advance permission, whatever news was going on. And I brought a kind of seminar standard to the classroom. We didn't have to understand, for example, everything about Aristotle to have a lively discussion about some of his ideas, and to show that much of what he was driving at were current topics in kids' minds.

The way the administration saw it, this was a deviation from the educational curriculum, but your own experience showed that this gave reality and aliveness to learning.

You're quite right. But I think that the dynamic at work here is worth exploring, because it's not as simple as the administration just opposing it. What's happening is that each level of the system that has to give permission is on thin ice. So that the buck is passed, and when the buck leaves the local precincts, it's passed between foundation project officers and certain university staff and on to policy people in Washington. The ball never returns to your home court, or if it does, it's invariably ringed around with all these restrictions that protect people who make their living in the system. I'm not alleging that this is a conscious process, but it happens, to the point that you don't want to do it anymore.

Would you comment on how grading on the curve, which I presume most schools do, imposes a kind of bell curve stratification on the larger society?

The idea of the bell curve comes out of nineteenth-century Prussian Germany, from a series of debates that essentially concluded that a mathematized, predictable world is the best of all possible things to hope for. If you've read Hegel, you know all you need to know about this. In order to control everybody, certain strategic courses were undertaken in compulsory schooling. There had never been, prior to Prussia in the early nineteenth century, successful forced schooling in the history of the planet. Then suddenly, Prussia, in 1819, put all of their children in a two-stage system.

The first stage was designed to trivialize the child's most important learning years by filling them with balloons, songs, and funny games and to keep the intellectual or the moral part under the control of the teacher. Then around the age of twelve, the idea was to set everyone suddenly in competition with each other, and produce marks of rank on everyone, so that no matter how secure you were in your understanding of something, there would always be people visibly acknowledged as your masters.

According to Hegel and a number of other thinkers, this constant "alienation"—that was the word they used, and it was translated directly to American schools—this alienation would lead to a society which could be placed under the direction of experts that the state and the corporate world found safe and productive. The net result of this, Jerry, was that Prussia, a dirt poor country, within thirty or forty years, became one of the world's economic leaders. Horace Mann, and every other founder of American schooling before we had compulsory schooling, went to Prussia and came back with glowing reports of what the Prussians had produced, that is to say, a predictable society that could be disposed by the best minds.

So getting back to the bell curve. In the first place, we see it used at a moment when assessment is the wrong thing to do, it's inappropriate. And second, it's inaccurate, because people learn on private learning curves. Some people learn certain things instantly, and others learn them six years later. And I will tell you this—a kid who learns to read at five and a kid who learns to read at nine will be indistinguishable at the age of fourteen, assuming they both like what they're doing.

We can ignore this fact, we can say its too inconvenient or too expensive to allow that, and impose a learning curve in first grade that produces this wonderful bell. We can then assign the children on the flanges of the bell to special education programs and the people on the sides of the bell to dull course work and so on, and by simply doing that we can create a class system. Inside of a year or two, the kids will finish imposing this class system on themselves, and for some children, the humiliation of being a dull reader or bad reader will never wear off.

Compare this to 1812 or 1815, prior to the introduction of these ideas, when the founder of the DuPont fortune wrote to investors in France to say there was a miracle going on in this country—and they had better send money to invest in a gunpowder factory—because everyone here could read and debate like a lawyer. Or look at De Tocqueville's famous 1835 analysis, when he said that the classical Greeks are children compared to an American dirt farmer's kids. Look at the bestsellers of that day. I encourage everyone to get an unedited version of James Fennimore Cooper's *Last of the Mohicans*, especially if they have one or two college degrees, and see what an impossible book it is to read. And yet, it sold the equivalent of ten million copies!

Are you saying that as education has increased in this country, literacy has declined?

That's exactly what I'm saying. Now when you try to reconstruct the intellect of a thirteen-year-old kid, which is essentially what my classroom was about, you're dealing with social resistance which is quite unbelievable. And yet I just got a call today from a kid who, at age thirteen, had sixteen criminal charges against him and was filed as a functional illiterate by his school. He's now working on his second college degree and trying to decide between three or four interesting work offers. This is a boy that wanted to have a gun at thirteen, less than ten years ago.

So what miracle happened? Well the miracle that happened was that he was given himself back. And it didn't take a New York State Teacher of the Year to do that. I'm not claiming any particular insight, other than what was once common knowledge. This country was once unique in world history, because it took ordinary people, people who were considered trash in Europe, and made them independent, hard-working, self-respecting people. To deny what is unique about American history is just nuts, because in there we have the skeleton key to unlock the problem of our schools.

What you're saying is that there was a tremendous amount of literacy before the average person graduated from grammar school. My own grandmother went to school until the sixth grade, but she was quite a reader well into her nineties. Now we have a world in which the President is saying that everyone is entitled to at least two years of college, in the same way that a sixth grade education was assumed to be necessary at the beginning of the century.

I hope that he's just a dupe, Jerry, I really hope so. Because the way the game works is that we say our problems in education exist, A, because we don't have enough money and, B, because we don't have enough of the kids' lives to work on them. We've watched schooling go not only from twelve to fourteen weeks and producing a totally literate nation—

—twelve to fourteen weeks or twelve to fourteen years?

Twelve to fourteen weeks! That used to be the school year. And kids who went for longer than that didn't go every day, or even every week; they came and went. And furthermore, most of them were taught by one woman who had six, seven or eight ages with class sizes of sixty to eighty. That's an impossible situation according to the way we do business today. But in fact, as soon as you change the teacher-student ratio from the teacher being ninety percent of the solution and the student ten percent, to the reverse of that, the student ninety percent of the solution the teacher ten percent, then you can see how very large classes and mixed classes with mixed experiences can work. The kids become responsible for teaching each other.

What I'm hearing here is that one of the key building blocks in the development of a society of dependent, obedient people is the school. The mechanism of conventional schooling, enshrined as a secular religion, now reaches children at earlier ages and extends itself to older ages. So if the goal is independence, self-reliance, critical thinking—all the attributes that

Abraham Lincoln, Benjamin Franklin and others held up as important values—then somehow this whole schooling mechanism needs to be radically transformed. And I want to get that very clear, because there is a childlike devotion to the school system that reminds me of the devotion to the Blessed Mother at St. Brendan's Grammar School fifty years ago.

The various media have encouraged that idea. I'm not suggesting there was a cabal, but simply that the system we have is a result of the way ideas have been presented to people, especially those with the power to define this mechanism. Flattering luncheons were held where the decision was made to take that wonderful woman who ran those one room schools—which she ran so well without an administration—and put her under the direction of an apparatus of men, not just a single layer, but infinite layers, which are still being spun out.

It almost sounds like the apparatchiks in the late stage Soviet Union.

That's an excellent parallel. The question is whether this grows naturally as a result of certain fundamental decisions. MIT makes mandatory reading, I believe, a book called *Autonomous Technology,* by Langdon Winner, which was written about twenty years ago. Winner says that once you start with certain premises, it is inevitable that a system will eventually control all its personnel. The apparent leaders will remain only as long as they serve the system, and if they don't, they're marginalized and gotten rid of and someone else is put in.

Whether it happens naturally or not, I've been able to track an absolutely intelligent group of people in the field of education, representing a number of interests, that believed that the family was the barrier to a sane future. These people wrote extensively about their vision of the future and what it would take to get there, and schooling was the mechanism to utopianize. The ideologues communicating these ideas—that schooling is the means to get children away from the family and the mechanism to utopianize—perpetuate themselves from generation to generation because they control hiring at universities and foundations, and they hire people like themselves.

I'm going to quote something that you've said, and I'm going to ask you how to attain what you're suggesting. "We have to radically decentralize government corporate schooling, return the power of designing and assessing programs to the local level, and ensure that every form of training for the young aims at producing independent, self-reliant minds, good characters, and individuals who get fighting mad when called a 'human resource' and told their main function is to be part of the work force." Okay, great, I accept that. So how do we get there? Who do we attack and what do we build?

First, the schema has to be seen clearly. As long as the economy is built up of very large corporations, very large institutions, and very large government agencies, by necessity all the approved training leads toward some position on the pecking order of these giant employment pyramids. I'd like to contrast this scenario with two groups who have never participated in this type of economy, and who have had a continuous record of success. I'd like to do this in order to independently verify that success is possible when we rethink what a good life is.

Johns Hopkins University has been tracking the Amish phenomenon for a long time. They've published several mind-blowing books about what has happened in Amish America. At the beginning of this century, there were 5,000 Amish, now there are 150,000. So the group itself has retained its integrity and grown thirty times. Secondly, one hundred percent of the Amish, or very close to that, have independent livelihoods, divided approximately into fifty percent small entrepreneurial businesses and fifty percent small farms.

Now consider the drawbacks these people labored under. The government of Pennsylvania had been their sworn enemy through the century. They don't use telephones; they don't use computers; they don't use cars; and they're schooled only through the eighth grade because the Supreme Court cut them a deal allowing that in 1976. So with all these presumed drawbacks, you still have a community that, for all intents and purposes, has no crime at all, that takes care of its old and young, mixing them together in the active life of the community, and is amazingly successful, amazingly wealthy, and amazingly unschooled.

Many people would say that it's that religious glue, that pious glue, that gives the Amish their advantage. So I'd like to jump to a group that's as resolutely, militantly free-thinking as any that's ever existed—the Mondragon Cooperative, in the Basque country of northwest Spain. Their population is almost equivalent in size to the Amish, and they aim for exactly the same grownup solutions. Everyone there will have an independent livelihood, or they'll be a part of a small group that makes its living doing something valuable for the community. Their schooling is resolutely directed toward developing the same kind of independent, self-reliant, tough-minded characteristics that Amish education also stresses. So here we have two groups that are small, but not that small, who manage to uphold Lincoln's idea for America—that independent livelihood is where it's at.

Back in the 1840s, it was nearly impossible to assemble an American work force of over forty people, because people would only work for you long enough to get a little stake and then cut off on their own. If you taught them too much, they'd set up in competition with you! When we look at the history of New England factories during this time, we see a situation where a significant pool of labor existed among young, unmarried women, who were also very well-educated. As an incentive to attract these women into the workplace, factories sponsored concerts and dances; they set up libraries, and promoted activities such as literary societies.

As soon as these young women could bring some stake to their marriage from the wages they had earned, they left the factories. That was the American Dream—that you could write the script for your own life. Very, very gradually that dream was converted, not by evil people, but by people who understood that their wealth depended on their ability to command labor. Until they could assemble large groups of labor, they were never going to be wealthy in the way that Europeans reckoned wealth.

Okay, John, I'd like to encapsulate what you're saying. You've stated that the accumulation of great wealth requires the ability to command labor. You cannot command labor if it's independent and critical, therefore, you need a schooling system that operates in a manner similar to an obedience school for dogs—they have to be taught not to pee in the house, to heel at their master's beck and call. And in effect, the entire schooling enterprise, and there are obvious examples, is a huge obedience school run on the kennel model.

You've given two examples of groups operating outside of this system: Amish-Americans, a traditional, God-centered, family-based community, stressing strong moral character, and the more secular, perhaps, Mondragon worker-owned cooperatives in Spain. These two poles are totally at variance with the consumer-based, mass obedience operation which is cheerleaded all the way from the political Left to the political Right to the local chamber of commerce. So if I hear you right, what we really have to face up to is the absolute need for a critical distancing from a whole educational status quo which seeps into our deepest aims.

Absolutely. That's a perfect abstract of the matter. And we can eliminate Marx's idea that evil or venal people are doing this. The people who are doing this have convinced themselves "scientifically" that this is the only way it can be. This is what parson Thomas Malthus, biologist Charles Darwin and polymath Francis Galton all said. This is what the book, *The Bell Curve,* a couple of years ago said. This is the way they wish it to be and it can't be any other way. So they have to overlook Jaime Escalante in California, Marva Collins in Chicago and even John Taylor Gatto in New York. They have to overlook the Basques, and they have to overlook the Amish, because they don't fit the theory.

There are others here who would like participate in this discussion. Michael?

Michael: We are a homeschooling family and have been for many years. I know there are exceptions; there are many good teachers in the system who really want to educate kids in the truest sense of the term. But the school system, at its heart, even though it's there to—in some sense—educate the children, at its heart it's really there to break their spirits. That is what I think all the time. We've had some experience with our own children for short periods of time at local schools, and it has only confirmed and reinforced this idea.

Michael, consider this. The most influential U.S. Commissioner of Education that ever existed was William Torrey Harris, and in a book he wrote back in 1906, *The Philosophy of Education,* he said that the purpose of schooling was to alienate children from their families, their churches, their neighborhoods, and themselves. I mean, it wasn't a secret. It's just that people who walk their dogs or watch the sun come up in the morning, they don't have time to read books called *The Philosophy of Education.* Of course it's about breaking the spirit.

Anne, you have a question?

Anne: I see a contradiction between the purpose of the school systems as they now stand and the belief that they can be fixed without also altering the primary purposes of society. In other words, with corporations wanting a docile work force, and with a government needing a military to engage in wars that many would consider to be against the interests of those who are asked to fight, why would people in control of the schools—ultimately the politicians—want to change the system so that it would, in fact, produce critical thinkers?

I think you're hitting it right on the head, Anne. You're going to need to

195

change a lot more than just the schoolhouse.

Let me speak to that. One of the great ways that people are held in place is by their own fear. Because these enormous employment pyramids control the flow of money and the flow of information around the whole country, you might assume that nothing can be done. But the truth is, these forces have almost no internal cohesion at all. They hate each other!

Look how fast the Soviet Union came apart. I would like to just tell you that I sat with Jeanne Kirkpatrick about two weeks before the first signs of the crack took place. There were a few other people in the room, and she said in that cold, steely, flinty voice of hers, "Let me tell you that it won't be for a hundred years that you'll see a crack in the Soviet Union, because they have a personal dossier of every citizen, and they have mathematical ways of telling where the fault lines will appear." Two weeks later the Soviet Union was dying, and a short time after that, it was dead.

Learning in the Stream of Life
Susannah Sheffer

"What would we do for young people if we were truly trying to help them pursue their interests and their goals and figure out what they wanted to do with themselves in this world? School would look very different."

When we step back and observe education in America, we see that it assumes that people come into the world basically helpless and ignorant and in need of something called schooling, something that must be provided in a place set apart from adult life, organized in groups of fifteen to forty children, divided up by age, with pre-determined information arranged in orderly bits and pieces that take no more than sixty minutes to explain. The process lasts eight or twelve or sixteen years, until finally, the "educated" person is prepared to enter the real world.

From this perspective, one begins to get a sense that the whole arrangement is something to be questioned, that there must be a more natural way to learn, that better fits the way people live and think. This is the issue I wanted to explore by talking with Susannah Sheffer, who helps young people to learn in a very special way. Sheffer has been working in the area of homeschooling for more than a decade, as a teacher and mentor of students and parents. An educator in the lineage of John Holt and Ivan Illich, she is the editor of the magazine, Growing Without Schooling, *and the author of* A Sense of Self: Listening to Homeschooled Adolescent Girls.

Susannah, tell me a little bit about how you began your involvement with homeschooling?

I entered this world through John Holt, the author of a book called *How Children Fail,* which is his story of being a fifth grade teacher and wondering why the students in his classroom weren't learning what he was trying to teach. I was a fifth grade student myself when I picked up that book, and I thought, "Wow! How does this guy know so much? How does he know what school is really like for us? Why does *he* know it when my own teacher doesn't seem to have caught on?" I read his other books over the next few years and began corresponding with him. I thought he really knew something about young people and about learning. We continued to correspond, and then I began to get involved in the work of homeschooling.

What does that work consist of?

For the families who do it, it consists of helping kids find pathways into the world. For me, and for others who are involved in it as their daily work, it involves helping families directly, it involves some legal work, and, for me, it involves editing the magazine, *Growing Without Schooling,* a magazine through which parents and children actually talk to one another about learning and what helps it and what makes it difficult.

Someone might wonder, "How can homeschooling work if the parents are not so smart? What if they haven't graduated from college? What if they don't remember a lot of the courses they took in high school?"

There are two ways to answer those questions. The first is that your very questions show how much we think that schooling is synonymous with knowledge. The way you phrased it was, "What if they haven't graduated from college?" There are lots of smart people who haven't graduated from college, and the very notion that people doubt themselves, that they think they could never teach their own kid, that they've got to turn that over to somebody else, that's part of the whole problem. But after all, parents have been helping their children learn for quite some time. Schools weren't always as common as they are now, and even today, every parent helps their children learn in myriad ways. So you don't need to be certified in education in order to help a child learn about the world.

On a very practical level as well, it's important to understand that homeschooling is not about keeping kids at home, sitting at the kitchen table with their mother or father and doing school work with them. That's not the sort of thing that I'm describing at all. It's about kids learning in many, many different ways. They have access to so many other adults, so many other experiences, so many other ways of learning on their own steam, that they don't need their parents to know everything. If their mother doesn't happen to remember some high school subject that the young person is interested in, that young person has many other options for learning it. The parents just need to be parents. They need to be good parents—supportive, attentive, helpful, and so forth. They don't need to be formal teachers.

How, then, do you understand the formal schooling operation? You've spent ten years talking to people on the outside, so that should give you an interesting perspective on why this institution occupies ninety-nine percent of the children of America.

Yes, indeed. And I'm building on the work of so many people whose thinking has come before, most especially, John Holt. Holt looked very insightfully at what he felt were the primary and secondary functions of schools. The primary functions are the things that, if teachers don't do them, they get fired—getting through the math books and giving tests, and so on. Then there are the functions we don't like to think too much about, such as the function of keeping kids off the streets.

The major function of school for a lot of people is that it puts kids somewhere all day long. We don't really know, as a society, what to do with kids if they aren't kept somewhere. When I was in ninth grade, one of my teachers actually confessed this to us. He said, "You know, you're here because nobody knows what else to do with you." That's the number one function of schooling for a lot of people, so their questions about homeschooling are often logistical questions. What do you do with kids if they're not sitting in a building somewhere all day long?

Some people call that the "holding vat" function.

Sure, you can call it that. But I have to say, so that we don't just speak of this glibly, that there are some very real reasons why that function is so attractive in our culture. It is very difficult to figure out what to do with children throughout the day if you don't send them away somewhere.

A third function of schooling—to state it very frankly and boldly—is to separate out winners from losers. In school, you have some who succeed and some who fail. It's not okay for everybody to do well. Now a skeptic listening to that might say, "But every teacher is trying to help all the kids learn," and I think that's true. A good teacher is. But try to give all the kids in your classroom the grade of A, for example. I've heard too many stories from teachers who get in trouble for doing that. They get taken to task and, perhaps, eventually get fired for it.

It makes you wonder what the goal is really supposed to be. What if you're a teacher and you decide to give all your students A plusses because they all learned what you taught? Let's say you're a good teacher and it worked. Why should people get in trouble for that? One reason is that school is not set up so that everybody can win. There is a fear that the grade of A would be devalued, and if everybody in the whole school gets an A, your A must not be worth that much.

And the result is we teach inequality.

Well, yes. One can speculate about why the society has developed a need for that, for the notion that some kids must succeed and many must fail, but there are other things that school teaches as well. There is a quote from Ivan Illich, that "school teaches the need to be taught." In other words, it teaches us that we need to be taught things in order to learn them; that we need to go to a special place and have a whole formal arrangement in order to learn what we want to learn, particularly as we get older. Homeschoolers challenge that. Homeschoolers, the young people themselves, are learning in all kinds of ways without those arrangements.

I want to talk about that, but first let's get a little deeper here on the proposition that you just articulated, "Schools teach the need to be taught."

Listen to how people talk when they want to learn something. So often, people talk in terms of taking a class. They say, "I want to learn Spanish, so I'm going to sign up for a Spanish class." I'm not saying everybody says that, of course, but quite a number of people, when they want to learn how to do something, they think in terms of taking a course. They don't necessarily think of the other options. That's just one example.

We learn in school that if you want to learn something, you need to have it formally taught, not in an authentic situation where you have a relationship with somebody and you work together on something, in the course of which you learn. The notion is that you need to go to a special place where nothing but learning happens. When you ask kids why they go to school, they will usually say, "To learn." They might think, privately, that they go because they have to, but the accepted answer is that they go to learn, and the implication is that they don't learn in other situations. What Illich and Holt and others are saying is that you don't need to go to a special place to learn, that learning is something that happens in the stream of life through the various work and activities that people do.

The lesson is also that learning occurs in a place where you don't control things.

Yes, that's certainly part of it.

And it's not where you live. It's not where real stuff happens. It's a kind of "getting ready place" that is not determined by you, but by a leadership group called teachers.

Let's not blame the teachers for this by the way. Teachers are doing what the structure of schooling asks them to do. It's not that teachers walk in with evil intentions—in no way do I want to imply that that's remotely the case. But teachers are in a situation where they're faced with people who didn't choose to be there, haven't had the chance to think through what they might want to get out of the situation, and haven't had a chance to make a connection between what they want out of their lives and what is in the curriculum.

All sorts of things happen once that connection is made, once a young person realizes there's a reason for learning to read, or write, or study history, or whatever it might be. Then there are all sorts of things that a young person will be willing to do and all sorts of rigor that a young person will submit to. I've seen this repeatedly, but the trouble is, in school we don't give them the chance to make that connection. Here's a way to think about it: What would schools look like if they asked the young people who came, "What can we do for you? How can we serve you? What are your interests? What are your goals? What are you worried about? What do you want out of life? How can we help you?"

If I can remember back to the time when I started school—I'm not sure that I can—but my dim memories are that if my first grade teacher, Mrs. Whitecart, had asked, "How can I serve you?" I wouldn't have had the foggiest idea. We were just told we had to go to school, so we marched in and the thing started. Then the bell rang after an hour or so and we ran out to play and that was the most fun. The notion that there's some kind of quasi-autonomous learner here with some people there to serve him or her, that's a pretty foreign thought.

Right, and that's what I wanted to illuminate by posing those simple questions. Many very well-meaning people want to help young people in that way. They go into education because they want to help young people make sense of the world, and find their particular pathway through it, and so forth. But is that what school is really all about? What would school look like if it were about that? What would we do for young people if we were truly trying to help them pursue their interests and their goals and figure out what they wanted to do with themselves in this world? School would look very different. In my capacity as a friend and mentor of many homeschooled young people, I see how it would look, and it is very different.

I'm just reflecting as you're speaking. If what you study is not what you have an interest in, for whatever reason, but is what the curriculum forces you into, and if you do that day after day for ten, twelve, fourteen years, you learn to accept an externally imposed set of practices and inquiries that can separate you from a sense of what you truly need and want. You also lose the ability to discipline yourself to follow your own path wherever it might lead you. This really puts you on a kind of automatic pilot in your schooling, and then in work. You settle into a world that's constructed for you, not intimately connected to your own being in the world.

Separation is a really good word here. Too many young people—but by no means all—who attend traditional schools have learned to make a distinction in their minds between the stuff that other people want them to do and tell them to do, and the stuff that they really want to do and would choose to do on their own. What they really want to do has been devalued and they're not supposed to do it until they have finished their homework. Maybe they even feel a little guilty for spending time on it, or if they spend too much time on it, they feel like they're not being a good student. The alternative to all this is a much more integrated life.

I'll tell you a real quick story that illustrates it about as well as anything I know. It comes from a young woman, a seventeen-year-old, who has never been to school. In other words, she's been learning independently in what we call homeschooling for her entire life, and she is very serious and dedicated about a bunch of interests and one of them happens to be writing. She works with me on her writing, sending me her essays and asking for my critical comments—that's something that I offer to homeschoolers.

One day last summer, she had a friend from the local high school visiting her at her family's summer place, and this young woman, a teenager, was working on an in-depth, fairly long essay about a book that she had read. She was working on it of her own choice, and with quite a bit of commitment, and her friend from the high school could not get over the fact that she was working on this essay during the summer. In other words, this is not something that you do. This friend could not make sense of this. "Why are you working on an essay in the summer when no one's making you do it, when it's not connected to any schooling?" He just could not get his mind around it, and he found it very difficult, and almost threatening and unsettling.

The young woman who'd never been to school, found her friend's attitude equally strange. She couldn't understand why he had such a hard time understanding why she would choose to do this. For her, there isn't a distinction between the school year and summer, between the time when you focus on learning and the time that you don't, between work and play, and so forth. Whether it was July or January was not really an issue for her. That's the sort of thing that really fascinates me in the young people I know who have never been to school, and it's the sort of thing that deeply saddens me when I see it in high school students.

You're suggesting that schooling has a certain element, maybe a critical element, of repression and conformity, which, if it works, leads to a resentment of learning.

The resentment comes from being told in a hundred different, not-so-subtle ways that what you really want to do and care about is not important. The funny thing is that young people who do not grow up that way often choose to do things that school thinks is important, such as writing a good essay. That's why I think that particular story is so compelling, because this is a young woman who is writing an essay of a caliber that every high school would love to see in their students.

If you let young people choose what to do and do what they want, it's not true that they're going to watch television all day, which is the image that's often conjured up when we talk about letting young people direct their own education. On the contrary, I have seen it enough times to be very confident saying that young people will choose to do all manner of serious activity.

If homeschooling is not just about reading a book around the kitchen table with Mom, then what are the other possibilities? How do you distinguish between activities that constitute learning and those that might be considered just goofing off?

We're back to that same distinction between work and play. A little two-year-old doesn't think, "Now I'm doing serious work. Now I'm goofing off." That's an adult distinction that we learn to make. For the two-year-old, everything is serious. Everything that two-year-old does is done with as much dedication as that two-year-old can muster, and yet it's also joyous. You see, that's the thing: learning is not miserable. Watch a child learning to walk, watch the way that young child throws herself into the task, watch her tolerance for failure, which is much higher than many of ours, and try to decide then, is she doing work or play? The same thing can be true in a different and perhaps more sophisticated form in older kids and teenagers.

But you were asking what young people do when they don't go to school, and I should make that somewhat concrete. To speak generally about it, it involves things that young people might do on their own, such as reading, writing, drawing, doing math problems, doing experiments, any one of a number of things. It involves activities with others, such as having a writing club where students all write together and offer comments on each other's work, or having a science group where they do experiments together. These are some examples.

It involves getting out in the community and hooking up with adults who do the things they're interested in doing. In the case of young people interested in writing, it might involve volunteering at a newspaper or magazine, or working with someone else who acts as a writing mentor. In the case of science, it might involve doing field work with a scientist. I know young people that have gone with scientists into the field, or volunteered in a lab, or simply gone out observing. So it's a mixture of getting together with others, doing certain projects and activities on one's own, and in one way or another getting out to the community.

Just listening to you, I can hear people saying, "That's all very well, but it's a bit utopian. When you have to be with a kid hour after hour, it's just too much. I've got to have a break."

Think of the scenario I just described and tell me where you see any one adult with that kid hour after hour. After all, if you've got a kid whose week involves some time in the house doing activities, some time with other homeschoolers in various group activities, some time at the library, some time with an adult mentor working on math, and another day of the week volunteering at a museum, there is no obligation for the parent to be with that child day in and day out. It is certainly true that homeschooling parents tend to enjoy the company of their children and not find it as onerous as the American public often seems to. But even so, there's no need to burden the parent completely, because there are so many other things that these kids can be doing, and that's especially true as they get older.

Can you make a claim that homeschooling will bring parents and children closer together?

It often does. Young people, particularly teenagers who have been in school for most of their lives and then turn to homeschooling, report that it brings them closer to their family. They find that it brings them closer to their parents, in part because they just get to know them better. They're not separated all day long, so kids get to see, let's say, the pressures that made Mom grumpy today, or whatever it might be.

I hear some really wonderful things from homeschooled young people about their parents and their respect for them and their understanding of them. They say, as well, that when they've got conflicts and problems with them, they can't run away from it, so they have to work it out. Homeschooling families have all the family stresses and problems, but they can learn ways to deal with them because they are together more.

I spoke recently with Suzanne Arms about childbirth, and how, in America, it is a process of separation of mother and child. There is the separation to the hospital nursery, to the baby bottle, to infant daycare, to the car seat, to the other bedroom. It's a process of separation and isolation of the child at the earliest stages of life that has long-term implications for the child and for society. As I reflect on what you're saying, I get the sense that schooling is just a continuation of this larger process that imparts to young people a sense of alienation.

Yes, and what's ironic about that is that many people, if you ask them what school's about, particularly in the upper grades, will say it's about preparing young people for adult life. Homeschooled young people often find that funny or kind of bizarre. How do you prepare for life by removing yourself from it? In other words, homeschoolers find that their friends in school don't have a clue about many aspects of adult life because they are so segregated from it. It's the homeschoolers that are more likely to be in the stream of adult life, out and about in the community during the day. It's a strange notion to think that we need to take someone out of the stream of life in order to prepare them for reentry into it.

What about this idea of segregation by age—having all the twelve-year-olds together, the thirteen-year-olds together? What dynamic does that support?

It's a way to organize. Once school takes on a custodial function, you need to keep the kids somewhere, and then you need a sequential curriculum where you try to teach one group certain things, and another group something else, and so forth. Once you have that notion, then naturally, you almost have to group them according to age. Now, in all fairness, a number of schools are experimenting with some relaxation of that. They are experimenting with vertical age grouping. They have older kids teaching younger kids, and are finding how effective that can be. Homeschooling, being out here in the world, allows that to happen on a grand scale and very naturally.

Perhaps dividing up children by age encourages a form of class consciousness—not poor versus rich, but younger versus older. It encourages students to accept their place in a group that is narrowly defined relative to other groups in a hierarchy.

That's a problem that comes up in many ways. The notion that kids in school are expected to learn to read at a certain age is one example. If you don't learn to read by that time, it becomes a problem. You're labeled "learning disabled," and you need to go to remedial class. But it only becomes a problem if you use that particular way of organizing learning. Schools organize learning in very rigidly structured ways, which aren't necessary if you recognize that it's okay for a young person to be a very advanced reader, but very rudimentary in mathematics, or whatever it might be. If you realize that people progress at all different levels, you don't need to have grade levels and all that stuff.

Now, in school, you have a problem if there are certain subjects you don't like. For example, it would be hard to graduate from high school if you've flunked geometry and algebra, wouldn't it?

It's not even so much whether you like it or not, it's also whether you can learn it in the way that it's being taught. This is something that comes up repeatedly. A young woman I know well was always considered a very poor reader in school. She never did well at it. It was a constant source of humiliation for her, because she'd have to read in front of the class and she wasn't good at it. A lot of people can identify with this sort of thing; many people have some subject about which they have night-mares. For her, it was reading, and so, as a result, she didn't like to do it, and she never did it if she didn't have to. A lot of that was because her particular learning style didn't mesh with the way reading was taught in her school.

After homeschooling for about a year, this young woman was able to turn that around, to become a confident, fluent reader and to see herself as a reader. Most important of all, she chose to read, to actually spend whole days reading challenging materials, which is the real key. It's not just how well you can read, but is it something that you actually choose to do and get meaning out of for yourself? So she was able to change that. Finally, when she was out of school—and she left school to become a homeschooler at age fifteen—finally in that situation she was able to learn in a way that worked for her.

Is it easier for a parent to homeschool a child five or six years of age as opposed to sixteen or seventeen? Is it easier younger or older, or is that even a meaningful question?

There are just too many other factors influencing the situation to be able to answer that. A five-year-old child is more likely, perhaps, to be curious, full of questions, and so forth. It can be a real pleasure to an-swer his or her questions, and it may feel less intimidating to a parent because the parent might think, "Well, this is not algebra, which I didn't do well in. This is something I can handle. I've helped my child learn so many things thus far. I can help him go just that little extra distance at age five." On the other hand, with a five-year-old, there are more issues of logistics, more questions of direct child care than there are for an older child. There needs to be somebody responsible with the child at all times.

With an older child or a teenager, they're able to be so much more independent that logistical questions become much easier. I had a discussion group with five homeschooled adolescent girls, three of whom lived in single parent homes with the parent working outside the home, and it was not a problem for them. As teenagers, they didn't need their parents' direct custodial care all day long. Had those kids been younger, there would have been the need for more creative arrangements. So I would say there are wonderful things and particular challenges about homeschooling at any age.

When a teenager is homeschooled, and then tries to move into college, how does that happen?

The quick answer is that homeschoolers have an amazing track record at getting into college. They are applying into every kind of institution, from selective private universities to state universities, to community colleges. And they're doing very well because they are, by-and-large, the kind of interesting, self-motivated young people that colleges claim to want. You can follow up with any homeschooling organization and get a great deal more detailed information about that. We've had many articles in *Growing Without Schooling,* and there are whole books now on college admissions for homeschoolers.

Susannah, it seems like parents and children need a good support system to do this. They need lots of support from the community, and to really prepare and organize things in an ongoing way so that their child has things to do on a daily basis.

That's absolutely true. And that's one reason why there are so many support groups and support resources among homeschoolers themselves. The magazine that I edit is one on a national level. Let's say you were homeschooled and you've got a problem or a concern—you're really feeling stuck. You could write to *Growing Without Schooling* and ten people would write back with ideas for you.

Supports exist locally as well. There is a directory of homeschooling families all over the country who are willing to get in touch with and help each other. Support groups exist in every state, and in many cities and towns. These resources exist for just the reason that you described. But families get support or involvement, as well, from all sorts of people that may not be specifically involved with homeschooling. Again, it's the scientist with whom your kid volunteers, the helpful librarian that refers good books to you, and that sort of thing. People in the community take an interest in young people and are willing to help.

Opposing Privilege and Power
Noam Chomsky

> "Jefferson warned later in his life that if 'the banking institutions and moneyed incorporations'—what we now call financial and manufacturing institutions—took over power and authority, the Revolution would be lost."

Modern society is deeply influenced by a set of assumptions—often un-stated—that intensify privilege, perpetuate poverty and encourage environmental destruction. Understanding and attacking these ideas is the work of philosophers and social critics. No one performs the role quite like the noted linguist and political observer Noam Chomsky.

Chomsky is Institute Professor of Linguistics and Philosophy at the Massachusetts Institute of Technology, and the author of more than a hundred books and articles, including Language and Mind, Manufacturing Consent *and* The Minimalist Program, *to name a few. In February 1996, Professor Chomsky and I explored the ways in which institutions, myths, propaganda and notions of respectability shape society.*

Noam, I just read a transcript of one of your recent speeches, where you describe how throughout history honor has been given to those who speak on behalf of the powerful. You conclude with the observation, "Rending these chains is a first step toward freedom and justice." Maybe we could start there.

Well, we can go back to the earliest recorded texts in our canon—take the Bible, for example—and we'll find that those who have served power have always been rewarded with respectability. It's as close to a historical truism as you can find. There were a lot of intellectuals in the Bible. They didn't use the term, "intellectual"; they were called prophets. But they played the role that intellectuals play in the modern period. They gave geopolitical analysis, social critique; they expressed moral judgments and so on.

The prophets of the Bible came in two types, types that in the Soviet Union used to be called commissars, and those that were called dissidents. The commissars, the people who served power, were the ones who were later considered false prophets. They were the people, however, who, in their own time, were respected, honored and protected. They served power. There was another group of people, seemingly off in a corner somewhere, who exposed the corruptions of power. They're the ones who were reviled, imprisoned, driven into the desert, and so on. It was only much later that the evaluation was reversed and they were recognized as the true prophets.

That pattern just perpetuates through history, and for perfectly good reasons. If you serve power, authority and privilege, you'll end up, by and large, with respectability. And if you undermine them, whether it's by political analysis, moral critique, or anything else, they're not going to applaud you for it.

They're not going to applaud you for it, because you're not validating the power structure.

No. What you're doing is, in fact, speaking up for the interests of the general population and for what the people themselves see as right and wrong. That's not what privilege and power want. History isn't physics, but this pattern is about as close to a true historical generalization as you can find.

What we're up against today, perhaps, is nothing different from what has prevailed for ages.

The details are always different because circumstances are different, but there are some things that remain constant because they just have deep institutional roots.

In society it seems necessary to have a certain mythology in order to prop up privilege, and oppress dissent.

It is necessary if you're in charge. And you have to undermine these powers if you're trying to expand the sphere of freedom and justice. That's why there was an American Revolution,

Revolutions represent one outcome of these tensions. We had the French Revolution, the Russian Revolution, the American Revolution—

—and every one that you mentioned—in fact, every revolution I know of—was a very complicated affair. Revolutions are, in part, civil conflicts, and usually it turns out that these civil conflicts are not two-sided as we're taught, but three-sided. There are the two powers fighting each other, but a large part of the population, often a considerable majority of the population, have something quite different in mind.

Let's take, for example, the first modern democratic revolution, the English Revolution of the seventeenth century. We're taught in history books that it was the King and Parliament that were fighting. That's true. But then there was the population, which was publishing their own pamphlets and had their own spokesmen—itinerant preachers, mechanics and others. What they were calling for was something else. They said, we don't want to be ruled by a King or by Parliament. We want to be ruled "by countrymen like ourselves, who know our wants, and know the people's sores." And the same was true in the American Revolution. The rebellious farmers weren't at all happy by what came out.

The United States was really designed, much more so than other countries. It was designed on a principle enunciated very explicitly by James Madison, one of the most influential framers at the Constitutional

Convention, who explained and stressed and urged that the primary responsibility of government was, in his words, to "protect the minority of the opulent against the majority." Therefore, democracy is a threat. We must make sure that the wealthy, what he called "the more capable set of men," are in charge, and that the rest of the population is marginalized, fragmented and dispersed. Well, a lot of people didn't like this perspective, and there was plenty of conflict about it, but that's part of the origin of our constitutional system. Actually, Madison himself didn't like the outcome and condemned it pretty bitterly a couple of years later.

Adams and Jefferson were also embittered in the last years of their lives.

Just like Madison. By 1792, Madison condemned what he called the "daring depravity" of the time. He was pre-capitalist. He thought that a class of enlightened aristocrats would develop, but it turned out to be a class of grasping businessmen, who, as he put it, were becoming "the tools and tyrants" of government. They were "overwhelming" the government with their power, and they were being "bribed" by it as well. Tools and tyrants. Madison didn't like that. And in fact, that is a pretty good picture of what is going on in Washington right now.

So, in other words, the mythology of an enlightened aristocracy was a good cover for grasping businessmen.

Well, it's a little more complicated. Madison, like Adam Smith, was pre-capitalist, meaning he was anti-capitalist, in essence. Like Adam Smith, he saw the early stages of rising industrial capitalism. Jefferson, who was the one real committed democrat of the whole group, and, incidentally, was not part of the Constitutional Convention, was an even stronger anti-capitalist. Jefferson warned later in his life that if "the banking institutions and moneyed incorporations"—what we now call financial and manufacturing institutions—took over power and authority, the

Revolution would be lost. We would just have a new form of aristo-cratic rule. Later in the century, that happened to an extent that was worse than his worst nightmare, and people fought against this devel-opment.

There was a very lively independent press, working class press, right through the nineteenth century, in fact well into the twentieth century. Right around here where I live in New England, which was the center of the industrial revolution, artisans, mechanics and young women from the farms had their own press. They bitterly condemned the rise of in-dustrial capitalism, which they saw turning them into slaves and un-dermining republican principles. They denounced what they called "the new spirit of the age: Gain wealth, forgetting all but self." That's what we're supposed to admire these days, but it would have been bitterly opposed by the people we've been discussing.

In many of your books, you have referred to the "vile maxim" of Adam Smith, "All for ourselves and nothing for other people." What did he have in mind? What's the context for that comment?

He had in mind the basic principle of the rising capitalist classes, which is what the working people of New England paraphrased a century later without having read Adam Smith, "Gain wealth, forgetting all but self." This idea of all for ourselves and nothing for anyone else was, Smith argued, the "vile maxim of the masters of mankind." He pointed out that this impulse, sometimes, incidentally, happens to help people, but he certainly wasn't impressed. In fact, the historical Adam Smith, who was also rooted in the Enlightenment and anti-capitalist in many re-spects, is rather different from the image of him that's been constructed, as is the case with Madison.

So, in late twentieth century America, do you see some kind of revival of those who oppose "the moneyed incorporations?"

There's a continuation. This fight has been going on for hundreds of years. It takes different forms all the time. The current period, for example, is very much like the 1920s. In the 1920s, they were calling it the end of history. History had reached perfection; business rule was total; inequality was extraordinary. In fact, we're beginning to approach that level again. Labor had been crushed and smashed; labor had almost no role in what was going on. It was the great period of mass production and automobilization, and so on. It looked like pure business rule with nobody interfering with it. Then, along came the 1930s, and that proved not to be true. That kind of cycle's been going on all through modern history.

I recall someone saying in 1955, when I started college, that there was really nothing more to be done. All the liberal issues had been resolved.

Daniel Bell, a very smart sociologist, wrote a famous article and a book called *The End of Ideology* around 1959, arguing that ideological issues were over. He argued that they finally understood everything, more or less. It was just a matter of a little bit of tinkering around the edges. Economists, incidentally, were saying the same thing. Paul Samuelson, the leading economist at the time, was writing that it would take an idiot not to be able maintain a steady three-percent growth with very low unemployment. From now on it was just a matter of tinkering. Well, a couple of years later the economy had totally changed, the country was up in arms and there was tremendous ferment. These cycles go on and on.

A hundred years ago, William Morris, the famous artisan and revolutionary socialist, gave lectures, telling English working people how all the leading thinkers were saying that society had reached perfection and that nothing could be changed. If this is so, he argued, civilization would die. He just didn't believe it. Well, he was right. People kept struggling and changing, and a lot has been achieved.

Do you consider the debates about the revolutionary struggle that characterize our current period to be particularly sterile and one-sided, or is this pretty much history as usual?

Well, again there are cycles and changes. You can certainly find analogs to the current period. The 1920s and the 1950s were partial analogs. The Gay 'Nineties, the last decade of the last century, were very similar. These were times, like now, where enormous power was shifting towards very narrow sectors of wealth and privilege whose goal was to undermine functioning democracy, to convert the society into roughly a two-tiered society—a small sector of great wealth and a lot of people whose existence ranges from suffering to absolute misery, a Third World structural model, if you like.

These wealthy sectors also want to move the power to make decisions into hands that are invisible and unaccountable to the public. In a sense, this is a realization of the fundamental principle of American democracy, the Madisonian principle that I quoted, that the prime responsibility of government is to protect the minority of the opulent against the majority. However, when we quote Madison, remember that he was talking about something that hasn't existed for two hundred years, namely, a pre-capitalist, enlightened aristocracy. But his phrase now means exactly what the words say, and there is a very sharp shift in that direction.

Inequality is getting pretty close to level of the 1920s, right before the stock market crash. Democratic forms are functioning less and less well, and what's more, the population knows it. Over eighty percent of the population now says, in polls, that the government is run for the few and for the special interests, not for the people. That figure used to run a steady fifty percent for many years. It's just shot up to over eighty percent, revealing a tremendous alienation and cynicism.

At the same time, there is also a lot of confusion, since public discourse is very narrowly controlled. This is a business-run society, dedicated to marketing, to propaganda, to what they call "control of the public mind." It includes not only the media, which a lot of us talk about, but also schools, the entertainment industry, just about anything you can think of. And business doesn't kid around. This society spends about a trillion dollars a year on just plain marketing—one-sixth of total gross domestic product—with billions of dollars a year just spent by the public relations industry. This spending has a purpose. It's to control the public mind—in their words, to fight "the everlasting battle for the minds of men," to sell them free enterprise and "indoctrinate them with the capitalist story."

One of the things business wants to train people to believe is that the government is their enemy. Now, there are plenty of bad things about the government, but what they don't like about it is what's good about it—namely, that the government is potentially, and sometimes actually, influenced by the public. In fact, it could be influenced to quite a large extent by the public. On the other hand, if you can shift power into the hands of what amount to private tyrannies, for example, IBM and General Electric, you don't have to worry about disruptions of power. These corporations are unaccountable to the public and the public has no way of influencing them. You can adapt to them, like totalitarian states, but you can't do anything about them. That's the direction in which things are going.

Incidentally, there's a little scam going on here, too. The same people who are drilling into your head that the federal government is your enemy are also saying we have to strengthen it—but only that part of the government that pours money into their pockets. So the Heritage Foundation, the right wing foundation that, more or less, sets the budget and agenda for the right wing, wants to increase the Pentagon budget—against the will of the population. The population is opposed to that by about six to one, but the Heritage Foundation wants it because they know something that you're not supposed to know. That secret is that the system is primarily functioning, and has been for fifty years, to transfer funds from the general public to advanced sectors in high-technology industries. That's how Newt Gingrich ends up getting more federal subsidies for his rich constituents than any other suburban county in the country, outside of the federal government itself.

What role do you see the school system playing in preparing people to be-lieve the messages that prop up the privileged? To what degree is there any liberating element in the school system?

Let me answer with a few facts. Back in the 1930s, the business world was outraged over the fact that the public was actually getting involved in the public arena. What the business community thought they had achieved in the 1920s was over. The New Deal measures weren't a gift to the people—they were a result of public action, the creation of the CIO, the Congress of Industrial Organizations, a lot of public organiza-tion and pressure. And the U.S. moved into the mainstream of the in-dustrial world then. Well, the business press was infuriated over this public action. They talked about "the hazard facing industrialists" in the "newly realized political power of the masses," which we have to suppress.

Right after World War II, a huge campaign of corporate propaganda began, which went after everything, including the schools. By the early 1950s about a third of the material in schools, meaning textbooks and so on, was straight business propaganda. That's one third of the total material, and the rest was very heavily influenced by it. Well, even the most dedicated teacher is going to be heavily influenced by that kind of pressure. It makes a difference. The schools, by and large, now instill obedience and acceptance of the doctrines preferred by those who have the power to fight what they call "the everlasting battle for the minds of men." This pattern goes right through college and through the profes-sions.

How would you compare the propaganda system in the so-called free world to an authoritarian system? What are the differences?

There are differences. Let's take the Soviet Union, which was our opposite extreme when it existed. It was the most totalitarian society among
the major societies, and we're arguably the most democratic. The propaganda systems were run very differently. In the Soviet Union, it was
as Orwell described—there was a ministry of information, rather like a
ministry of truth. Everyone knew where the propaganda was coming
from. It was crude, direct, and didn't allow very much in the way of
deviation, but people could identify it. They knew what it was.

In fact, it's unclear how much attention they paid to it. In the 1970s,
the United States government did studies together with Russian research
centers in major U.S. universities to figure out just how Russians got
their news. They found that a large majority of the population—perhaps three quarters of the population—was listening to foreign broadcasts. Of the more educated sector, around ninety-five percent received
their news from foreign broadcasts. This means they were getting their
news from the BBC, not from *Pravda*. Not many Americans listen to
foreign broadcasts. We get our news from one source—corporate propaganda. The studies also found that *samizdat*, the technically illegal
underground literature, was reaching about half the educated population, and a little less than fifteen percent of blue-collar workers, throughout the country.

Well, the analog to *samizdat* here in the U.S. is something like *Z
Magazine*. The total probably doesn't reach even one percent of the
population. Here, our sources of information aren't controlled by the
state the way they were in the Soviet Union, but our information sources
happen to be very narrow. We're trained not to go outside of these chan-
nels, and we just keep to them. These information sources have a very
definite point of view that they instill in you. They do have and, in fact,
even try to create, a certain range of debate and discussion for all sorts
of reasons, one of them simply being professional integrity, which you
can't dismiss. But there are other institutional reasons. One of them is
to give you the illusion of debate, but if you look closely, you'll see that
the debate is within very narrow bounds.

Let's take for example the latest Pentagon budget. I don't recall much significant debate about it at all. Clinton signed it at $265 billion. The only issues that were talked about in the media were the banning of HIV-positive enlisted personnel, and the banning of abortions at military clinics. In terms of the $265 billion and how that stacks up against other countries, I don't think I saw anything in the mainstream press at all, and I saw nothing about foreign aid.

Let's take a look at both of these issues. The Pentagon budget, right now, is running at a level equal to the peace-time Cold War average. It's not as high in real dollars as it was at the peak of the Vietnam War or the peak of the Korean War, but if you take the years when there wasn't a major war going on, the current Pentagon budget is about the same. Well, there was supposed to be a Cold War then. We had this big enemy, the Soviet Union, and the enormity of those budgets shows you just how seriously they were taken.

Right now the Pentagon budget, in real dollars, is higher than it was at the end of the Nixon presidency. It's going up over the objections of the population, and here the margins are really huge. It's about six to one in opposition. In fact, the Pentagon budget is going up beyond even what the Joint Chiefs of Staff want. They don't want it to go up that fast because it's going to get them in trouble. But it's going up for another reason. There's a reason why the Heritage Foundation, Gingrich and the rest want that budget to go up, and it's the reason that I mentioned. That Pentagon budget is part of the funnel by which public funds are transferred to the high-tech industries.

Take a look at the functioning sectors of the economy—computers, electronics, aeronautics, metallurgy—these dynamic sectors of the economy are very heavily subsidized by the public, and much of it flows through the Pentagon system. The Pentagon funds much of the research and development, and they provide a cushion, a kind of stable market for excess production. During the Cold War period it was always possible to claim that we do this because of the Russians. Well, now you need other excuses, and it's intriguing that instantly, as soon as the Russians were gone, the excuses changed. Now we need it, not because of the Russian threat, but as the Bush administration put it in March 1990, because of the "technological sophistication" of Third World powers. That's why we need it. So the Pentagon budget has got to remain the same, or even go up.

This Third World argument doesn't even merit ridicule. In fact, a large part of their technological sophistication is the arms that we sell them. And the public pays for that, too, through subsidies. In fact, right after the end of the Cold War, when Pentagon procurement was starting to go down, our economic policy changed. Now the public has to subsidize arms sales to Third World dictators—that's where most of them go in the Third World—in order to keep the domestic economy functioning. Under Bush and Clinton, this trade-off has been almost open.

Take as an example Lockheed Martin, the biggest military supplier, which, incidentally, has its headquarters in Newt Gingrich's district. We pay Lockheed Martin—you and I, the public—to upgrade F-16 fighters so that they can sell them, at public expense through loans from the Export-Import Bank, to the United Arab Emirates, or Indonesia, or wherever. And then Congressmen such as Newt Gingrich, or the propaganda agents for Lockheed, come along and say, "Look, there's a real danger out there. The technological sophistication of Third World powers. Now they've got all these upgraded F-16s. We, therefore, have to build the F-22 to defend ourselves from them." The F-22 happens to be produced by Lockheed with the same corporate headquarters. And remember that when you're building an F-22, or an F-16, or a Raytheon missile, or any of this other stuff, almost all of this is dual-use technology, which means the corporations involved, who are getting the payoff, can adapt it to commercial markets too, and they do.

Have you seen any debate on this?

Try to find it.

So, if you combed The New York Times *or* The Washington Post *or* Time *or* Newsweek, *you wouldn't come across this discussion.*

Well, if you really look carefully you can find some facts and a little discussion. But let's take, for example, Newt Gingrich—a dramatic example. Here he was in the fall of 1994 smashing the Democrats, denouncing them for being in favor of welfare, and talking about the need for personal responsibility and getting rid of "the nanny state"; he's been doing it ever since. Yet Newt Gingrich is the biggest welfare freak in the country. He gets more federal subsidies than any other Congressman in a comparable district. Did you hear any debate about that? No, you didn't.

Do you think there is a racial element involved in the question of who gets the benefits of government welfare programs?

There certainly is a racial element. It's part of the really vicious propaganda that has been developed in order to sell the corporate welfare programs that transfer funds to the rich. One way in which this has been done—this goes right back to Reagan's crazy anecdotes about black welfare mothers driving Cadillacs and breeding like rabbits—is by engendering race hatred.

Public policy for about twenty years now has been directed to very anti-social ends. It has been specifically directed to establishing a sharp divide between a small sector of the very rich, and a large mass of people whose incomes are either stagnating or falling—the majority of the population—while cutting out public services such as transportation, environmental protection, and so on. When you're doing that to people, you don't tell them what you're up to. You've got to get them to accept the cuts somehow, and there aren't a lot of ways to do that. What you do is get people frightened, get them to hate each other, in order to turn their attention away from the real power and towards fearing and battling each other. The welfare mother, by implication black, has been used for that purpose.

Furthermore, this whole war against crime thing is a concocted political campaign for exactly the same purpose. Crime—which is bad, of course—has been rather steady for about twenty years. It is the perception of crime, which is fanned by propaganda, that has increased enormously, and the number of people in prison is just zooming. It's about triple what it was during the Reagan years. The United States is way ahead of the rest of the industrial world, maybe all the world, in imprisoning its own population. That's for population control. None of that has anything to do with crime.

Some prisons are now run by companies that are listed on the stock exchanges. And you've got states like Texas, building surplus capacity and then using brokers to bring in prisoners from other states, using their lower salary base to house prisoners for forty dollars a day rather than eighty dollars a day. This system is working so well. Some people might say that this increase in prison population is a conspiracy, because it seems to be working almost perfectly for those with extra capacity for sale.

Everything you said is correct, but I still think that the major goal of this fabricated war on crime—which is not affecting crime, incidentally—the major goal is to frighten people, and to make them hate and fear each other. When people are separated from one another, frightened and suspicious, then they're not looking at what's really happening to them. The United States, incidentally, is the only country I know of where crime is considered a political issue. In other countries it's considered a public problem. Here it's a political issue, and that's because it follows the Madisonian idea of fragmenting the population, in this case by fear and hatred.

On the other hand, everything you said is exactly right. Criminal justice is part of the state sector of the economy that is growing very fast. The same kind of people who want to rip off the Pentagon, or for that matter the National Institute of Health, for profits, also want to make what they can from this rapidly rising sector of the state economy. Even the high-tech companies are getting involved. This is not on the scale of the Pentagon yet, but they see it as another cash cow for high-tech surveillance equipment and so on.

So, Noam, in all these debates, we need to look beyond the diversionary campaigns of the two political parties, beyond what we see on television and in the newspaper.

That's right. We need to look beyond whoever reflects the interests of power—that means the corporate media and the respectable intellectuals that follow the party line. To put it metaphorically, we need to look for the prophets who have been driven into the desert.

The Mythologies of Global Development
David Korten

"Part of the sickness of our society is that we've given
up so many of the non-financial relationships, the
things that we used to do for each other in the family
and as members of the community purely out of love
and affection. So much of that has broken down;
we've lost the balance between monetized activities
and what we might call 'the economy of affection'."

*David Korten has been involved in issues of Third World development for
more than three decades. A former faculty member of Harvard University's
graduate schools of business and public health, he also served for many
years as a Ford Foundation staff member, and as advisor to the United
States Agency For International Development (AID). In these roles he
managed economic development projects in Central America, Africa and
Asia, including the establishment of university programs to disseminate
Western business management ideas and practices.*

*Korten's ideas about international development and the global
economy have evolved dramatically over the years. He is now an outspo-
ken critic of programs like those he once helped establish. He is President
of the People-Centered Development Forum, an alliance dedicated to the
creation and maintenance of just and sustainable societies, and the author of* When Corporations Rule the World.

*David, as I read your book, I just happened to have on my desk a book
called "The Great Transformation," by Karl Polanyi, published in 1944.
Polanyi writes about England and the industrial revolution, and he says
something that I think is a good entry point into your work. "At the heart*

of the Industrial Revolution of the eighteenth century, there was an almost miraculous improvement in the tools of production, which was accompanied by a catastrophic dislocation of the lives of the common people."
Polanyi goes on to explain how, for centuries, the people of England had used common fields that were open to all. With the industrial revolution, landowners decided to enclose these fields and turn them over to sheep production for the textile mills that the steam engine had made possible. The result, of course, was to drive peasants into the cities, into the horrible circumstances that Dickens and other writers describe so well.

I think this helps put in context this contradiction between what is described as progress by those who are in control of the media, the jobs and the capital, and the human suffering of individuals who lack the power and resources to protect their particular station in life.

As you know, Jerry, I've spent much of my life and career in the business of development, trying to bring the supposed benefits of economic growth to people in Third World countries. I'm embarrassed to admit that it was somewhat late in life that I began to see the phenomenon that Karl Polanyi was pointing out.

The fact is that, historically, periods of extraordinary economic growth have also been periods in which a majority of people is pushed into increasing impoverishment. This has been the process of the industrial revolution. The industrial revolution has been built around massive technologies that have made it possible for a very few people to capture control over far more than their share of the world's wealth. And in taking development out to the Third World, we have been perpetuating the myth that this is the way to bring universal prosperity to people throughout the world.

Here's what Polanyi has to say about enclosure, the fencing in of the common land on which the peasants grew their food and raised their livestock:

Enclosures have appropriately been called a revolution

*of the rich against the poor. The lords and nobles were
upsetting the social order, breaking down ancient law
and custom, sometimes by means of violence, often by
pressure and intimidation. They were literally robbing
the poor of their share of the commons, tearing down
the houses which hitherto, by unbreakable force of
custom, the poor had long regarded as theirs and their
heirs'. The fabric of society was being disrupted.*

Doesn't that sound a little bit like some stuff going on today?

Very much so. And in a sense, what was going on was the colonization
of the rural areas of England. Then as the industrial system required
more and more resources and markets, it spread out to colonize other
parts of the world. Part of my awakening came when I began to realize
that the development efforts that I was involved in were, in many ways,
an extension of this process. I began to look at the kinds of projects that
the World Bank funds, and saw that, at any given time, anywhere from
one-and-a-half to two million people were being driven off their lands
to make way for them. And people were being made increasingly dependent on products that global corporations provide.

*When you were at Stanford getting your Ph.D., what was your perspec-
tive?*

I was a Young Republican in college, and when I went to business school,
I was very concerned about poverty in Third World countries. At that
point, many of us were concerned about the spread of Communism,
and it hit me that if we were going to fight that process, we had to bring
prosperity to people. I believed that the way to do it was through business—through training business managers and getting corporations to
invest in poor countries, so that they could live the same kind of affluent life that we do. The early part of my career in development was fo-

cused on setting up business schools. My wife and I helped set up the business school at Hailie Salassie University in Ethiopia, and I spent three years in Nicaragua as the Harvard Business School advisor to the Central American Management Institute.

So, tell me, how did you evolve from someone who was pushing ahead this project of managerial capitalism to your current perspective and work?

There was no particular sudden awakening. It was a very, very long process. We started looking at various projects in Central America and Asia that involved grassroots development efforts, and we began to see that industrial expansion into rural areas was disrupting people's lives, and that the government and the economic system were not working. So we got increasingly interested in the public sector organizations through which development assistance was delivered and through which we were supposedly bringing benefits directly to the people. We worked on the issues of managing those organizations for quite some time, and became aware that very often, what they were doing was displacing people and taking over control of their lives.

A lot of our work in The Philippines, for example, centered on irrigation. In many parts of Asia, farmers have developed their own irrigation systems for centuries. They have constructed them sometimes under intensely difficult situations. They control and manage them, and they're often at the heart of the social structure of the community. Then the development project comes in, often funded by the World Bank or the Asia Development Bank, and completely obliterates the systems that the farmers have built, leaving them dependent for their irrigation water on massive central government bureaucracies that don't work very well. Of course, part of what's behind that are the construction companies that are getting big contracts on World Bank loans.

Were you at all impressed or moved by the Alliance for Progress as John Kennedy outlined it?

Well, yes, at the time it seemed to be a very positive initiative. It expressed our development commitment. But I've come to take a very dim view of foreign aid. Many AID people are very, very committed to making projects work and do it from a deep belief that this is going to benefit people. It's only when you step back and begin to look at it in the larger perspective that some of these other dynamics start to become clear. I've come to the conclusion that, on balance, a majority of our aid is benign, and most of the rest is gravely harmful.

So what do we get from our AID work?

We get very little. What it took me years to realize is that any foreign exchange we provide is only useful for buying things abroad. So no matter what the nature of the project is, what you're really doing is encouraging the country that receives foreign aid to become more dependent on the global economy. This is exactly the opposite of the philosophy that many of us advocate. Development needs to be about people getting greater control of their local resources, and helping them use them more effectively to meet their own basic needs.

How about this argument that, by the process of aid and transnational development, we enable people of the Third World to become citizens of what's called the global village.

Well, at one level, I think there are some very positive things happening in the world. The growing sense of being part of one world and dependent on one ecosystem, for example, is a very important piece of progress in human evolution. But at least two things are terribly distressing: one is that as we draw others into the global economy, we make them increasingly dependent on global corporate power; the other is that the culture that we're bringing to these countries, through our mass media and so forth, is a corporate consumer monoculture, which essentially conditions people to buy the products of these relatively few corpora-

tions. The penetration of McDonald's and KFC and other fast food companies, for example, is just massive. So people come to identify themselves less as members of a community or of a country than as part of
the Pepsi generation. They begin to lose contact with their community,
with basic values of any sort other than consumption values.

Another tragedy of this is that economic growth, in almost in every
case, leads to increasing pressures on the Earth's ecosystem. We have
increased global economic output anywhere from five to seven times
since the 1950s, much of it as a consequence of the kinds of development processes that I've been involved in. That has increased our burden on the environment from five to seven times, and we're now up to
the limits of what the ecosystem can sustain. We must come to grips
with the fact that it is impossible for everybody in the world to live the
kind of high consumption lifestyle that is the goal of development.

*Is the theory of these global corporations that the invisible hand of the
market is able to transmute individual choices into a very efficient
system of allocation that works to the common good?*

That, of course, is the theory they espouse; that's what you learn in a
basic economics course on the theory of the market. The problem is
that what we have is not a market economy. It's a corporately planned
and controlled economy, very different from the kind of competitive
market economy comprised of local small producers and buyers that
Adam Smith advocated. We have a world in which a handful of corporations, detached from any link to any place or community, have extended their power beyond the reach of most governments, and are
making the world's major resource allocation decisions based on the
demand that they face from the global financial system to maximize very,
very short-term profits.

*This reminds me of the chapter in your book, "The Decline of Democratic
Pluralism," where you compare free market capitalism to Marxist regimes.*

You indicate a couple of very close parallels between the corporation and the Marxist state. For example, both the corporation and communism lead to the concentration of economic power in a centralized institution. Both create economic systems that destroy living systems of the earth. And both produce a disempowering dependence on mega-institutions that erode the social fabric.

Yes. And as we tout the victory of the free market economy over communism, we ignore the fact that of the world's hundred largest economies, fifty are corporations. Now, the economy internal to a corporation is not a free market economy. It is a centrally-planned economy, and in many ways, is more tightly controlled than any state-planned economy that we've seen—in terms of the ability of management to shed workers, to buy and sell plants, and to dictate the terms of people's lives.

Would you say then that the corporate captains are in charge, or are they caught in a game based on producing at the lowest possible cost?

They're trapped in a system. This is a point that I argue with people who talk about voluntary codes of conduct and business responsibility, and so forth. That's a nice idea, but it neglects the reality in which corporate managers live. Over the last three years, the Standard and Poor's 500 largest corporations have increased their profits at an average rate of twenty percent a year. That has become the basic expectation of the financial markets. If you're a corporate manager, if you're doing your job, you'd better get your profits increased by twenty percent this year. There are only a few ways you can do that: find cheaper sources of labor; bid down wages; replace more of your workers with technology; find more buyers; find ways to get around environmental regulations, and so forth. One of the best investments that a business can make these days is to buy politicians to get them special subsidies and tax breaks and relief from environmental and labor standards.

What about the argument that the new economy can generate commodities that will give all the people the benefits of a modern way of life instead of the traditional one that has sustained them in the past?

Here's what you see—the springing up of international airports and cities with skyscrapers and mega-shopping malls and superhighways with Mercedes Benz cars. But you need to realize that that's a very thin veneer. Only a tiny percentage of the population enjoys that.

In The Philippines before we left, there was a massive building boom in air-conditioned mega-malls selling all the latest consumer electronic equipment from Japan, and designer clothes from Italy, and so forth. But this was at a time when roughly sixty percent of the people were living in absolute poverty. So, in fact this was evidence of a growing gap between a very small number of people enjoying very nice luxuries, and the rest of the people, who were losing hold of their means of livelihood, being driven out of the forest lands, unable to find basic employment, being driven into slums of the city, working in very, very low wage jobs, or scrounging around selling a few cigarettes on the street corners at stoplights.

If we looked at the debates in the U.S., or the U.N., or England, or France, or Japan, would we see any strategy or plans coming out of the established quarters that will help us get back on the right track; or are they full bore in the wrong direction?

I see absolutely nothing coming out that would give us hope. I was very struck a few weeks ago when the front page of *The New York Times* had, side by side, an article on global warming and how strong the scientific consensus was that this was a terribly serious problem, and right next to it an article on what Congress is doing. Congress is fighting over balanced budgets, in a way that shows almost no recognition of the realities of what's happening in the global economy, what's happening to the poor, what's happening with the environment.

So it's just a complete gap between policy makers and what you consider to be the real crisis. Is that a fair description?

Absolutely fair. The way the political system has transformed itself, particularly as television advertising has become such a key factor in campaigns—it's enormously expensive. The only way you can raise the money to win an election is by appealing to corporate interests, which then means you're in their debt and have to focus on their agendas. This is why I think useful action is not talking to members of Congress, but getting the word out among the public, breaking this veil of silence, helping people recognize that we've become trapped by a series of myths. As long as we believe those myths, the economic system will maintain its control of our lives until it leads us right over the cliff.

Okay, let's talk about what can be done. How do we respond to a situation that is not going to get any better unless we can move the ball in a very different direction?

Well, we have to act at many levels. At the international level, we should seriously consider closing the World Bank.

I haven't head that one from by anybody from the Harvard Business School in a while.

We talk about the problems of AID, but the World Bank is far worse than AID. It's much bigger and more powerful, but also, the aid that it extends is debt. The biggest barrier that the poor in Third World countries face is their debt, yet every action that the World Bank takes increases that debt.

And what about the International Monetary Fund?

Well, there is probably a need for an international organization that helps countries maintain international liquidity. But the main thing that the IMF has been doing, in league with the World Bank, is going out to countries that are deeply in debt and imposing policies of structural adjustment that are geared mainly to making sure that the international banks are protected.

You've suggested that the IMF be replaced by a United Nations organization that will manage the process of disposing of international debts. That's similar to what Julius Caesar did upon coming into office, and I believe in the Old Testament there was something called the Jubilee year, in which people's debts were canceled or reduced.

Well, we need to take this thing apart. You know much of that debt is private and involved all kinds of shenanigans. The World Bank and the IMF have been socializing that debt, turning it into public debt so that the government has to repay the debts of a lot of corrupt business people. The burden of debt relief should fall squarely on the backs of those who created and benefited from it.

What about individuals in their daily lives. What can be done at that level?

Each of us can examine our own lives in terms of what really contributes to our quality of living. We can concentrate on those things and reduce our unnecessary consumption, especially of the things big corporations produce. That's a piece of it. We can also get involved in the process of public education about the realities, helping people to penetrate the myth that growth and GNP are valid measures of human well-being and progress, the myth that unregulated markets efficiently allocate society's resources, the myth that trade benefits ordinary people. There's a lot of re-education that we need to do to help people focus on policies that improve the well-being, the quality of living, of people in balance with the earth. It's a very different framework from the policies that are most suited to increasing corporate profits.

Part of the education we need is about how to organize our living spaces. Developing our living spaces around urban sprawl and suburbs with single family homes all spread out is enormously energy inefficient, in part because all sides of the house are exposed to the elements. We need to look at reshaping our communities so that we can get higher population densities, become less dependent on the automobile, and use more public transportation. And we need to find ways to organize our living spaces around green areas and walkways, and get our jobs closer to the places where we live.

Now I happen to live in New York City, in Manhattan, and it's the first time in my life I haven't owned an automobile. There are a lot of things in Manhattan that one could improve on in the quality of life, but the fact that I don't need an automobile, that most things I need are within walking distance, and we have excellent public transportation— to me it feels like being liberated from the expenses and the burden of an automobile rather than making a sacrifice.

So we need to get involved as citizens in public policy decisions and in public discussions of what kind of cities we want. There are some interesting initiatives. For example, in Portland, Oregon, there's a group called Coalition for a Livable Future that has made enormous progress in developing urban growth boundaries around the city, and in getting changes in land use patterns, so that they begin to get higher urban concentrations. They are involved in planning public transportation, and stopping highway proposals that would undermine the development of public transport. In this way they are promoting an increasing urban density that preserves the rural spaces around the city.

What you're talking about is people organizing to demand policies that fit into the criteria of sustainability.

Absolutely. We can't allow our communities to be managed in a way that's driven by the imperatives of corporations to continually increase profits. This is why we've got to build a new political movement in the

United States built on a new sense of what kind of society we want. We've got to realize that the only power that either the institutions of government or the institutions of the corporation have, is the power that we as citizens yield to them. And we can take back that power. That's what we have to do.

You talk about replacing the power of the state with the power of the global corporation as an act of collective suicide. What do you mean by that?

Well, for all the failings of government and the democratic process, governments are, at least in theory, responsible for the whole and, to the extent that our democratic mechanisms work, accountable to the whole. As we have, in effect, dismantled the state, as we have dismantled national borders and passed on power to corporations as the dominant institution in the global society, we've passed on power to an institution that has no pretense of being responsible for the good of the whole. In theory and in practice, the predominant responsibility of the corporation is to increase the wealth of its shareholders. And its only real accountability of any consequence is to the *largest* of its shareholders, who are the people who control the biggest piece of the wealth pie.

The other way it's suicidal is that a huge portion of corporate profits and corporate operating costs, which include the outrageous salaries of CEOs and very expensive corporate overhead, involves the extraction of wealth from societies—as corporations trash the environment, pay people less than a living wage, and destroy their health and physical capacity through bad working conditions. We're not only transferring the wealth of society from the large population to those who control corporate power, but we're also depleting the natural and human capital of society. That's where the suicide comes in. It's almost like the institution of the corporation is at war with life and with people, and is destroying the very foundation of life on the planet.

You're referring here, I believe, to what you call "externalized costs." In your book you quote Ralph Estes, the author of Tyranny of the Bottom Line, *who talks about an estimated $2.6 trillion in externalized costs per year. What does that mean?*

If we look at the theory of the market, we'll see that the whole claim that the market allocates resources efficiently is based on the premise that the firm internalizes all its costs, that the full cost of the production and use of a product is borne by the firm and passed on to the consumer. Now, what Ralph Estes has pointed out is that there are a whole bunch of industries—the most obvious being cigarette companies—where the production and use of their product entails enormous costs that are borne not by the company, but by society. And anything that restricts the ability of these companies to externalize these costs, they consider to be an unfair restraint.

The list of these real costs is long: work place injuries and deaths, unsafe vehicles, long-term environmental illnesses, the loss of crops, the loss of forests, and on and on. Ralph Estes has calculated a total figure of $2.6 trillion in externalized costs, and that doesn't even include direct corporate subsidies from governments, or the subsidies that are embodied in special tax breaks for corporations. So you start to get the picture. Total corporate profits are on the order of $515 billion; compare that figure to $2.6 trillion in externalized costs, and that means that the costs of the corporation to society are about five and a half times the amount of their profits.

Now, it is hard to sort all of that out, and these are of course rough estimates, but Estes has compiled them from a number of legitimate studies. Part of what this tells us is that all is not as it seems in the economy. It helps quantify a general perception that, in many ways, life is not getting better. We're suffering from more congestion, many of our friends are dying from cancer and other kinds of illnesses, we find the environment deteriorating, forests disappearing, and so forth.

You make the point in your book that we need to "delink" from depen-

dence on the big institutions of the global economy. What exactly does that involve?

Most of our communities throughout the United States and throughout the world are concerned about strengthening their local economies to provide more jobs and so forth. Now, you've got some very major choices there. You can go out and do what Alabama did—you can give away all sorts of tax breaks and land and subsidies to get a Mercedes Benz plant to bring 1,500 jobs to your community at a cost of $200,000 per job. Or you can look around trying to figure out what things are needed in the community. What are your own local businesses, what are their needs? How can you put people to work in your community using local capital, local businesses, local materials, and so forth, to meet more of your local needs so that you begin to build up an interlinked local economy that is less dependent on the vagaries of the global market? It's a lot cheaper.

Okay, let's just take something that hits a lot of people in this country, and that is running shoes. Can we really get any local running shoes?

Delinking may get down to simplifying our lives. The first thing is to not be swayed by all the advertising, and hype, and swoosh. Be a little bit clear about what you really need—an adequate pair of shoes will do. It might even be possible for a group of folks to figure out how to set up a small shoe factory in their own community. I don't imagine it really involves all that sophisticated a technology.

That's a very interesting question. Could people start to get back to more of a village economy, as opposed to this hyperconsumption that we're all hooked on in one form or another?

Yes, absolutely. Part of the sickness of our society is that we've given up so many of the non-financial relationships, the things that we used to do for each other in the family and as members of the community purely out of love and affection. So much of that has broken down; we've lost the balance between monetized activities and what we might call 'the economy of affection'. But, you know, we can begin to recreate that.

Now, another of the really interesting things that has been happening around the world is a revival of community currencies. That's quite an interesting development because it involves a recognition of what money really is. This is another area where we get hypnotized. We get so focused on money that we begin to think of money as real wealth, or money as a resource, or money as the thing that defines who we are and what we can do, when in fact, money is not a resource at all, Money is an accounting chip, it's a claim on resources, it's just a piece of paper that we create to facilitate exchange.

A lot of communities that have people that are unemployed or that have un-utilized resources in their local businesses believe that this is because they don't have enough money. But these communities, in fact, could just turn around and say, "Hey, money is the easiest thing of all to create. Let's get together and agree that we're going to create and accept our own community currency." They can then create it, distribute it, and start getting their economies moving. This is another technique of delinking.

I wonder whether the state or the city could actually pay a part of their salaries in local money. For example, in many U.S. cities a large percentage of city employees live in the suburbs. If one were to say, "We're going to pay you, in part, in currency that is only accepted within the city limits, in the community that has generated and continues to generate your livelihood." That certainly would be a type of delinking.

Of course, and the local government would also have to accept the local currency for payment of taxes.

Here we see one of the interesting social characteristics of money—that its value is based entirely on a social consensus. It's one reason why the boundaries of the territory within which a particular currency is valid become important in building social fabric and maintaining the sense of being part of a shared enterprise.

What about the idea of delinking by halting the unloading of cargo shipped to the U.S. from foreign sweatshops. There was a time when the United Farm Workers were able to win the support of unions in Canada and Europe and Australia to the point where boycotted grapes coming out of California were simply left on the dock. Could you ever conceive of some kind of movement to boycott identifiable cargo that represents the destruction of the environment, or the mistreatment of human beings?

As a practical matter, it's a question of whether labor unions are strong enough to pull it off and not be replaced by the large pool of unemployed people who'd love to have those jobs. The larger point is that as long as we are dealing with a global economy, it's very hard for people to address these kinds of issues, whereas if you have more localized economies, it's a much more manageable task.

Now, some people will complain that you're not considering the needs of those poor workers in China and Indonesia. Having spent most of my life working in Third World countries on issues of poverty, I know that is nonsense. A major part of the problem of those countries is that we have structured their economies so that their labor and their land are being used to produce cheap products for export rather than producing food for their own people. And you have plenty of people in China and Indonesia and elsewhere where this food is being produced who'd like a little something to eat themselves, so they've got the same problem and the same issue. If they could localize their economies and devote that land and their labor to producing their own food and their own shoes, ultimately, we would all be much better off.

Let me get back to the money issue. What about a city credit union? Could the people of Greenwich Village or Oakland or a city in Connecticut, could they band together for a credit union and withdraw from this international banking game.

They certainly could. Credit unions, the idea of community banks—this is another piece of the potential delinking. It delinks you from the money market institutions that essentially suck up the money from the community and then take it out to play in the big global casino. So these kinds of financial mechanisms make a lot of sense. There's also the question of jiggering the banking rules back in the direction of smaller, local firms rather than toward bank mergers and consolidation. And this brings us back into the whole area of campaign finance reform. As long as campaign finance works the way it does, you're just not going to have a lot of politicians standing up and pointing fingers at the corporations.

You've also introduced the idea of negative interest on money. Why is this important?

One of the very interesting characteristics about money is the fact that we expect that our money will produce a rate of interest return without any effort on our part. It makes it a very peculiar kind of asset. Most any other asset we have, such as a house, deteriorates over time. We've got to keep investing in it. In terms of its actual viability, aside from market inflation, it actually requires continuous investment just to keep it whole. And even if one simply holds gold, there's a carrying charge. You've got to hire a bank vault, or otherwise protect it.

Money is just about the only asset that we expect to just sort of normally replicate, and yet it's the one asset that in itself has absolutely no use value. So we have this peculiar situation, where the people who control money are able to claim society's real wealth at a continuously expanding rate. This leads to a discounting of the future; because converting an asset into money in the future is less valuable than converting it into money today and gaining an effortless interest return.

Now, if you were to introduce a negative interest rate on money, then it would become like other assets—if you just held on to it, it would deteriorate in value. A negative interest rate on money would also increase the value of holding real assets that produce real productive output. For example, if you invest in a forest that's going to be producing over generations, it would make more sense, financially, to let it do so than to cut all the trees down and put the money in a bank in order to earn interest.

So David, you want to disrupt the money system.

What I want to do is urge people to rethink our institutions in every aspect. I'm not wedded to the idea that a negative interest rate money system would work or would be the answer. But I think it is one of many, many things that we need to look at seriously. We need to break out of the tyranny of our assumptions and the conventional wisdom that the way things are is the only way that they can be. There are lots of other ways that things can be if we apply our imagination.

The Colonial Exploitation of America
Judi Bari

"They pay as little as they can, they rip off the resources, they take the profits elsewhere, and then they invest in other timber lands around the world. Our county is being robbed by these corporations and the value of these trees is not being saved for future generations."

From 1988 until her death in 1997, Judi Bari was a powerful force in the fight against corporate destruction of redwood forests in Northern California. The environmental group of which she was the most visible member, Earth First!, took the lead in saving thousands of acres of old-growth redwoods, through such tactics as demonstrations, political initiatives and negotiations, and by literally chaining themselves to trees designated for cutting.

Judi's story is tragic and heroic. Her car was bombed in 1990, leaving her partially paralyzed. The response of the U.S. criminal justice system was to charge Bari herself with the crime, forcing her to sue the FBI for false arrest and violation of civil rights in a case which is still pending. She fought breast cancer for the last year of her life, but her personal battles never diminished her energy in fighting against those who would sacrifice the redwood forests in exchange for money.

I spoke with Judi first in August 1995, then in 1996, on the eve of a mass rally in Humboldt County that brought the nation's attention to the liquidation of the Headwaters Forest. It was a context for speaking out against the mindless, nineteenth-century industrial thinking that threatens what we now recognize as the interdependency of all forms of life.

Judi, let's start with an update of what's happening in Mendocino and Humboldt counties.

The assault continues up here. When you talk about trees—and up here that means coastal redwoods—you're not only talking about a magnificent species; you're also talking about the life support system of the Earth. Trees are the ecological life support. In the city it's not always easy to see that, but out here you can't miss it. And it's really hard to live here and see these trees going by, truck after truck, beelines of them, hauling tiny trees from Mendocino and giant trees from Humboldt, and not be profoundly affected by it, and feel that the Earth's life is being ripped off.

Let me share this with you. Someone brought to my attention a recent advertisement from the Ukiah Daily Journal *that reads as follows: "Timber, Timber, Timber. 169 acres of redwood and fir. Remote timber land on Indian Creek. Log the trees and get the land for free. $350,000. Agent." What do you make of that?*

That's pretty horrible. There's not much land left to log on Indian Creek and most of that is corporate. Only about a third of it is private, and that's an ad for private land. Our campaigns have focused on corporations, because they're the ones who have done such a horrible job and are really at fault. That kind of marketing is disgusting and when something is really blatant enough, we will challenge private land owners. But the real crimes against nature are being committed by corporations.

When you say corporate, you're distinguishing a land owner who has, say, twenty-five or one hundred acres from these behemoth corporations that have hundreds of thousands of acres?

Yes, and I'm distinguishing a real person from a corporation, especially if it's a land owner who lives locally. They have an interest in the community and in the community's future.

In Mendocino County we have about 300,000 acres of corporate timber land. About 200,000 acres are owned by Louisiana Pacific and the rest by Georgia Pacific. So we have two corporations, both of which are multinational, who not only own timber land around the world, but also control two-thirds of the clear-cut redwood lands in our county.

Does the President of either Louisiana Pacific or Georgia Pacific live in Mendocino County?

Absolutely not. One lives in Georgia and one lives in Portland. The profits also don't stay in this county. These corporate heads make huge salaries, they extract the profits from Mendocino Country just like a third world country, and they pay people as little as they can. They bust the unions; there are virtually no unions in timber in this county anymore. About one-third of the timber workers are immigrants, often illegal immigrants from Mexico, getting paid abysmally low wages to do the most dangerous job in the United States.

So they pay as little as they can, they rip off the resources, they take the profits elsewhere, and then they invest in other timber lands around the world. Our county is being robbed by these corporations and the value of these trees is not being saved for future generations. We live in a rural poverty area with poverty levels and social problems that are surprisingly similar to what you will find where you are in Oakland, and in many other urban areas.

It sounds almost like a colonial arrangement where the absentee owner depletes the resource, sucks the money out, and fails to reinvest, because there is no real connection to the soil, to the trees, to the traditions and to the people.

Also in colonial style, Louisiana Pacific is very aggressive politically. When I first started working with Earth First! here in 1988, we had minority support on our county board of supervisors. Four supervisors would vote for Louisiana Pacific on any issue, and one would vote for the community or the Earth. We now have a three-to-two majority. Because of our political work, in and outside of the system, we've actually managed, in a timber-dependent county, to get a majority of supervisors who oppose this liquidation of the forests by out-of-town corporations.

In the most recent election, Louisiana Pacific invested $80,000—this is the company itself—in a supervisor race for which no one had ever spent more than $10,000. They wanted to unseat the environmental candidate so that they could control the county government. They didn't succeed. We still control the county government, and we've managed to pass special county forest rules to try to reign in this corporation in particular. They are stricter than the state rules.

According to the California Forest Practices Act, if a county can prove depletion of the forest, they're allowed to pass special county rules. That's why Santa Cruz has their own rules, for example. Well, we are a timber-dependent economy and this is the mainstay of the economy, and Louisiana Pacific is this very powerful political force. So while we were in the supervisor's board room, promoting these county forest rules, which the supervisors eventually voted in favor of, the head of Louisiana Pacific was in Sacramento meeting behind closed doors with Governor Pete Wilson. As soon as we finished passing these rules—it was a six-year process—the state overruled them under pressure from Louisiana Pacific.

Now have you gone to court to test whether that's legal for the state to take precedence over the County of Mendocino?

The county would not sue, but I don't think it was legal. We had a similar incident several years ago. We passed a law through a citizen's initiative to ban timber companies from aerial spraying of toxic herbicides. The same thing happened. It was preempted by the State.

I remember that very well. As a matter of fact I was Governor during one year of that dispute. The California State Supreme Court at the time said that the county can overrule the state. Then after I left office—at least I hope it was after I left—the state legislature passed a law establishing the power of the state to preempt local authority, specifically with respect to aerial spraying.

In that case, however, we created so much political pressure that the timber companies "voluntarily" decided to stop aerial spraying of herbicides. Now, instead, they hire miserably paid crews to do ground spraying with very inadequate safety equipment. At any rate, we did create the political pressure even though we didn't have the legal authority.

What's the confrontation right now? What's the big issue in Mendocino and Humboldt in terms of preserving the forests?

The whole issue is this liquidation of the remaining forests. Ours is a focused, anti-corporate movement where we have defined the problem as the corporation versus the community. In Humboldt County, you're probably familiar with the Houston-based MAXXAM Corporation. Charles Hurwitz, the corporate raider and major shareholder, is now trying to cut 2,000-year-old trees—the last little island of primeval forest that's left of the redwoods.

What's going on in Mendocino County, where I live, is almost as bad. What's happening here is Louisiana Pacific, our largest land owner, the "Snidely Whiplash" corporate entity here, is on the other end of the liquidation scale. They've cut virtually all of the old growth. There is almost no old growth left in Mendocino County at all. There are a few residual smaller trees, and that's what they're cutting.

So Mendocino County is what you get if MAXXAM gets what they want in Humboldt County?

Right, because they don't stop. After they cut the old growth, and the trees grow back to a certain extent, they cut them again. They've cut the second growth, they've cut the little baby trees that begin growing after that, and now Louisiana Pacific is logging the understory.

When you cut down all the conifers, all the firs and the redwoods, which are defined as "commercial species," the trees that made up the understory of the natural forest remain. They're called "tan oak," and these tan oaks are little scraggly things. Louisiana Pacific is now going back to their cut-over land and taking off the tan oak. They're chipping them up and using them to make fax paper or to burn for electricity. They are virtually throwing them away. They are the only things holding the soil in place right now, but they're deemed a non-commercial species by the California Department of Forestry, so there are no regulations at all to control their use.

Aren't there logging restrictions that aim to protect the soil integrity and prevent erosion?

This is unregulated, absolutely unregulated, and that's one of the issues. The California Forest Practices Act does not address this problem at all. So they're cutting these little tiny trees which the loggers call "pecker poles." These not only include oaks and things like that, but they also include baby redwoods that are just beginning to grow back. Louisiana Pacific fought and won a law suit to allow them to cut redwoods that are as young as twenty years old. These are trees that don't even reproduce until they're one hundred years old. They're just literally stripping the forest floor.

The logging companies seem to be saying that trees are like carrots or broccoli or corn. You plant them and harvest them. It's a crop and people want them and everything's fine.

Yes, but of course that's not true at all. Trees are part of interacting ecosystems. They're not just seeds that you plop in the ground one season and pull out the next. Old trees need to give to the soil, and young trees need to take from the soil. Maybe the forests would be renewable if they waited a thousand years until they logged again, but they cut down a thousand-year-old tree and then they're back again in twenty years to take any stump sprouts that may have come out of it. They never let them grow back. So their practices are just liquidation. That's the only word for what they're doing.

They take any little scrap of biomass that they can find. Pecker poles are too small to saw into a log, so they chip them up for pulp or for waferboard, and make an inferior kind of plywood out of it. I've literally sat and watched this chip mill they set up in Ukiah. There's a truck every five minutes entering that mill from somewhere in the county. It's really horrible to watch, because all that they have left to truck in is these scraggly little trees.

We thought this was the worst they could do. But Louisiana Pacific, always innovative, has come up with what is the final insult to the Earth, and to our county. They've rented dumpsters, industrial-size dumpsters—it doesn't seem believable but it's true, I've seen it with my own eyes—and they put them in the middle of the clear-cut. They scrape the ground clean of anything that's too little to put on a log truck, and this is also going to the chip mill. They're taking the future from the soil, anything that could provide nutrients for the forest to grow back. They want to talk about a renewable resource here, but they have no intentions of staying.

What about the idea of letting trees grow for seventy or one hundred years and then selectively logging. Is Louisiana Pacific doing any of that?

Of course not! But even seventy to one hundred years is not long enough for redwoods. Redwoods don't reproduce until they're one hundred to one hundred fifty years old, and if you cut them before they reach reproductive age, you're not only taking all the trees but you're actually ruining genetic diversity.

The logging corporations say, "We replant." But what they replant are these genetically-identical clones that are engineered to grow quickly and then be cut. There is no genetic recombination going on because these trees don't reach reproductive maturity. They don't make viable cones by the time they're cut. So while they're greatly changing the conditions in which ancient redwoods grew—things like how much sun, how much wind, how much moisture—they're also eliminating natural genetic recombination. Even if you don't see it in our lifetime, what's really going on is redwood genocide.

How do you answer the charge that Earth First! people put spikes in the trees?

We publicly renounced and denounced the practice of tree-spiking in 1990. We oppose tree-spiking. It targets the wrong person. It targets the worker who is not to blame, but is himself a victim of this corporate economy. There was this fantasy put out that if you spike the trees they won't cut them down, but that has not been the case. If the trees are spiked, they go ahead and cut them anyway, and if they hurt a millworker running it through the mill, they don't care. The companies also relish the anti-Earth First! publicity they get, so we have found this to be a failed tactic. We don't do that at all, and we stand up, sometimes to lethal force, with non-violence.

Tell me, is the marbled murelet up in your area?

Not any more. It used to be before they cut the trees down. The marbled murelet is only in the ancient redwoods. It's a very delicate balance in the first-growth ecosystem that allows this bird to survive.

Are there other species that are being undermined by this type of dumpster harvesting?

There are hardly any species left up here! A few spotted owls remain, but the species that is most impacted is the redwood forest itself. But because the law is written in such a screwy way—we can't fight them on the liquidation of redwood trees—we have to fight them on the liquidation of the owls and the murelet. But it's the forest and everything about the forest that is at risk.

The theory of the law is that the trees belong to whoever has title to the land, whereas the wild animals are held in public trust by the people at large. The only way that the people can stop the cutting of trees is to tie in the disappearance of the trees with the disappearance of the wildlife, which, in effect, does not belong to the landowner. That's the kind of indirect legal framework that creates such difficulty in stopping the massacre of the ancient forests.

It really does, but all of these legal concepts are illegitimate. If you liquidate the forests, you impact all kinds of public trust values—things like breathable air, drinkable water, the fish populations. Even the climate is impacted.

Judi, I just want to bring into higher relief the differences of opinion here. Earth First! advocates leaving trees to grow for at least 150 years. That might well be incompatible with the financial structure of Louisiana Pacific and Georgia Pacific and MAXXAM. Is that a fair statement?

It's absolutely incompatible.

So you have a choice here. If you're going to argue for a forest that preserves the character it has had for tens of thousands of years, you can't allow the free working of the market, you can't perpetuate some of the corporate structures that now run this country.

That's right. One of our tactics, for example, has been to urge the county use its power of eminent domain to seize timberlands and operate them in the public interest. This is one way we could save both jobs and trees.

Some people, then, might argue that Earth First! is more opposed to corporatism or even capitalism than it is to the liquidation of the forest, that your main objective is ending capitalism and using the environment as a means for that?

On this question, Jerry, I'm not the typical Earth First!er. I tend to lean more toward the political left. Before I was involved with Earth First! I was a union organizer, and I'm personally against corporatism and capitalism. But, Earth First! is decentralized. It doesn't have a strict political ideology. If you want to know my personal opinion, I believe Earth First! may be too singularly focused on saving the trees without talking about the causes of why they're being liquidated.

Let me just offer my own perspective here, Judi. Your work touches upon some fundamental issues and I think it's important to follow them in a few directions. Perhaps what we're talking about isn't right or left, or socialism or capitalism. It's about how our economics fit into the inexorable biological laws that nobody repeals and everyone is subject to.

Capitalism has been with us for just a couple of hundred years and has evolved, it hasn't remained the same. As you look out and see the proliferation of inequality and the continuing assault on the environment, you see that the successes at the material level of the capitalist economy are running into some major contradictions. These contradictions are forcing very drastic changes in our understanding of capitalism and how it works. I really don't believe that our images of nineteenth-century capitalism are going to be reliable guides to what is going to work in the next few decades

What I see here is that the notion of the sanctity of property has obscured the fact that no person created the wildlife or the redwood trees. They were around before America ever became America. So some humility and respect for the larger picture is in order.

Now we do have regulations and many of them would be hard to argue against, even for most free-market capitalists. If you put up a tannery next to someone's backyard in San Francisco, you'd be run out of town. In the same way, you can't destroy timber in Humboldt County in a way that creates erosion, silts up the streams, destroys the salmon spawning grounds, and, in other ways, impacts the larger community and the world.

None of us is an isolated monad with this bundle of private property rights outside the fabric of these larger obligations. So I very much believe that it's time to take another step in the evolution of capitalism. Right now, I don't think the federal government can make that happen. It can't even operate what it owns, so they're not the answer. But we're on a track of real destruction socially and ecologically, and we have to understand that as clearly as we can in order to come up with a better set of rules.

I think, also, Jerry, people need to reexamine the ways they use what we have. People, after all, are buying the wood that comes out of this county.

We're all implicated in the cutting of redwood trees or trees of one kind or another, and that's another area for creative change. We can use other materials; we can use them more conservatively and re-use them when we're done. There are lots of revolutionary changes needed to support this kind of shift, this change in the way we occupy this space on earth.

You can look at it theologically or you can look at it scientifically, but the wisdom that goes into these trees and all the thousands of species that interact and coexist in an ancient forest grove—we don't know all the dynamics of that. Nobody does. And understanding the underlying wisdom that creates that reality is something that human beings ought to be about.

The Design of a Sustainable Future
Wolfgang Sachs

"It's time to concentrate technological progress much more on saving nature rather than on saving labor. And it seems to me that we have enough creativity and enough intelligence to make quite a number of breakthroughs in this area."

Wolfgang Sachs might, with equal accuracy, be called an historian, a theologian, a sociologist, an environmentalist or a futurist. Educated in Tübingen, Munich and Berkeley, and a former faculty member of the Technical University of Berlin, he is Senior Research Fellow at the Wuppertal Institute for Climate, Energy and the Environment in Wuppertal, Germany.

The author of For Love of the Automobile, *and editor of* The Development Dictionary, Global Ecology, *and* Greening the North, *Sachs, who has worked with Ivan Illich and many of his friends, poses the following question: "How can we extend hospitality to all the people on the planet, expected to double in numbers, without jeopardizing the natural resource base for subsequent generations?"*

Wolfgang, first of all, let me just ask, when was it that we first met? Was that 1983?

Yes, in 1983, in Mexico. We went to a restaurant together in Cuernavaca, and I was embarrassed that half of the people at the restaurant recognized you. I thought, "I shouldn't come too close to this guy, everybody recognizes him."

Well, that has its pluses and minuses. Anyway, lots of water over the dam since the early 'eighties. At that time you were working on the manuscript that ultimately became For the Love of the Automobile. *What were the questions that led you to write that book?*

Our little research group was wondering at the time how Germany got trapped into a high energy consumption society. We were looking, in particular, into cars and how Germany, as all western nations, had gotten stuck in a highly automobilized society. I asked myself, "How did we get into that corner?" And since I liked that kind of perspective, I decided to produce a history of the automobile.

I was not looking at the automobile as a technical artifact because a car is much more than a car. A car is wrapped into desires, needs, hopes, lifestyles, and everything. A car, in effect, is a means of communication. You speak to yourself and you speak to others. So I thought I should look at the history of the car as a cultural symbol.

I went out and tried to understand, for instance, what people thought a hundred years ago as the first cars appeared on the streets. What did they think? How did they react? What did they project into the future? I tried to trace the symbolic place the car took in our societies. I tried to trace that through history until today, focusing on the increasing disenchantment with cars over the last twenty years after eighty years of enthusiasm. I looked at the rise of the project of motorizing society, the enthusiasm, and then after a turning point in 1970, the history of disenchantment, of getting stuck in a situation that nobody knows exactly how to get out of.

So the automobile had an image at the turn of the century very different from what it has today. It was an instrument of liberation, of expansion, of delight.

To be more precise, in Europe, where the automobile first took hold, the automobile was perceived by the political and cultural elite of society as bringing back the privileges of the carriage after the train had taken these away. Imagine. The train of the nineteenth century was powerful, speedy, so even the aristocracy were compelled to take the train. But the train forces you to stick to a schedule, it forces you to stick to a certain route, and it forces you, as contemporaries said, to mingle with the masses. So it was a decrease, if you want, in the quality of elite life.

Then the car comes on to the stage of history. And suddenly, people say, "The car gives us the advantage of the train. It is motorized and at the same time restores the privileges of the carriage. We can go on our own. We are independent in terms of time tables, in terms of routes, and we can keep to ourselves. We don't have to mingle with the masses." So that experience constituted the original enthusiasm for the car.

And then in Germany, in the 'thirties, came the Volkswagen. What was the Volkswagen's particular significance?

Until the early 'thirties, the car was a luxury good. In fact, technologically speaking, the only cars available until 1928 were huge and heavy—limousines in a way. In February 1933, four weeks after he became German Chancellor, Hitler went to the opening of a new highway, and made one of his first promises to the German public. He promised that the car would not remain a luxury good, that it would become a popular good for everybody in society. It was one of the typical essential promises of fascism which aroused the enthusiasm of the people. So you had a consent in German society to the project of Hitler because of these kinds of promises. He promised modernity for everybody.

The Volkswagen was constructed and designed by Porsche according to the indications given by the Nazi government; it should be a cheap, sturdy, simple kind of car. But they never got around to doing it because the first two hundred Volkswagens produced in 1938 immediately went into the German army. So the promise was never even faintly carried out.

There's a funny story about this. In 1936, Hitler started a subscription program. You could subscribe to purchase, in two or three years, one of these German Volkswagens. You had to pay a certain amount of money every month, and there were about 300,000, 400,000 people doing that—paying every month to get the promised Volkswagen. But their Volkswagen never came.

After the war, there was a law suit before the courts. For ten years people tried to get back the money that they had invested in the 'thirties. In 1959 they finally succeeded, and the Volkswagen corporation allowed them to purchase new cars at a lower price.

Is there some essential connection here between the promise of modernity, the automobile and the promise of speed, on the one hand, and fascism and authoritarianism, on the other? Is there some Trojan horse here? This promise wasn't just made by Hitler. It was delivered in the United States by Henry Ford who was an admirer of the fascist operation.

And Hitler was an admirer of Henry Ford.

And what did they mutually admire in each other?

Well, I don't know what Henry Ford admired in Hitler, but I know that Hitler admired Ford's ambition to provide the entire population with simple and sturdy cars, which was of no concern to the European car makers at that time. We don't want to discuss German Nazism here, but one has to be very clear that the fascination Hitler met in large parts of the population has to do with the fact that he promised a modernist popular project. He promised to bring modernity to everybody and not just to the well-to-do. That was an important part of why people believed in him. So it served the attempt of the totalitarian state to get a grip on society.

As you observe modernizing projects in the world today that are operated by multinational corporations without much interference from national

governments, do you see fascistic elements there? There are certainly enor-
mous changes imposed without the consent of the governed.

Well, I see two tendencies. One, is homogenization. Any project that designs a large economy will eventually bring peoples tastes and aspirations into a common frame. They will differentiate, but nevertheless, they will be in a common frame and in interaction with each other. So it's a homogenizing kind of exercise. At the same time it is a very undemocratic exercise, in the sense that the powers that are increasingly acquiring a grip on world society are not controlled by anybody—certainly not by the people. And that basically is what democracy is about.

As corporations grow their power grows, and they are only influenced by people in their role as consumers. But what I think is even more important is that through global markets, the space for the self-determination of each country is shrinking. Democracy needs a certain kind of space. Democracy means that people have the right to handle their own public affairs. Now, if you say "their own public affairs," you're implying a certain defined space, a community which occupies a certain territory. But as globalization increases, it's perforating borders; it's making national communities unimportant and irrelevant; it becomes clear that globalization is, in this way, at odds with the space requirements of democracy.

I want to go to another aspect of your work and that is development. You edited a book entitled The Development Dictionary: A Guide to Knowledge as Power. *This book is a dissection and demolition of the very idea of development. You also criticize environmentalism. I'd like you to just elaborate on some of this—maybe we could start out with the idea of development. Certainly, development has a very positive ring for many.*

Development has a positive ring for everybody, but that's where the clarity stops. Nobody knows what development is, so that is all that development is—just a positive ring.

Development has been the key word in shaping and interpreting the relations between North and South. However, we were struck by the fact that this has only been the case since the postwar years. We saw that development was a certain way of looking at the world and we wanted to look at these fifty years of development since the Second World War as a cultural history. We wanted to understand what kind of glasses one puts on the moment one speaks about development. How is reality colored? What things stick out and what other things are left in the shadow?

Now, if you speak about development, you are bound to use words such as poverty, resources, production, equality, aid, and all of that. These are the words which fall into your lap when you open any United Nations document. So we decided we'd better go out there as historians and anthropologists and look at these words. Basically, *The Development Dictionary* is a portrayal of twenty words—aid, production, development, and so on—that, according to us, make up development discourse.

You state that development discourse started in 1949. Can you really identify it as a speech by Harry Truman, in that particular year?

It was the 20th of January, 1949, in President Harry Truman's inaugural speech. Then after the inaugural speech, he sketched out his so-called Point Four Program. In that program, which was directed towards what later became known as the Third World, Truman, for the first time in history, called half of the world an underdeveloped area. So there it was, the word underdeveloped, a word that has become so natural to us. In fact, we cannot understand the world without using that word. That word is, in a way, younger than I am; what has become so natural today is of a very recent date.

So the development era for us began with Truman. He was the first one, at least from a prominent political stage, who looked at the planet and saw a few nations— the United States and some other Western countries—running along a common race track and running way ahead, with many other nations lagging far behind. The big imperative then is to catch up. And basically, development is about catching up with those who are running ahead. Sure enough, the image was there before Truman; colonialism had these kinds of notions. But the new thing after the Second World War was to project the self-understanding of Western societies as an economic entity upon the rest of the world, and at the same time to say that it is feasible to bring entire societies on to the path within a couple of years, or at least a couple of decades.

I remember the election prior to January 20, 1949. It's the famous election of 1948, when Harry Truman had his great upset. How old was I? I was ten. I can remember Dewey, the man on the wedding cake, and Truman with his whistle stops. "Give 'em hell, Harry!" And then the consequence of all that showmanship is this incredible process called development. In what sense can we say the American people were voting on this development project when they picked Harry Truman over Thomas Dewey?

I don't think that the American people ever elect a President because of issues of foreign policy.

It's interesting to reflect on what people vote on and what we get.

The entire philosophy out of which development emerged, out of which the United Nations emerged, out of which the international, multilateral field of thinking and action emerged—that, of course, has a long history. But it came to a head during the Second World War as the Americans in particular, but also others, were thinking about what the world should look like after the capitulation of Germany. The question that the United States was confronted with after the Second World War was how to design an order for peace in the world.

Don't forget that the United States also had to be the successor to France and England. Until the Second World War, the world was shaped by these colonial empires, and the U.S. came along as a non-colonial power. The United States was always proud of not being a colonial power. So the kind of order they would project could not be the old colonial power. They couldn't simply step into the shoes of France and England.

To propose economic development as the new horizon for the world had a charm to it, and it also had a nice advantage. The advantage is that by calling for economic development, you establish a prerogative for the United States without calling for territorial occupation. It created a world order without the leading nation going out there and occupying other people's countries like the English and the French did. And, in fact, in the years after the Second World War, the hegemony of the United States was almost solely based on economic development. Only at extreme moments did the United States feel forced to resort to old-fashioned, colonial means of occupying other people's territory.

It's kind of a de-territorializing colonialism.

I would call it an anti-colonialist imperialism.

I'm thinking back to the Nazi era, where the mythology of the ancient Germanic peoples was used to promote the radically modern—the embrace of technology and modern integration. Then how for the American project, a new form of colonialism and hegemony was promoted with anti-colonial imagery and rhetoric. In both cases it seems to reflect the thought of Mao Tse-Tung, or maybe it was Lao Tzu, who said "When you're going to move in the East, make a sound in the West."

Yes. But I would not formulate it in a way which assumed an intention. There's no intention there. I don't think it was a mischievous kind of enterprise. It was a new phase of history.

Wait a minute. Don't you think the architects in the State Department or other places had the idea of containing communism? They wanted to divide up the world to make sure the United States was protected with buffer states, which basically meant the rest of the world outside of the Soviet Union and its satellites.

Certainly, but the containment of communism was understood as a project which would protect the freedom of economic development. Economic development was at the core of it.

You see, there has been a move in history by which power is increasingly wielded not through territorial claims but through economic claims. In the nineteenth century, to establish power meant to invade somebody and take their territory. Increasingly in the twentieth century, power means to control the economic apparatus, to have free movement of capital, and goods, and what have you. That was established with the hegemony of the United States. So they didn't have to go out there and occupy a country. The point was to guarantee a free space of movement for American capital and for Western capital.

You said earlier that development is a very new project, and that now the lenses through which we see the world are colored by it. If I understand you correctly, when I think about "underdeveloped" countries or "poor" countries, that very phraseology, that imagery, is a construct that has within it all sorts of premises that I don't notice. I'm already embedded in a view that forces me into a false way of seeing myself and others.

Yes. I have a nice anecdote to that. The experience you describe struck me like a thunderbolt. It was fifteen years ago—at the time we met, more or less. I was taken by a friend through the neighborhood of Tepito in Mexico City.

The thieves market.

Exactly. We walked around, and I visited courtyards, the markets, and talked to people who carry out their everyday survival there; there were families; we ran into a fiesta. One got the impression it was a difficult life there, but also relaxed and dignified. At the end of the day as we stood together—our Mexican friends had gone away—I said, "Well, it's all nice here but these are poor people." And this Mexican friend stepped back and said, *"Somos Tepitanos, non somos pobres."*

Suddenly, the message was driven home to me that by calling them poor, I insulted them. I had put as the most prominent definition of them a lack. I called them poor as if it were the most important feature of their life, while, of course they would say, *"Somos Tepitanos. That* is our first characteristic."

Whenever you call other people or other countries poor, you take as their first definition a lack. You say to them, "You are a deficit. You consist of a lack." And that is, of course, an insult to anybody. You cannot define somebody in the first place as lacking something. Not even handicapped people. A handicapped person wouldn't permit that. So speaking in terms of development implies, by necessity, that we look at others in terms of a lack, and not in terms of what they are and what their aspirations are. Therefore, I think it's deeply insulting to look at other countries in terms of development.

But it's a habit that stands on a long tradition. In the old days, as long as society saw itself as Christian, it would see the other as pagan. As society during Enlightenment times saw itself as a highly accomplished civilization, it would see the other as savage. And with the development era, what our societies have thought about themselves is that we are wealthy, productive and rich, so others are poor, underproductive and miserable. We are increasingly moving into a situation where we consider ourselves as secure societies, rational societies, stable societies, while others are risk factors, with potential chaos and instability, and we have the right to intervene. If we follow this thread of argument, it might clearly identify why today the Development Age has come to an end.

You're asserting that development is dead.

The Development Age which was opened at the end of the Second World War is dead, and I will be precise about the sense in which it has come to an end.

That age was running on two promises. The first promise was that the entire world could eventually become like the United States. So it had a promise of justice across the world. And secondly, it had the promise that along this path, there would never be any end; development would go on infinitely. So there was a promise in terms of time. It could go on forever.

Now, take these two promises. After half a century now, they are not valid anymore. The gap between rich and poor nations in the world is deeper than it was at the end of the Second World War, so inequalities have increased across the globe. Second, and even more importantly, the ecological crisis has brought home the insight that this type of development cannot go on forever because it has already reached the Earth's biophysical limits. Only a small minority of the world population can enjoy the fruits of development.

So inequality is inherent in the development concept.

Right. We have created forms of wealth which are inherently oligarchic. They cannot be generalized to everybody; they're reserved only for some parts of the population.

If you look at today's discussions, I would say there are these two poles. On the one side, there are those who say we can go on with development more or less as ever. We might have some environmental modifications, but they take it for granted, implicitly, that this development will not be for everybody. So they shrug off the large majority of the world. On the other side are those who aspire to create conditions in the world of a good global neighborhood, which increases the space for less powerful countries and societies to gain in dignity. These are the people who deeply criticize development and are clear that development, in the form we have gotten to know it, has come to an end.

If development's dead, then we in the developed, rich world can't hide behind the notion that we're just rich for a little while, until our poorer and darker brothers and sisters catch up through our efforts. That's quite a disillusioning reality sandwich that you're asking us to bite into.

You can say it in other ways. For fifty years, the kind of justice we have held out to the world was that there was a growing pie, that because the pie of economic wealth was growing, those who were poor could eventually get a larger share and we wouldn't have to renounce anything, because our share was also growing. Now the idea of the growing pie is over, because economic development is no longer a matter of a growing pie. For biophysical reasons, the pie cannot grow beyond a certain limit, therefore, justice cannot be promised anymore in these terms.

Perhaps it's time now to talk about responses to the end of development, about what we actually can promise. Some of the responses, and one that I know you have been involved with in Germany, fall under the category of plans, and a particular species of plan known as a green plan or a sustainability plan, formulated under the shadow of Agenda 21. That was the agenda adopted at the Global Environmental Summit at Rio de Janeiro in 1992. So I want to first ask, what should one be wary of in the whole embrace of a green plan. Because it's a plan, and isn't that again the shaping, the manipulation, the attempt to control large classes of people in the inhuman way that we've been criticizing?

Well, I am not afraid of a plan as such, because it depends very much who is planning in what way. And even those, Jerry, who attack green plans are themselves planning quite a bit. Any kind of corporation today has a planning horizon of five, ten, even twenty years. So following someone's plan is on the agenda anyway.

In any case, what we are trying to do in Germany is not so much lay out a plan. Therefore, I wouldn't accept the word plan in that sense. It is rather a kind of thought experiment. We're trying to seriously ask ourselves what a sustainable Germany could look like, and then trying to lay out a number of avenues to help us arrive there. That kind of perspective has plural elements to it. It is not addressed simply to government actors. It is addressed basically to the public at large. So I wouldn't even call it a plan, because it's not clear who is going to be the actor as such. It's not clear who is going to be acted upon. It is a proposal, a perspective, which can then serve as a basis for debate and for a common search in the various quarters of society.

So let me push this a bit. What is sustainability? What are we sustaining? Is that even possible given the way we're living today?

I don't know if it's possible, but in my view, it is the challenge at the threshold of a new century. Many people are speaking about the future and all kinds of discussions are going on, and I find it quite ridiculous to reduce the debate about the future to the information highway, genetic technology and international competitiveness, at the moment when everybody who is in his or her right mind will have to recognize two things. One is that the crucial experience at the end of our century is that we have to calculate biophysical limits into our equations of further development of industrial civilization. Second, it's pretty obvious that there is a deepening chasm which runs through the world between the world's rich and the world's poor. So, if you want to think of the next century, it's pretty obvious that these are going to be the deep running conflicts which will shape our lives to a great extent. So when I speak about sustainability, I speak about a kind of political perspective which tries to give some sober, careful response to these two basics.

I think for many people it's hard to get the feel of the world you describe. Your German sustainability plan calls for a reduction in what we're using and extracting and creating as waste by a factor of ten. That in itself says we are living in extreme excess. But the conditions of daily life make it very hard for many of us to see the extent of the problem. The urgency of the situation seems very remote and implausible.

Fair enough. But if it were a Sunday walk, we wouldn't need to speak about it. It is, in fact, a deep running and profound historical challenge. Today the German economy is weighing much too heavily on the planet and on other peoples. So to put it in a simple way, the objective is to lighten the German economy by a factor of ten, meaning that within fifty years, Germany must bring down the throughput of nature, energy and materials, by eighty to ninety percent.

Of course, Germany generates far less greenhouse emissions, carbon dioxide, and waste than the United States, so we have even a bigger challenge.

Probably.

In order to convince anybody of this we're going to have to have a strong scientific foundation. So when you talk about biophysical limits, how do you prove them or how do you demonstrate them? If you want a radical restructuring of my personal existence along with that of several billion people, I've got to have a pretty powerful argument here. Give me some threads to weave my rug.

Well, I don't exactly accept the premise that the task is so daunting. There are many people who have the common sense to see that what has happened in the last two or three generations cannot be the normality for the next three or four or five hundred years. There are enough people out there who very much recognize that we have gone through an extraordinary phase of history in this century—America since the 'twenties, and Europe since the 'forties or 'fifties. So it's only two generations or three maybe that we speak about.

Think back on the tremendous transformation which has taken place during that time. Even pretty normal people, without any complex data, have a sense that you cannot extend these kinds of transformations for the next two or three hundred years, nor to all countries in the world. That is not going to work. We can speak about the availability of land, the availability of water—all of that. There is a certain common sense there.

Now, you can, of course, also resort to science. There are many, many approaches, but it seems to me simplest to speak about the greenhouse effect. As you know, the International Panel of Climate Change—two thousand scientists from around the world gathered by the United Nations and the World Meteorological Organization—were asked to provide the state-of-the-art in scientific evidence about climate change. Last year, a very large majority concluded that there is a human effect present in current climate change. There is an enormous consensus in the community of meteorologists, and of people who deal with large-scale ecosystems, that we are confronted with a potential crisis whose repercussions we have no way to gauge.

The conclusion is that even though we cannot spell out the consequences to the last detail, we have to organize our way of living and of producing in a way that we do not overstep certain limits of risk and of possible threat. Now, there have been people debating that, but there is probably no better organized and better equipped community of scientists out there than the IPCC. Keep in mind that it is normally impossible to have irrefutable knowledge, because nature out there is much too complex and has its own inscrutable feedback mechanisms. We are faced with the limits of our knowledge.

So it is prudent, it seems to me, to design a preventive politics. To design an economic system, and to reinvent styles of life, which don't systematically overstep possible limits. It's obvious. If you are driving a vehicle and you see that your vehicle is running towards an abyss, you try to correct your course; you don't ride at the edge all the time. You keep a certain distance in order not to fall down in a moment of lowered attention. That is what everybody does in normal life. So society is required to try a path of prevention, of receding back in a certain way from the dangerous edge of the abyss.

Let's return to this reduction by a factor of ten. That's not ten percent.

No. It works out to an eighty to ninety percent reduction in the overall inputs of nature that we consume, which means materials like topsoil, wood, copper, bauxite, and the overall quantities of energy, such as oil and natural gas. Another critical factor is land, which may be kind of unimaginable for Americans because they have a huge land mass. But think of Europe. Europe is a continent where things are pretty dense. We cannot afford, in the long term, to go on at the same pace paving over our land for parking lots, roads, construction, and so forth.

Here in California, projections show a massive and continuing paving of the prime agricultural land in the Central Valley. The building of houses is so much more profitable in the short term than the production of food that the market drives people to pave over their land. After all, the food can be grown in Mexico or it can be grown in Asia, it can be grown in Spain, wherever.

It's profitable because for many years now, nature has only been minimally present in the market. The market thrives on the fact that nature doesn't cost anything. Our bookkeeping seems so positive because the assets of nature do not show up in our accounting books. But at some point, even nature, with all its power, will be exhausted in many different ways and will make itself felt. So one approach to correct the parameters under which the market works would be to give more consideration to the value of nature.

In the last few years, there's been a mounting chorus call for the elimination of barriers to global trade. This is the GATT, the General Agreement on Trade and Tariffs, which opposes any barrier to the movement of goods across borders. What this is calling for is energy consumption, extraction, and more and more possession of stuff— chemical, plastic, whatever— with almost no real recognition of the issues of overconsumption.

I don't recall anyone at G-7 saying we should be "less weighty" on the world in the coming years. It doesn't even show up. Everything seems to be moving toward more container ships, more things in them, more port expansion, more railroad cars, more trucks, more subdivisions, more garages, and all that is the absolute opposite of what you've said.

The market will produce an efficient equilibrium only if all factors are calculated in. This, by and large, is not the case. The factor of nature is systematically undervalued. Therefore, the outcome is bound to be inefficient. Second, politically speaking, we have this schizophrenia in international politics. On the one hand, they are pushing free trade. On the other hand, they are urging international summits like Rio de Janeiro, like the population summit or what have you, where in various ways, leaders call for environmental policies. But these two strands rarely meet. That is the state of the world at this moment.

In your discussion of a green plan for Germany, you point out that the rich countries consume eighty percent of the world's resources, and that the remaining vast majority of people are going to have to consume more.

Sure enough. Given that they're in a powerless and underprivileged situation now, they need to have some room to recover.

They need more. We've got to take less. Now, when we take less, is there some technical fix available, where we can get a little minicomputer and without using a lot of resources, have our happy indulgent ways? Or does this mean we become more ascetic?

Both. There are technical fixes, *and* you're going to change. So, let me address the first issue in particular, because what we're speaking about is giving technological progress a new direction.

For a hundred years at least, technological progress, to a large extent, meant concentrating on increasing labor efficiency. We tried to make labor superfluous. Now, it's time to concentrate, let's say for the next couple of decades, not on making people superfluous, but on making kilowatt hours superfluous, making barrels of oil superfluous, making liters of water superfluous. It's time to concentrate technological progress much more on saving nature rather than on saving labor. And it seems to me that we have enough creativity and enough intelligence to make quite a number of breakthroughs in this area.

Less nature used for a given unit of output. That's being lighter on the planet. A lot of that would seem to be dependent upon computers, but you've said that the production of computers generates enormous waste. So do we have to be careful of computers?

Certainly, we have to be careful about computers. There is no doubt about it. A computer seems to use a small amount of energy because you just think about the electricity needed for operating it. But that's not the whole case. Most of nature is being invested during the process of production, and there are highly sophisticated materials contained, toxic materials. You have to move lots of nature in order to obtain these materials. The present mode of computer production is clearly unsustainable given the high rates of turnover. The turnover is enormous. Every two or three years you have a new generation of computers, creating huge mountains of electronic garbage that involves enormous amounts of toxins and enormous waste of materials.

Now, much can be done on that and is being done. It is possible to design computers to be much more durable, and to design internal components which can be exchanged as the technology improves. All of that is possible, and that is one example of the direction we are going to move as objects begin to be designed in a radically different way—in a way that they last much longer, that they can be repaired much easier, and that they have higher longevity so they can be exchanged for new products, rather than discarded.

Is it true that in Germany there is a requirement that a car be totally recyclable?

Not yet. But that's the goal. There are steps being taken in Germany, in a long term fashion, so that we might have a certain class of products—very durable products such as computers, or cars, or washing machines—which remain the property of the producer. Consumers would lease them on a long term basis, and then these products would go back to the producer. Now, because these goods are the continuous property of the producer, who will be obliged to take them back, there is a very powerful incentive for him or her to think of the end of the product at the beginning, at the design stage.

Then, of course, there's another class of product, which we think of as biodegradables. There are quite a number of things we use in everyday life, such as shirts or shoes, which we are able to make biodegradable using current technology. That means that these things can be made to return to the earth without harm. And there's a third class of product we would like to entirely get rid of, which are toxins.

We've got a long way to go here.

Yes, a long way to go, and a way which will require all the imagination of the engineers.

And it's not just the engineers. It's also a moral turn, a conversion of how we view what the good life is and how we live it.

It's a moral turn and it's also an overall awareness about what the historic juncture is. The historic juncture is to bring that project of modernity on to an entirely different plane, a plane where it is in the right measure with respect to nature.

Let me come back to product design, because that brings me to another frontier. Another frontier, certainly, is that you have to design the proper parameters for the market. One has to shift the tax base in a way that the consumption of nature—energy, materials, and land—costs more. So you put taxes on land, on energy and materials, on the one hand, and you try to reduce the tax burden on labor. That follows a very simple rule. Any finance minister will tell you. You put taxes on things you don't want and you relieve taxes from things you want. We don't want continuous destruction of nature, and we do want more possibilities for people to work. So that's the only rational way to go about it.

Now, what about the way we've organized our lives. In laying out your green plan, you talked about different conceptions of time and space.

Let me begin with the dimension of volume. There's no doubt that we have to think of a society where the overall volume of consumption is reduced. Now, how can one do that? How is that possible without necessarily damaging well-being?

In answering these questions, it has been very important to discover that there is a hidden contradiction in our lives. On the one hand, we try to increase our wealth in goods, while on the other hand, we are always decreasing our wealth in time. You cannot at the same time increase your wealth in goods and your wealth in time, and you need time in order to conduct a good life.

So there is an argument here that we should increase the possibilities for people to choose the length of their working time and to choose the income they would like. We should make it possible for people to ask themselves, "How much money do I really need?" If it were possible to fully exercise our sovereignty over time, then a path would be paved for more people to trade more money for more time.

So, you're talking about a less material way of living.

Sure enough. Because the first question, when it comes to choosing what you want to do with your life, should be, "What is well-being for me?" The biggest chunk of your life goes into working for other people, into going out and earning a salary. One earns a salary, and then turns the salary into commodities. But we've become accustomed to a broken spin cycle, by which we work and work and we have a certain income and then we go out and buy a number of products and then we get used to the products, which again forces us to go out and work and work.

Now is it possible a little bit to interrupt that cycle? Surely enough. It is possible the moment you have the right to choose the length of your working time. You can say, " I'm working only half a year and the other half of the year I will devote more time to my three-year-old daughter. I don't know how to speak French, so I will concentrate half a year on learning French because that is much more important to me." This would require the art of getting by with less money, but it also suggests the possibility that we can reduce the levels of global overconsumption by offering people more autonomous time.

For people who are at the lower end of the income scale, that's impossible.

Agreed. As in many questions, the dimension of inequality comes in. But one could think of schemes, for instance, where you have a reduction of working time for lower income people without a reduction of income. Then the more you go up the income ladder, the reduction of working time is more closely linked to a reduction of income. One can think of these kinds of things.

This is a radical assault on the borrow/spend economy. Two-thirds of the economy is consumer purchases and purchases are driven by obsolescence, fashion changes, and all the rest.

On the one hand radical; on the other hand, not at all. Because there are many people out there who have learned how to get by with less money already, to organize their life in a way that they don't sacrifice everything for earning income but keep some space of their own. So that notion is already jingling around and many people are used to it and becoming more artful at it.

What you're really calling for is some pretty serious self-limitation here and a collective conversion. It almost sounds bigger than Christianity or any kind of major upheaval in people's understanding of life.

Well, let's not exaggerate. Because, it is totally wrong to think that our society is stable. We are undergoing incredible transformations every ten years in our society, in our economies. We are all the time pushed by ever new ways of transformation. So the point is simply to use those dynamics and to give them a different direction.

Rehumanizing the Beginnings of Life
Suzanne Arms

"The thing that's important to remember is that for a
baby, birth and the first hours, days and weeks
afterwards are its first impressions. We know how
important first impressions are, but neurologically,
we are patterning people for insecurity and addiction
and mistrust."

*Suzanne Arms is a photojournalist who, since the birth of her own child in
1970, has studied and traveled extensively, exploring how, in different historical times and different parts of the world, children have been born and
nurtured in their earliest years. Arms is the author of seven books on pregnancy, birth and bonding, including* Immaculate Deception, *published
in 1975, and a sequel,* Immaculate Deception II: Myth, Magic and Birth,
*published in 1997. She is a crusader for a more natural way of childbirth, a
return to a more human, connected, feminine and less technological passage into life.*

I spoke with Suzanne shortly after the publication of Immaculate
Deception II, *and we talked about how the medical profession continues
to misunderstand the dynamics of birth, missing the very fundamental
point that the body has an innate capacity to thrive, to rebound, and to
create. Childbirth in America today is more artificial and alienated from
life than at any time in history, and one result is the gradual dissolution of
the bonds that tie the human community together. Suzanne's work demonstrates that the first steps in reestablishing these bonds are realistically
within reach.*

Jerry, I remember you in 1978 standing in your office—I guess it was the Governor's office—when a group of us who were lobbying for midwifery and the right of midwives to attend birth legally in California had a chance to talk with you. You set up a commission to study alternative birth practices and I was appointed to it. So we go back a long way.

We do, and I remember the bill that came out of that, allowing women who weren't part of the medical establishment to assist at birth. It's kind of a preposterous notion that midwifery had to be legalized, but nevertheless, we tried to do exactly that. In response, the California Medical Association made the bill its number one attack item. And one of the people in the state Senate who was supposed to vote it out of the committee changed his mind. He'd received, and has received since then, tens of thousands of dollars in donations from the CMA. So while we may talk about childbirth, this subject is certainly embedded in the whole system of politics, and the money and the corruption that goes with it.

That's right.

We met at another time too.

Yes, we did. The night of the 1989 San Francisco earthquake at a mutual friend's house. She was getting ready to have a home birth with a midwife.

And it worked out okay.

Oh, yes. She went against her social class and the belief that she should go to a private hospital and a private physician, and she chose home birth with a non-nurse professional midwife.

So where do you begin when it comes to talking about something as fundamental as childbirth?

Part of the problem in talking about childbirth is that it has such a big context for us to think about. So let me just delineate some of the aspects of it. The first is that because childbirth is a crucial, primal time in a woman's life, and it's a baby's first experience of extra-uterine life, it has a profound importance in laying down patterns in the neurological system of the body. A woman, because of her hormone and endocrine system, is rendered wide open and vulnerable in pregnancy, during birth, and then afterwards in the postpartum months. And so is a baby.

When you effect a mother and a baby at this crucial time in life, you're not just effecting their birth. You're effecting the patterns that get established in years to follow regarding how they feel about their own capacity and power—how much the mother trusts her body and her baby, how much the baby trusts or doesn't trust its mother and other people, and the development of both of them.

So when you give a woman the best care possible in birth, or the worst care possible, you've really affected the entire culture. And you've also affected women on the other side of the world who, today, model themselves after middle-class, white Americans. The problem is that we make choices that we don't understand, choices that are not based on scientific evidence, and which have a long political history that lacks respect for the feminine and appreciation of both the need and the capacity of women and babies to birth normally.

When we talk about birthing normally, isn't it a fact that, historically, many women died in childbirth and that half of the babies didn't survive childbirth?

The problems women have in childbirth are most often directly related to chronic disease, to socio-economic factors such as poor nutrition, to having children too closely spaced together, or to stress. For the last couple hundred years, because of various religious injunctions and social pressures, women have had babies every year or two years. Their bodies could not recuperate. In addition, they were often malnourished and working too hard. They were not getting the rest they needed, and therefore, were prone to exhaustion in labor and prone to hemorrhage. But labor and birth itself are nowhere near as dangerous as people have come to believe.

If you study people in other cultures, as the World Health Organization has, you learn that the two most common problems in birth are the woman bleeding too much, and the baby having breathing problems. We have built an entire system of care around emergency and first aid treatment that believes that those two things will occur, that they will be catastrophic in nature, and that they cannot be handled except in high-risk hospitals by the most highly-trained professionals specializing in disease.

But the fact is, a simple hormone shot or hands on compression of the uterus will usually stop a woman from bleeding too much, and a ten-dollar ambubag—a little bulb that squeezes oxygen into the baby at a small rate—in the hands of a skilled person, can get a baby breathing well. So it isn't a matter of professionalization.

Now, there are people from Southeast Asia, I believe it was the Hmong, who have a high incidence of poverty, as they call it, but a very low infant mortality rate.

Right, but they probably have good nutrition. One of the things to understand is that every year, the U.S. ranks among the worst in the world in infant mortality and perinatal mortality. We rank well below countries like Japan, Sweden, Denmark, Holland and England, all of which use midwives at the core of their health care system.

Is our high mortality rate particularly because of the problems of poor women?

It's due to several things. It's due to the socioeconomic inequities in this culture and the fact that many women aren't getting cared for. And

I don't mean just prenatal care. Women aren't getting the food, housing or emotional support they need. A woman's emotional state greatly affects her chances for prematurity and low birth rate.

These are not our only problems. Middle-class women are having cesareans at a rate of thirty to forty percent. For women in their thirties who go to private physicians, eighty or ninety percent of whom are having epidural anesthesia, we're seeing different kinds of complications. They seldom end in death of the mother or baby, but they definitely end in complications.

I had the opportunity to witness and document births in Kingston, Jamaica, at the second largest maternity hospital in the Western Hemisphere. Often fifty births a day, 14,500 births a year. They don't even have sheets on the bed. They have one huge, four-foot oxygen tank which they roll to women who need oxygen, if they can. And the interesting thing is, here's a group of women who are two generations away from home birth—the British institutionalized hospital birth as the routine—but midwifery is the care they get. And they birth well.

The difference is that midwives have an expectation of normalcy, and they observe the entire labor process expecting things to go well, not catastrophic things to happen. These women labor ten and fifteen to a room, three to a bed. They have to walk to the delivery room carrying a bag that has their own sheets, their own food and climb up on the bed. These women are often hypertensive, overweight, or malnourished. They give birth often to small babies or low birth rate babies. But they push their babies out and their babies thrive.

The vast majority of babies have no problems because they don't separate the mother and baby after birth. There is an expectation that women are competent, and the pair is kept together. The mother and baby are together, and women breast feed immediately and for a long time. So this is a case of a Third World country that, even in the hospital, hasn't lost normalcy. You've got midwives at the core of their care.

Here in America, we have 33,000 obstetricians compared to seven thousand practicing nurse-midwives and professional non-nurse midwives. Holland, on the other hand, which has among the finest infant and maternal mortality and health statistics in the world, has a reverse ratio. They have five times the number of midwives to obstetricians.

Still, infant mortality rates in the U.S. are falling, particularly for the afflu-ent middle class and above. What are the issues that we need to be con-cerned about?

Because we have come to depend upon hospitals as our primary source of "health," we've come to depend upon highly trained sub-specialist physicians as the people who can keep us healthy. So women giving birth today in America have an inverse relationship in terms of the amount of trust they have in their body to how much education they have. The woman with the greatest amount of college education and the greatest amount of professional skill is the least likely to be confident in her own body's ability to birth. So women who are well-educated and are among the healthiest in the world are having the highest rate of epidural anes-thesia—that's anesthesia where you're completely numb from the waist down—the highest rate of interventions of all kinds, the highest rate of cesarean surgery, and the lowest rate of breastfeeding.

Let's go into each of those issues and what the implications are.

The most important thing to understand is that we exist in a continuum of either separation or connection to our world, and to each other, and to our own bodies. That continuum begins in the womb. And if we have the opportunity to be connected in a deep way to one human being at the start of life, then we have relatedness and connection to other care givers, to family, to the community, and to the Earth and spirit.

But the way we're approaching birth and child care today is by sepa-ration. As a result we are seeing a country that has the largest percent-age of incarcerated people in the world, high rates of learning disor-ders, depression, anxiety, violence and addictions to all sorts of substances. That's middle-class people, as well as people of low income.

Addiction to food, addiction to buying.

To work, to the computer, to the television, in lieu of relationships. We're spending more and more money on quick solutions. But very few people are looking at the beginning of life. How we treat a mother-baby pair in pregnancy, at birth and afterward, how we treat them in relationship to the father, the family, and the community, effects the very patterns that set their life in motion. If we look at it closely, we see a continuum of disconnection, alienation and loneliness.

Let's go right to the early stages. How do you believe a woman should prepare for having her baby?

The most important things besides good health are social support and feeling good about your body. Studies were done as early as the 1920s that showed that very little medical prenatal care has to be given to the healthy woman. Studies, for example, in Canada, show that one home visit in the course of a woman's pregnancy has much more opportunity to positively change her thinking and her well-being than does all of the prenatal care the average woman is given. We need to focus prenatal care on women who have identifiable complications of pregnancy or come into pregnancy ill.

Now, who is going to figure that out? Is that a midwife, is that the woman, or is that a doctor?

Well, the Dutch system is a model. When a woman is pregnant in Holland or thinks she's pregnant, the first person she goes to is a midwife. It's a neighborhood or community midwife. If she doesn't like the one who's nearest her, she can go to any midwife. The midwife makes the referral to a physician if the woman needs it. However, most women never need to see a physician in the course of their pregnancy, birth, or postpartum care.

Wait a minute. How's she going to get a sonogram then?

There's no evidence-based documentation supporting routine use of sonograms in pregnancy, intravenous fluids in labor, electronic fetal monitoring, artificially stimulating labor, episiotomy, or drugs or anesthesia for pain. There's no scientific evidence on the value of any of it, except in the case of specific complications.

I want to say something about sonograms. A lot of women think that they're seeing a picture of their baby. But what they're seeing, in fact, is a computer-generated image that is part of a whole technological reshaping of their consciousness of their body and themselves.

You're quite right, and it's really interesting because you get women taking the sonogram video home from the doctor's office, putting it on their television, and sitting there on the couch saying, "Oh, look at our baby out there." But the baby isn't out there. The baby is *in here.* More and more of what we do to women in pregnancy is making them more and more anxious about their own body and more separated from it, and therefore more separated from the entire experience of childbirth.

It's as if the artificial creation on a screen influences people to lose the sense of their own true being.

It's very much similar to the virtual community that people are talking about on computers. You cannot have a full relationship with another unless there's eye contact, and unless there's a visceral feeling of touch, and smell, and all of the things that have to do with being in our body.

So there's the beginning of it. The woman in pregnancy is alienated from her body, she's alienated from her baby, she's made to feel that her body is unsafe. She's given all sorts of prenatal tests to supposedly assure "perfection." And then she starts to worry about how she's going to care for this baby after birth because we have no routine paid postpartum maternity leave. So women start to disconnect from their babies even in the course of pregnancy, as they plan and arrange for daycare, which they know they're going to have to use, because most of them are going back to work three weeks to three months after birth.

So the sense that a woman has of her body today—given all the programming by medical technology, the imagery, the narrative that forms in our own imagination—it must be very different from what a woman conceived of and imagined a hundred years ago.

Very. But the interesting thing is it's also very different from a country like Holland, which is as industrialized as we are, and yet has not lost the belief that birth is a healthy normal process, that one should expect normalcy. Midwives are the bulwark of the system there, while physicians and hospitals are a great keep-it-in-the-back-pocket part of the system that is used rarely and only as needed.

In Holland, for example, a woman is fully covered by insurance for birth at home if she's fully healthy. Fifty percent birth at home. If a woman needs to go into a hospital, she's also totally covered. But if she chooses a hospital birth and an obstetrician-attended birth and she doesn't medically need it, she has to pay extra. Now, isn't that interesting?

Let's go to this whole issue of pain. Women are certainly not just promiscuously demanding painkillers. There's some suffering and some fear here that's real.

Yes, pain is a critical issue in birth. And our approach to pain involves feminist, as well as feminine, issues.

Can you distinguish between those two words?

Feminist is the political context that says a woman has a right to her own body, the right to make her own choices, to make decisions about whatever she wants, even if it's choosing drugs for pain relief that may complicate labor and cause problems for her baby. That's one issue. The feminine issue, which is sometimes at odds with the feminist—and I am a strong feminist—is that birthing is a primal raw force. In order for a woman to let go and birth this baby, she has to be not in her head, but down in her body, moving around, making noise, squatting, sweating. Labor is very primal work, and requires that a woman let go.

When a woman is taught to be a good girl and be compliant, which is what she's taught growing up and in most prenatal classes, she's learning to be the very opposite of what she really needs to be in birth, which is to be instinctual, unfettered, and give free reign to her body. Instead we're strapping her to electronic fetal monitors, giving all sorts of symbolic cues to her brain, to unconscious aspects of her psyche, that say, "You are not well. A catastrophe is about to happen." Then we expect her to open up and push this baby out under the eye of the clock. "Oh! It's been an hour and you haven't progressed one centimeter!"

So the issue of the feminine is that birthing is a primal, unfettered, wide open, embracing of everything that is in life. And in order for the feminine to do its work, paradoxically, it needs enough structure around it to feel safe.

Picture in nature a group of elephants encircling the mother elephant in labor, protecting her from harm because, at the end, she has to lie or be pushed over on her side in a very vulnerable position to give birth. She can't do that unless there's a ring of support around her. The ring of support that the feminine needs at birth is the watchful eye of a midwife or physician, a doula, or family members, who inspire and encourage her when she thinks she can't go on. Now, that's one part of it.

The other part of it is pain. You can't talk about pain unless you talk about fear. Americans are phobic about pain in childbirth. And yet, we

don't medicate people for long hikes up a mountain. We don't medicate them for a painful, long-distance bike ride. There are all sorts of
things we expect to be strenuous and painful in this society if they're
recreational. But when it comes to birth, which is part of a woman's
natural physiology, she is not expected to be able to handle it. She is
expected to need drugs or an epidural. It's a very demeaning attitude
towards women, really.

A lot of feminists would insist that the issue around taking drugs
for labor pain is one of choice. But choice isn't the primary issue in
birth—it's awareness. All choices are not equal.

For me, in a society that is hell-bent on choice, where women demand, "I want my epidural," due to fear of pain, it's very difficult to ask
someone to take a look at what this epidural does to you and the baby
and the natural process. The fact is that epidurals tend to slow the baby's
progress down, lower the mother's blood pressure, and raise the
mother's temperature. All of these conditions can pose risks to the baby.
For example, when there is a fever in the mother, doctors and nurses
may suspect an infection, which could be dangerous to the baby. In response, they may separate the baby and mother and do a full septic
workup, including numerous blood drawings, a spinal tap and a full
course of antibiotics. All because the mother had an epidural.

Let's talk a little more about the pain.

Okay. I don't want to sidestep it at all. It's the foremost thing in most
women's minds, right? And I am someone with a very low pain threshold. The first thing to know about labor pain is that it is a normal physi-
ological result of the stretching of muscles and tissues. There is nothing
wrong with it. Second, if a woman is frightened, she adds anxiety to that
pain, which increases it.

Labor contractions are not continuous pain. They come in waves,
build to a peak and then dissipate. There is a break between them. The
contractions not only push the baby down the birth canal, they also

stimulate the baby's central nervous system. They awaken it, and ready it for the huge learning spurt that occurs as the baby comes out of the birth canal, and instantly changes from an aquatic being to an air-breathing being that has to deal with stabilizing its own temperature and breathing on its own.

One important thing to understand is that a woman who is well supported in labor usually feels no more pain at the end of labor than she does at the beginning. Why? Because her body creates all kinds of hormones, called endorphins, to take the edge off. As labor progresses, her pain threshold rises. If she's in a familiar, comfortable environment, with cues that say, "All is well"—I mean music, walking around, wearing her own clothes, with people around her who really support what she's doing and who she can lean on—then she experiences labor pain differently.

What about inducing birth?

Inducing labor has made a comeback in the United States. In the 1950s, we were inducing labor for the family's or the doctor's convenience. Now, we're inducing it for all sorts of reasons, such as the baby being three days past due. Well, a baby can be two and a half weeks past a due date. Most midwives don't even begin to worry until it gets to two and a half weeks past, but most obstetricians are starting to talk about artificially inducing labor within three or four days of the projected due date. So here's another example of women being set up for anxiety, which is the exact antithesis of the emotional state they need to be in order to have a normal birth.

So there's an assumption here that technology can improve on nature herself.

Ad infinitum. And we cut back on nurses in hospitals, and increase the amount of money we spend on equipment such as electronic monitors—which have never been proven either safe or effective. Listening with a stethoscope is much more effective. But we send women the message that specialists who control birth from a distance with drugs and machinery will safely deliver their baby.

How dangerous is inducing?

The big problem with every artificial procedure—and that includes inducing, episiotomy, all the drugs and anesthesia—is that you alter the course of the labor itself, and you tend to set in motion a spiraling effect of interventions where, because of this, you have to do that. You induce, the baby doesn't come, then what are you going to do? Well, then you're going to have to use Pitocin to artificially contract the uterus. The side effect of that is likely to be contractions that are too painful for the woman to handle and increased stress on the baby. So you give drugs or an epidural. Then, the baby's heart tones can shoot up or drop down and the next thing you hear, they're talking cesarean. So, the problem isn't so much the intervention itself as the role that intervention has in shifting the course of normal labor to a complicated labor.

So, what we're doing is substituting the power of progress and technology and modern medical science for this natural process that has been working for millions of years through all of evolution.

Every procedure we do is likely to alter the natural course of labor and increase the chance of complications. It's important that people understand the reasons for routine hospitalization for birth in the United States, which started in 1914 and then spread from here around the world. We had a shortage of doctors and nurses because it was World War I. We had high use of dangerous patent medicines and drugs that had been increasing ever since Queen Victoria took chloroform in labor. Victorian women wanted to escape from their bodies because of a legacy of shame and the messages that their bodies were not good. There was also a political campaign to eliminate midwifery.

It was felt that moving women into hospitals would enable better use of staffing and offer greater safety in the use of dangerous substances. In doing that, we created two teams of specialists: those who watch the baby, pediatricians, and those who watch the mother, obstetricians. Women were unconscious for birth. The baby couldn't be cared for by the mother and so someone else had to care for their babies.

The long-term consequences of this are that we continue separating mother and baby. We continue to "observe" babies in a nursery, rather than observing the mother and baby as a pair. We've lost the recognition of the primacy of this pair bond. And that's one of the most important things that's happening in modern society—kids are not sufficiently bonded to their parents and parents aren't sufficiently bonded to their kids.

Bonding is not the same as love. Everybody loves their child. Love is pulled out of us when we have a child. I think that woman who drowned her children in a car loved her children. But was she bonded to them? Bonding is a physical sense of connection to that other person as being so crucially important to you that you could no sooner hurt that person than you could cut off your left arm. That's bonding, and that's what we're compromising as we disconnect from our babies in pregnancy, disconnect from our own bodies in birth, and separate the mother and child in the first hours after birth. This disconnection continues when women go home from the hospital and put their kids in plastic car seats that become baby carriers, and sleep apart from their babies, and put their babies in full-time daycare when they go back to work. So, what I'm arguing against is this long term continuum of alienation and disconnection. It's never just one thing; it's the whole thing.

Now, you have not mentioned breastfeeding in this conversation yet.

Breastfeeding holds a great hope for the future. It's much more than nutrition. It develops the brain and the body and the nervous system of the baby and keeps the mother and baby physically connected. It can even repair damaged cells that drugs or trauma may have caused in the baby's brain. Breastfeeding has the greatest hope of strengthening bonding in this society.

How long should a child be breastfed?

A child should be breastfed for six months, minimum. Ideally, several years. It is six months before the baby's immune system begins to develop. Before that, breast milk protects it. But now less than twenty percent of babies six weeks old are fully breastfed. The rising amount of auto-immune disease in our society is one consequence.

Mothers were breastfeeding, weren't they, a hundred years ago?

Oh, yes. We didn't have any reasonable substitutes. People had tried to create formula for several hundred years, but not very successfully. We were giving babies gruel with sugar and any number of things in it; some babies would survive and many didn't. But the formula industry didn't really grow up until the 'forties. And then came mass marketing. It's difficult to market breast milk; nobody's going to make any money off of it. So formula is everywhere, along with bottles.

Women have been led to believe that it's at least as good as breast milk. And when they have difficulty getting started breastfeeding, which is a learned skill, they quit in frustration.

Do you have any knowledge of how native peoples or people in Africa or Latin America raise their children.

Traditionally, around the world, babies are worn on adults' bodies for many, many months. They are fed continuously, because we are a continuous feeding species. We need to have just the right amount of protein and other elements in our nutrients, in our diet, for the first months to develop the brain. Children sleep with their mothers throughout the early years.

People today who have to work eight or ten hours away from their baby would be well advised to sleep with their infants as well, to give them as much full body contact as they possibly can in the hours they are together. But instead, we are being taught how to use behavior modification to get babies to stop crying in the night, babies who haven't had enough close physical contact during the day.

At what age do you think children should be moved to their own separate room?

That's a developmental question and a matter of preference. It depends, in part, on whether that baby has an extra need for touch and closeness, whether that baby has experienced trauma in the womb or at birth, whether the baby has a very delicate nervous system. It's a very individual thing. Why don't we wait until a child begins to want his or her own separate place?

We are constantly pushing people apart in the belief that that makes people more independent. What research shows, clinical experience shows, and the wisdom that's inherent in the body shows, is that it produces insecure people. Insecurity is not independence. The way to create an autonomous human being is to allow that human being to be very dependent at the beginning of life. I've heard people say, "We're putting our baby in daycare. We want him to get socialized." You can't socialize a baby at six months. What are they going to learn? They're going to learn that they have to share attention with six other babies.

What does the word socialization mean? Does it mean that children tend to be isolated, and if you put them in a group with other kids, they're going to learn how to play with them? Is that the theory?

The idea is that they're going to be overly selfish and they're going to dominate your life, but if they are socialized, they will learn to give up what they need for the good of the group.

It's important to understand that every culture has warped childbirth to some degree or another. They've made decisions about whether babies look more beautiful with their heads flattened or their ears pierced. Culture tends to warp things in its own interest. But traditionally, all cultures understood and valued the need for babies to be dependent and cared for by their mothers.

The ancient part of our brain, which is nurtured in the child's first years, is developed through sensation, through touch. It is not secure; it is not calm; it does not feel a sense of trust. Without enough close physical contact, we are malnourishing the ancient brain and hyperstimulating the neocortex with all of the intensity and devices of modern life, in the belief that we're going to get some healthy, intelligent human beings.

You see what we're getting. People don't trust each other. People behave as if they have no connection to the Earth or to spirit. And the evidence is there that it starts at the beginning of life, when we are not allowed to be dependent, and to fully develop our ancient brain.

So physical contact, bonding, touching, is the foundation of our basic sense of trust.

It's the core of everything. That's right. It's the belief that in the next experience that happens to me, I will be safe, because the last time I was safe. The thing that's important to remember is that for a baby, birth and the first hours, days and weeks afterwards are its first impressions. We know how important first impressions are, but neurologically, we are patterning people for insecurity and addiction and mistrust.

Listening to you, Suzanne, it seems that right from the beginning, we're established in a way of life that keeps us very dependent on the technological and on the elite professional.

Right. And there's huge profits generated this way. Every time a baby is put in a hospital nursery just for observation, that's three hundred to four hundred dollars a day going to the institution. That money could be used to help mothers and babies postpartum at home. When you have a cesarean, you triple the cost of birth.

We have four million births a year. Childbirth is the major condition for hospitalization in this country. We are talking about a fifty-billion dollar a year industry, and that money is not going to feed and clothe and nurture pregnant women, or care for mothers, fathers, babies and families after birth. This is a lot of money that could be used in better ways to serve society.

Now, how about the health maintenance organizations. They are not going to profit theoretically from extra service. Those entities win by doing less. How do you think that's going to impact the birth process?

We're going to see more management and more control until the HMOs recognize that it's less costly in the long run to have midwives, to have most births out of the hospital, in birth centers and in homes, with follow-up care for everyone in the home. Once that is recognized, there will have to be a massive retraining of obstetricians and neonatologists, because we have too many of them. Instead of a twenty percent national cesarean rate, we'll have six or seven percent. Most births will be natural, so we'll have far less need for neonatal intensive care units.

So do you envision a system where home birth becomes a norm?

Home and birth center birth.

With the availability of high-tech assistance when that's called for, and practitioners who have the wisdom to sort out the appropriate places where children should be born.

Right. Studies in Holland show that you can tell who's most likely to have problems in childbirth ahead of time. You need to have a good transport system, which we do. When you have midwives caring for women through pregnancy and in birth, they see problems before they become serious and are able to handle them for the most part with very simple non-invasive measures, such as changes in diet during pregnancy, or shifting positions during labor. Instead of tracking the baby in labor by electronic monitoring, a caring, skilled human being is right there, addressing everything.

The assumption in the hospital is that a person doesn't need to be in the room with the mother because we've got the emergency technology and the operating room just down the hall. But a woman who has serious complications can often have a safer birth by calling ahead and going to a hospital than by mobilizing a speedy response while she is there. The hospital is not built for careful observation. We've put our money into electronic monitors instead of people. And it's been proven, by studies at Harvard and other places, that the electronic fetal monitor is not effective. But vast amounts of money are made from it, and now the legal system supports it, so everybody gets electronic monitoring.

But I can hear someone saying—and this is maybe not the best analogy— but saying that we've got the latest version of Windows. Why should we throw it out and go back to DOS.

We're going to use Windows '99, or whatever, when it is absolutely necessary. But we're going to consider technology to be a scarce resource that should be used only when necessary. And we will understand that whenever you intervene with a normal process, there are always long- and short -term implications. You don't want to do that for the healthy, normal birth. Save the hospital, physicians, medicine and technology for those who really need it.

I'm thinking of a quote—I don't know who said it—that the time for hu-

man beings is over. I found myself thinking of that line in the middle of this conversation.

But the good news is it's so easy to get back to basics.

Well, I don't know if it's so easy, because in so many different ways we're embedded in our ways of thinking and acting. Can we call a halt? Can we say we're going to have boundaries.

Can we use things with discrimination and discernment? Yes.

Can we? I don't know, because but there is a massive propaganda system that is invading our unconscious, and its message is that what you're talking about is romanticism. It feels good to talk about it, but we've attained this level of civilization and we don't turn around. The mass story is that progress is marching forward.

But I'm not saying we should go back to having no telephones or answering machines or airplanes, or that we should go back to having no hospitals.

Perhaps the real question, then, is can we take the good and leave the bad?

We can. But we're going to have to separate greed out of it, because in this country, birth has become a huge profit-making industry. And we have lots of educating to do, to give women back their confidence and authority in birth. Everyone will benefit.

Interview Dates

Jonathan Kozol—November 14, 1995

Vandana Shiva—April 11, 1997

Ivan Illich & Carl Mitcham—March 22, 1996

Gary Snyder—December 9, 1996

Sister Helen Prejean—February 6, 1996 and September 3, 1996

Lieutenant Colonel David Grossman—May 8, 1996

Donovan Webster—October 11, 1996

Thich Nhat Hanh—September 28 & 29, 1995

Helena Norberg-Hodge—January 9 & 17, 1997; April 16, 1997

Paolo Soleri—December 8 & 12, 1995

Alice Walker—June 5, 1997

John Taylor Gatto—March 25, 1997

Susannah Sheffer—February 25, 1997

Noam Chomsky—February 12, 1996

David Korten—April 8, 1997; January 9, 1996; January 29, 1996

Judi Bari—August 17, 1995; September 11, 1996

Wolfgang Sachs—April 23 & 24, 1997

Suzanne Arms—March 28, 1996

Bibliography

Suzanne Arms

A Season to Be Born, 1973
Adoption: A Handful of Hope, 1989
Bestfeeding: Getting Breastfeeding Right for You: An Illustrated Guide (with Mary Renfrew, et al.), 1990
Gentle Birth Choices: A Guide to Making Informed Decisions About Birthing Centers, Birth Attendants, Water Birth, Home Birth, Hospital Birth (Text by Barbara Harper, Photographs by Suzanne Arms) 1994
Immaculate Deception: A New Look at Women and Childbirth, 1985
Immaculate Deception II: Myth, Magic & Birth, 1994
Seasons of Change: Growing Through Pregnancy & Birth, 1993
To Love and Let Go, 1983

Judi Bari

Timber Wars, 1994

Jerry Brown

Thoughts/Edmund G. Brown, Jr., 1976

Noam Chomsky

After the Cataclysm: Postwar Indochina and the Reconstruction of Imperial Ideology (with Edward S. Herman) 1979
American Power and the New Mandarins, 1969
Aspects of the Theory Syntax, 1965
Barriers (Linguistic Inquiry Monographs Series, No 13), 1986
Cartesian Linguistics: A Chapter in the History of Rationalist Thought, 1983
The Chomsky Reader, 1987
Chomsky: Selected Readings; 1971
Chronicles of Dissent (with David Barsamian), 1992

Chumbawamba Live: For a Free Humanity (Audio CD), 1997

Class War: The Attack on Working People, 1996

The Clinton Vision: Old Wine, New Bottles, 1994

The Cold War & the University: Toward an Intellectual History of the Postwar Years (Editor), 1997

The Common Good, 1998

The Culture of Terrorism, 1988

Deterring Democracy, 1991

East Timor: Genocide in Paradise (The Real Story) (with Matthew Jardine), 1996

Essays on Form and Interpretation (Studies in Linguistic Analysis; Vol. 2), 1977

Fateful Triangle: The United States, Israel and the Palestinians, 1984

For Reasons of State, 1973

Free Market Fantasies, 1996

Global Contradictions: Political Power at the End of the American Century, 1997

Human Rights and American Foreign Policy, 1975

Keeping the Rabble in Line (with David Barsamian), 1994

Knowledge of Language: Its Nature, Origin, and Use, 1985

Language and Mind, 1972

Language and Politics, 1988

Language and Problems of Knowledge: The Managua Lectures, 1988

Language and Responsibility: Based on Conversations With Mitson Ronat, 1979

Language and Thought, 1994

Lectures on Government and Binding: The Pisa Lectures (Studies in Generative Grammar), 1993

Letters from Lexington: Reflections on Propaganda, 1993

The Logical Structure of Linguistic Theory, 1975

Manufacturing Consent: The Political Economy of the Mass Media, 1988

Manufacturing Consent: Noam Chomsky (VHS Tape),1996

Media Control: The Spectacular Achievements of Propaganda (The Open Media Pamphlet Series, no. 1), 1997

Modular Approaches to the Study of the Mind, 1984

Morphophonemics of Modern Hebrew, 1979

Necessary Illusions: Thought Control in Democratic Societies, 1989

Noam Chomsky on the Generative Enterprise: A Discussion, 1983

On Power and Ideology: The Managua Lectures, 1987

Peace in the Middle East? Reflections on Justice and Nationhood, 1974

Pirates & Emperors: International Terrorism in the Real World, 1995

Political Economy of Human Rights: The Washington Connection and Third World Fascism Vol. 1, 1979

Powers and Prospects: Reflections on Human Nature and the Social Order, 1996

Problems of Knowledge and Freedom, 1972
The Prosperous Few and the Restless Many (Real Story Series) (with David
    Barsamian), 1993
Questions of Form and Interpretation, 1975
Reflections on Language, 1975
Rethinking Camelot: JFK, the Vietnam War, and U.S. Political Culture, 1993
Rules and Representations, 1982
Secrets, Lies, and Democracy (Real Story Series) (with David Barsamian), 1994
Some Concepts and Consequences, 1982
The Sound Pattern of English (with Morris Halle), 1991
Studies on Semantics in Generative Grammar, 1972
Syntactic Structures, 1978
The Minimalist Program (Current Studies in Linguistics, 28), 1995
Topics in the Theory of Generative Grammar, 1978
*Towards a New Cold War: Essays on the Current Crisis and How We Got
    There,* 1982
*Turning the Tide: U.S. Intervention in Central America and the Struggle for
    Peace,* 1986
What Uncle Sam Really Wants (The Real Story Series), 1992
World Orders Old and New, 1994
Year 501: The Conquest Continues, 1993

John Taylor Gatto

Dumbing Us Down: The Hidden Curriculum of Compulsory Schooling, 1991
*The Exhausted School: The First National Grassroots Speakout on the Right
    to School Choice* (Editor),1993
One Flew Over the Cuckoo's Nest; A Guide to Understanding the Classics, 1975

Lt. Col. Dave Grossman.

On Killing: The Psychological Cost of Learning to Kill in War, 1996

Thich Nhat Hanh

*The Art of Mindful Living: How to Bring Love, Compassion and Inner Peace
    into Your Daily Life* (Audio Cassette), 1992
Basic Buddhist Wisdom (Audio Cassette), 1998

Be Still and Know: Reflections from Living Buddha, Living Christ, 1996

Being Peace, 1996

Beyond Self: 108 Korean Zen Poems, 1997

The Blooming of a Lotus: Guided Meditation Exercises for Healing & Transformation, 1993

Breathe! You Are Alive: Sutra on the Full Awareness of Breathing, 1996

Call Me By My True Names: The Collected Poems of Thich Nhat Hanh, 1993

Cultivating the Mind of Love: The Practice of Looking Deeply in the Mahayana Buddhist Tradition, 1995

The Diamond That Cuts Through Illusion: Commentaries on the Prajnaparamita Diamond Sutra, 1992

For a Future to Be Possible: Commentaries on the Five Mindfulness Trainings, 1998

Guide to Walking Meditation, 1985

Heart of the Buddha: An Introduction to the Teachings of Buddhism, 1998

The Heart of Understanding (Audio Cassette), 1987

The Heart of Understanding: Commentaries on the Prajnaparamita Heart Sutra, 1988

Hermitage Among the Clouds: A Historical Novel Of Fourteenth Century, 1993

Interbeing: Fourteen Guidelines for Engaged Buddhism, 1998

A Joyful Path; Community, Transformation, and Peace (with Arnold Kotler), 1994

Living Buddha, Living Christ, 1995

Living Buddha, Living Christ (Audio Cassette), 1996

The Long Road Turns to Joy: A Guide to Walking Meditation, 1996

Looking Deeply (Audio Cassette), 1987

Love in Action: Writings on Nonviolent Social Change, 1993

The Miracle of Mindfulness: A Manual on Meditation, 1992

The Miracle of Mindfulness: A Manual on Meditation (Abridged Audio Cassette), 1995

Moment by Moment: The Art and Practice of Mindfulness (with Jerry Braza), 1997

The Moon Bamboo, 1989

Old Path, White Clouds: Walking in the Footsteps of the Buddha, 1990

Our Appointment With Life: The Buddhas Teaching on Living in the Present, 1990

Peace Is Every Step: The Path of Mindfulness in Everyday Life, 1992

Plum Poems (with Svein Myreng), 1998

Plum Village Chanting Book, 1998

Plum Village Meditations: With Thich Nhat Hank & Sister Jina Van Hengel (Audio Cassette), 1997

Present Moment, Wonderful Moment: Mindfulness Verses for Daily Living
    (with Mayumi Oda), 1990
The Raft Is Not The Shore (with Daniel Berrigan), 1975
Rose for Your Pocket, 1987
Stepping into Freedom: An Introduction to Buddhist Monastic Training, 1997
The Sun My Heart: From Mindfulness to Insight Contemplation, 1988
The Sutra on the Eight Realizations of the Great Beings, 1987
Taking Refuge in L.A: Life in a Vietnamese Buddhist Temple (with Don
    Farber), 1987
Teachings on Love, 1997
*Teachings on Love: How Mindfulness Can Enhance Your Intimate Relation-
    ships* (Audio Cassette), 1996
Thundering Silence: Sutra on Knowing the Better Way to Catch a Snake, 1993
Touching Peace (Audio Cassettes), 1995
Touching Peace: Practicing the Art of Mindful Living, 1992
Touching the Earth: The Five Prostrations & Deep Relaxation, 1997
*Transformation & Healing: The Sutra on the Four Establishments of Mindful-
    ness,* 1990
Zen Keys, 1995

Helena Norberg-Hodge

Ancient Futures: Learning from Ladakh, 1992
From the Ground Up: Rethinking Industrial Agriculture (with Peter Goering,
    et al.) 1993
The Future of Progress: Reflections on Environment and Development (with
    Edward Goldsmith, et al.) 1995

Ivan Illich

ABC: The Alphabetization of the Popular Mind (with Barry Sanders), 1988
After Deschooling, What?, 1981
Celebration of Awareness: A Call for Institutional Revolution (with Erich
    Fromm), 1971
Deschooling Society, 1971
Disabling Professions (Co-Author), 1978
Energy and Equity, 1974
Gender, 1982
H2O and the Waters of Forgetfulness: Reflections on the Historicity of "Stuff", 1985

Imprisoned in the Global Classroom, 1981
In the Mirror of the Past: Lectures and Addresses 1978-1990, 1992
In the Vineyard of the Text: A Commentary to Hugh's Didascalicon, 1993
Medical Nemesis: The Expropriation of Health, 1976
The Right to Useful Unemployment, 1978
Shadow Work (Open Forum Series), 1981
Tools for Conviviality, 1973
Toward a History of Needs, 1978

David Korten

Bureaucracy and the Poor: Closing the Gap (Editor), 1983
Community Management: Asian Experience and Perspectives (Editor), 1986
Getting to the 21st Century: Voluntary Action and the Global Agenda, 1990
Globalizing Civil Society: Reclaiming Our Right to Power, 1998
*People-Centered Development: Contributions Toward Theory and Planning
    Frameworks* (Co-Editor), 1984
*Planned Change in a Traditional Society; Psychological Problems of Modern-
    ization in Ethiopia,* 1972
When Corporations Rule the World, 1995

Jonathan Kozol

Alternative Schools: A Guide for Educators and Parents, 1982
Amazing Grace: The Lives of Children and the Conscience of a Nation, 1995
Children of the Revolution: A Yankee Teacher in the Cuban Schools, 1978
*Death at an Early Age: The Destruction of the Hearts and Minds of Negro
    Children in the Boston Public Schools,* 1967
Free Schools, 1972
Illiterate America, 1988
Night Is Dark and I Am Far from Home, 1977
On Being a Teacher, 1993
Outside the Dream: Child Poverty in America (with Stephen Shames), 1991
*Prisoners of Silence: Breaking the Bonds of Adult Illiteracy in the United
    States,* 1980
Rachel and Her Children: Homeless Families in America, 1989
Savage Inequalities: Children in America's Schools, 1992

Carl Mitcham

Philosophy and Technology : Readings in the Philosophical Problems of Technology (Editor, with Robert MacKey), 1983

Thinking Through Technology : The Path Between Engineering and Philosophy, 1994

Engineering Ethics Toolkit (with Shannon Duval), 1998

Ethical Issues Associated With Scientific and Technological Research for the Military (Annals of the New York Academy of Sciences, Vol. 577), (Editor, with Philip Siekevitz), 1990

Philosophy and Technology: Readings in the Philosophical Problems of Technology, 1973

Philosophy and Technology II (Boston Studies in the Philosophy of Science, Vol. 90), (Editor), 1986

Philosophy of Technology in Spanish Speaking Countries (Philososphy and Technology, Vol 10) (Editor), 1993

The Reader's Adviser : The Best in Science, Technology & Medicine Vol. 5 (Editor, with William F. Williams, 1994

Social and Philosophical Constructions of Technology (Research in Philosophy and Technology, Vol. 15) (Editor), 1995

*Technology and Social Action (*Research in Philosophy and Technology, Vol. 16) (Editor), 1997

Theology and Technology : Essays in Christian Analysis and Exegesis (with Jim Grote), 1984

Sister Helen Prejean

Dead Man Walking: An Eyewitness Account of the Death Penalty in the United States, 1996

Welcome to Hell: Letters & Writings from Death Row (with Jan Arriens), 1997

Wolfgang Sachs

The Development Dictionary (Editor), 1992

Global Ecology (Editor), 1993

For Love of the Automobile, 1992

Greening the North: A Post-Industrial Blueprint for Ecology and Equity (Co-Editor, with Reinhard Loske and Manfred Linz), 1998

Susannah Sheffer

Growing Without Schooling Magazine, for information call (617) 864-3100
A Life Worth Living: The Selected Letters of John Holt, (Editor), 1990
A Sense of Self: Listening to Homeschooled Adolescent Girls, 1997
Earning Our Own Money: Homeschoolers Thirteen and Under Describe How They Have Earned Money (Editor), 1991
Writing Because We Love to: Homeschoolers at Work, 1992

Vandana Shiva

Biodiversity: Social and Ecological Consequences, 1992
Biopiracy: The Plunder of Nature and Knowledge, 1997
Biopolitics: A Feminist and Ecological Reader on Biotechnology (Editor), 1995
Close to Home: Women Reconnect Ecology, Health and Development Worldwide (Editor), 1993
Ecofeminism (with Maria Mies), 1993
Ecology and the Politics of Survival: Conflicts over Natural Resources in India, 1991
Monocultures of the Mind: Perspectives on Biodiversity and Biotechnology, 1993
Staying Alive: Women, Ecology and Survival in India, 1988
The Violence of the Green Revolution: Third World Agriculture, Ecology and Politics, 1992

Gary Snyder

A Place in Space: Ethics, Aesthetics, and Watersheds, 1996
Axe Handles, 1983
The Back Country, 1971
Earth House Hold: Technical Notes and Queries to Fellow Dharma Revolutionaries, 1969
He Who Hunted Birds in His Father's Village: The Dimensions of a Haida Myth, 1979
Left Out in the Rain: New Poems 1947-1985, 1986
The Maidu Indian Myths and Stories of Hanc' Ibyjim (with William Shipley), 1991
Mountains and Rivers Without End, 1997
Myths and Texts: Paradise Lost, 1978
No Nature: New and Selected Poems, 1993

The Old Ways: Six Essays, 1981
Passage Through India, 1983
Practice of the Wild: Essays, 1990
Practice of the Wild (Audio Cassettes), 1991
The Real Work: Interviews and Talks, 1964-1979 (with William Scott.
    McLean), 1980
Regarding Wave, 1970
Riprap and Cold Mountain Poems, 1990
This Is Our Body, 1989
Turtle Island, 1974

Paolo Soleri

Arcology: The City in the Image of Man, 1973
Arcosanti: An Urban Laboratory, 1984
*The Bridge Between Matter and Spirit Is Matter Becoming Spirit: The
    Arcology of Paolo Soleri,* 1973
Fragments, 1981
Omega Seed: An Eschatological Hypothesis, 1981
Paolo Soleri's Earth Casting: For Sculpture, Models and Construction, 1984
The Sketchbooks of Paolo Soleri, 1971
Soleri's Cities (VHS Tape), 1996

Alice Walker

Anything We Love Can Be Saved: A Writer's Activism, 1997
Archbishop Desmond Tutu: An African Prayer Book (Audio Cassette with
    Desmond Tutu), 1996
The Color Purple, 1992
Finding the Green Stone (Catherine Deeter, Illustrator), 1991
Good Night, Willie Lee, I'll See You in the Morning, 1984
Her Blue Body Everything We Know: Earthling Poems 1965-1990, 1993
Horses Make a Landscape Look More Beautiful, 1986
In Love and Trouble: Stories of Black Women, 1985
In Search of Our Mothers' Gardens, 1984
Langston Hughes, American Poet (Catherine Deeter, Illustrator), 1998
Living by the Word: Selected Writings 1973-1987, 1988
Meridian, 1996
My Life As Myself: An Intimate Conversation (Audio Cassette), 1995
Once: Poems, 1986

Possessing the Secret of Joy, 1992
Possessing the Secret of Joy (Audio Cassette), 1992
Revolutionary Petunias and Other Poems, 1986
The Same River Twice: Honoring the Difficult, 1996
The Temple of My Familiar, 1993
The Temple of My Familiar (Audio Cassette), 1989
To Hell With Dying (Catherine Deeter, Illustrator), 1993
*Warrior Marks: Female Genital Mutilation and the Sexual Binding of
    Women*, 1993
Women of Hope: African Americans Who Made a Difference, 1994
You Can't Keep a Good Woman Down, 1982

Donovan Webster

Aftermath: The Remnants of War, 1996

Jerry Brown

A native of San Francisco, Jerry Brown studied at Sacred Heart Novitiate, and received degrees from the University of California at Berkeley and Yale Law School. In 1970 he was elected Secretary of State of California, and served as Governor of California from 1975 to 1983. He was elected Mayor of Oakland in June of 1998.

For more information about the We The People organization, please write to:

We The People
200 Harrison Street
Oakland, California 94607

Or E-mail: wtp@wtp.org.